MY SOCIAL-MEDIA LINKS

Email: attwood.shaun@hotmail.co.uk
Blog: Jon's Jail Journal
Website: shaunattwood.com
Twitter: @shaunattwood
YouTube: Shaun Attwood
LinkedIn: Shaun Attwood
Goodreads: Shaun Attwood
Facebook pages: Shaun Attwood, Jon's Jail Journal,
T-Bone Appreciation Society

I welcome feedback on any of my books.
Thank you for the Amazon reviews!

ACKNOWLEDGEMENTS

A big thank you to Barbara Attwood, Derick Attwood, Penny Kimber, Emma Bagnell, Jane Dixon-Smith

PABLO ESCOBAR
BEYOND NARCOS

WAR ON DRUGS BOOK 1

SHAUN ATTWOOD

For Zivi

GET A FREE BOOK

Sign Up For My Newsletter At:

http://shaunattwood.com/newsletter-subscribe/

MY BOOKS

English Shaun Trilogy

Party Time
Hard Time
Prison Time

War on Drugs Trilogy

Pablo Escobar: Beyond Narcos
*American Made: Who Killed Barry Seal? Pablo Escobar
or George HW Bush*
We Are Being Lied To: The War on Drugs (Expected 2017)

Life Lessons

*Making a Murderer: The Framing of Avery and Dassey by Kratz
and Other Parasites* (Expected 2017)

Two Tonys (Expected 2017)
T-Bone (Expected 2020)

CONTENTS

CHAPTER 1
EARLY YEARS

Pablo Escobar was born on a cattle ranch in 1949, the second year of The Violence, a civil war that saw millions of Colombians flee their homes and left hundreds of thousands dead. Slicing people up with machetes was popular and led to a new genre of slaughter methods with ornate names. The Flower Vase Cut began with the severing of the head, arms and legs. The liberated limbs were stuffed down the neck, turning the headless torso into a vase of body parts. A victim stabbed in the neck, who had his tongue pulled out through the gap and hung down his chest was wearing a Colombian Necktie. The turmoil affected nearly every family in Colombia. It accustomed Pablo's generation to extreme violence and the expectancy of a short and brutal life.

Pablo's parents were Abel de Jesús Dari Escobar, a hard-working peasant farmer who traded cows and horses, and Hermilda Gaviria, an elementary-school teacher. As her husband was mostly absent due to work, Hermilda cooked, cleaned and took care of her family. Pablo was the third of seven children.

One day, tiny Pablo wandered away from home. Hermilda found him under a tree, with a stick, playing with a snake.

"See, I'm not hurting you," Pablo said to the snake.

Gazing affectionately, Hermilda knew that Pablo was a sweet boy who loved animals.

The nearest school was so far away that Pablo and his brother, Roberto, had to wake up early. With no means of transportation, it took them an hour to walk there in worn-out shoes.

Rather that wear shoes with holes in them, Pablo decided to go to school barefooted. His teacher sent him home. Humiliated, Pablo told his mother that he needed new shoes to stay in school.

1

As she had no money, she deliberated her options and shoplifted a pair of shoes. At home, she noticed that each shoe was a different size. Disheartened, she confessed to a priest, who advised her to return the shoes and get them on credit.

She bought the shoes and arrived home, exhausted and anxious. With such a large family to feed, she complained about their lack of money.

"Don't worry, mom," Pablo said. "Wait until I grow up. I'll give you everything."

As The Violence between the Conservative and Liberal parties escalated, the family was warned to leave or else risk having their body parts re-assembled into art. But having no safe place to go, and loving the animals, the beautiful countryside adorned with wildflowers, and air that carried a taste of pine and resin from the forest, they chose to stay.

Pablo was seven when the guerrillas entered his village near the town of Rionegro, the Black River. Trembling, he heard machetes hacking the front door and threats of murder. He clung to his mother, who was crying and praying. His father said they would be killed, but at least they could try to save the kids. They hid the kids under mattresses and blankets.

The front door was so strong that the guerrillas eventually gave up trying to break in. Instead, they set fire to it. Wincing and coughing in a house filling with smoke, Pablo's parents braced to die. But soldiers arrived and the guerrillas fled.

With a burning building illuminating the street, the town's survivors were escorted to a schoolhouse. Pablo would never forget the charred bodies and the corpses hanging from the lampposts. Internalized in the terrified child, the horrors of The Violence would re-emerge years later, when he kidnapped, murdered and bombed to maintain his empire.

Growing up with six siblings, Pablo bonded the most with Roberto, who was two years his senior. Roberto was intelligent and had a passion for mathematics, electronics and cycling. Pablo enjoyed watching Roberto construct things such as radios, but rather than join in, he sat around for most of the day as if lost in thought.

Pablo and Roberto were sent from the family's ranch to live with their grandmother in the safety of Medellín, known as the City of the Eternal Spring due to a steady climate averaging around 22.2°C or 72°F. Downtown was a cluster of glass and steel skyscrapers separated by roads lined with trees. The surrounding expanse of houses grew more dilapidated towards the shantytowns, slums and garbage dumps – places crammed with displaced people where gangs of street kids, thieves and pickpockets roamed. The tough residents of Medellín worked hard to get ahead.

Pablo's grandmother was an astute businesswoman who bottled sauces and spices and sold them to supermarkets. Under her loving but stern hand, Pablo and Roberto had to go to church and pray every morning.

Although they loved the weather and the mountainous landscape, the second largest city in Colombia with all of its fast cars and over a million people intimidated the brothers, who were accustomed to the tempo of ranch life. They were delighted when their parents joined them, but their father disliked living in the city, so he returned to the countryside to work on other people's farms. Eventually, the brothers fell in love with Medellín.

The atmosphere at home was heavily religious. They had a figurehead of Jesus with realistic blood. After his mother told him Christ's story, young Pablo was so sad that when lunch was served, he put a piece of meat in his corn cake and took it to the figurehead. "Poor man, who made you bleed? Do you want a little meat?" This act convinced his mother that he was kind and religious. For the rest of his life, Pablo would always try to sleep with an image of Jesus nearby.

Hermilda enchanted Pablo with stories about his grandfather, Roberto Gaviria, who had smuggled whiskey. With long-range planning and a creative imagination, Roberto the bootlegger had outsmarted everyone, including the authorities. Pablo wanted to emulate his grandfather's success.

Growing up in a suburb of Medellín called Envigado, the kids built carts from wood and raced down hills. They made soccer balls from old clothes wrapped inside of plastic bags, erected makeshift goalposts and played with the other kids in the neighbourhood. It was Pablo's favourite sport. A popular prank was to stick chewing gum on a doorbell, so that it rang continuously.

On the streets of Medellín, some of Pablo's leadership and criminal traits started to emerge. Although the youngest in his group, he'd take the lead. When the police confiscated their soccer ball, he encouraged the group to throw rocks at the patrol car. The police rounded up several of the group and threatened to keep them in jail all day. Only Pablo spoke up to the commander. He told them they hadn't done anything bad. They were tired of the ball being taken and they'd pay to retrieve the ball. Some of the kids in the group ended up in business with Pablo later on.

In his early teens, Pablo was elected president of his school's Council for Student Wellness, which demanded transportation and food for indigent students. He learned about the US meddling in South America for its own advantage, which often increased the suffering of the most poverty-stricken people. He hated that the poor were the biggest victims of violence and injustice.

During this time, he absorbed anti-imperialist phrases which became mantras for the rest of his life. He heard rumours that the CIA had facilitated the assassination of Jorge Eliécer Gaitán, a leftist presidential candidate who had defended workers' rights and promised an equitable land reform. Gaitán's death had ignited The Violence that had threatened Pablo's family.

Pablo started to despise the way that society was structured: a tiny percent of the population owned the majority of the land and wealth, while more than half of Colombians lived in poverty. Determined to prevent that from happening to him, he claimed he would kill himself if he had not made a million pesos by the age of thirty.

According to his brother, Roberto, in his book, *Escobar*, Pablo developed an interest in history, world politics and poetry. At the public library, he read law books. He practised public speaking on student audiences at lunchtime or on the soccer field. Roberto remembers him speaking passionately about becoming the president of Colombia and taking ten percent of the earnings of the richest people to help the poor to build schools and roads. To create jobs, he wanted to encourage Asian manufacturers to build plants in Colombia.

In school, Pablo grew restless. Distrustful of authority figures, he felt more at ease with the street gangs. For money, he experimented with small scams. Believing that school was a waste of time, he dropped out for two years. On the dangerous streets, he refined his techniques and learned to avoid the pitfalls.

Hermilda convinced him to resume his education, so he could get the three grades necessary to graduate. As he adored his mother, he went back to school. But he ended up in constant arguments with his teachers whom he viewed as absurd and foolish. Eventually, he was expelled.

After his mother scolded him, he responded, "Mother, I keep on telling you: I want to be big and I will be. I'm poor, but I'll never die poor. I promise."

By sixteen, Pablo was displaying an extraordinary amount of confidence on the streets. With a comb in his pocket, he often gazed at windows to inspect his reflection. In later years he imitated the mannerisms of Al Capone and *The Godfather* played by Marlon Brando. His deep thinking was intensified by smoking marijuana. He grew quieter. When asked a question, he generally paused silently before replying. Some wondered whether he was imitating *The Godfather*, but it was a natural trait exacerbated when he was stoned.

Rationalising his banditry as a form of resistance to an oppressive society, he channelled his energy into criminal activity, which ranged from selling fake lottery tickets to assaulting people. With a rifle, he walked into banks and calmly told the staff to empty their safes. With a smile, he chatted to the tellers, while awaiting the cash. Unable to perceive that Pablo had shed his sense of fear, some mistakenly ascribed his bravado to drugs. The results he achieved from his cleverness and farsightedness – including eluding the police – boosted his faith in himself.

A formidable combination of intelligence and street smarts enabled him to rise above his contemporaries, some of whom sought his advice and joined his gang. Those who were nervous or frustrated felt safe in his company. He earned their respect by remaining calm and cheerful in dangerous situations.

One said, "He was like a God, a man with a very powerful aura. When I met him for the first time, it was the most important day of my life."

In *Killing Pablo*, author Mark Bowden described Pablo as an accomplished car thief by age twenty. Drivers were forced out of their cars by his gang and the cars dismantled at chop shops. He dictated orders from home, managing the logistics and collecting the cash.

His gang started stealing new cars, which were impossible to resell if they had been reported as stolen. To get around this, he offered the police bribes. After a year, his relationship with them was so strong that the police chiefs followed his orders. Complaints about him reselling stolen cars were ignored.

Money from selling car parts was used to bribe officials to issue car certificates, so that the stolen cars could be resold without having to be chopped. The officials receiving the complaints about what he was doing were the same ones issuing him the titles for the new cars.

He started a protection racket whereby people paid him to prevent their cars from being stolen.

Always generous with his friends, he gave them stolen cars with clean papers. Those receiving new cars were told to pick them up from the factory. If the factory workers detected the forged paperwork, Pablo's friends told them, "These titles were made by Pablo," which prompted the workers to hand over the keys.

Pablo and his cousin, Gustavo – who *Narcos* portrayed as

usually wearing a flat cap – built race cars from stolen parts and entered rallies. Suspected of stealing a red Renault, Pablo was arrested in 1974, but he bribed his way out of a conviction.

Pablo ordered the murders of people who tried to prevent his accumulation of power, including those who denounced him, refused to abide by his rule or declined his bribes. He discovered that murder provided cheap and effective PR. Focussing people on their mortality or that of their families brought their behaviour into line. He killed without remorse, just to increase his reputation and earnings.

Some of the people who owed Pablo money were kidnapped. If the debt wasn't paid by family members or friends, the victim was killed. This enhanced his reputation and helped his business grow in a world of opportunists and cutthroats. He also kidnapped people and held them for ransom.

Diego Echavarría Misas was a powerful industrialist who lived in a remake of a medieval castle. Widely respected in the higher social circles, he yearned to be revered as a philanthropist. But no matter how many schools and hospitals he opened, the poor were not fooled by his attempts to mask his malevolence.

The workers in his textile mills toiled endlessly in cruel conditions for a pittance. He fired hundreds of them in an abusive manner and without a severance pay. Like many wealthy landowners, he expanded his territory by forcefully evicting peasant communities. Attempting to defend their homes, some peasants were imprisoned or murdered. The rest were forced to settle in the slums.

Pablo had heard enough about Echavarría. One day, his kidnapping became news. His family rapidly paid the ransom, but his fate remained a mystery. After six weeks, his body was found in a hole near Pablo's birthplace. He had been tortured, beaten and strangled. The poor celebrated his death.

Although many people believed that Pablo had brought them justice, with no evidence linking him to the crime, he was not charged. On the streets, people stopped to shake his hand or bowed to him in reverence. They began calling him "Doctor Escobar" and "The Doctor."

Roberto has claimed that the early stories of his brother's brutality are untrue accusations made by Pablo's enemies.

Pablo started to apply his organisational skills to contraband, a thriving business in Colombia, a country steeped in corruption. Medellín was known as a hub for smugglers. Those who got caught typically bribed their way free. If they were unable to pay a bribe, the police would usually confiscate their contraband rather than incarcerate them. It was the cost of doing business and customary throughout Colombia.

With numerous police on the payroll of crime bosses, it was hard to differentiate between the police and the criminals. The police not only gave their criminal associates freedom from jail, but they also committed crimes for the gangs, including kidnappings and contract killings. Shootouts sometimes occurred between different police on the payrolls of rival gangs.

The court system was the same. Judges who earned $200 a month could charge up to $30,000 to dismiss a case. Judges who refused were threatened or beaten. Court staff could be bribed to lose files, which was cheaper than paying a judge. If that didn't work, the judge was killed. The court system was considered the softest target in law enforcement, and Pablo would master the art of manipulating it.

Early on, *Narcos* presented Pablo as a boss in the contraband smuggling business, but that was false. He was the underling of a powerful contraband kingpin who specialised in transporting cigarettes, electronics, jewellery and clothing in shipping containers from America, England and Japan. The goods were shipped to Colombia via Panama.

Having met Pablo at a soccer match, the kingpin asked him to be a bodyguard, in the hope of reducing worker theft. He told Pablo that the way to make money was to protect the merchandise for the guy with the money, and that was him.

Pablo bought the poorly-paid workers seafood and wine. He

offered them half of his salary forever to work with him. If they stopped stealing, he'd come back and take care of them in two weeks. The workers agreed and returned the stolen goods they still had.

Specialising in cigarettes, Pablo drove across Colombia in a jeep ahead of half a dozen trucks transporting contraband. Along the way, he paid the necessary bribes to the police. Delighted with Pablo's performance, the kingpin offered him ten percent of the business. Pablo demanded fifty. The kingpin called Pablo crazy. Pablo said it was fair because the kingpin had sometimes lost more than half of the goods. Even after Pablo's fifty percent, the kingpin would still make more money because there would be no theft. The kingpin agreed to forty percent.

Through the contraband business, Pablo became adept at smuggling goods across the country, without paying government taxes and fees. Supervising two convoys a month earned him up to $200,000. He stashed his profits in hiding places in the walls of his home. He installed special electronic doors that only he could open. He recruited Roberto as an accountant, in charge of handling the payroll, making investments and depositing money into bank accounts with fake names. Over the years, money was invested in real estate, construction businesses and farms. As his brother was handling so much money, Pablo gave him a gun.

Giving half of his salary to the workers earned their respect and the name El Patrón or the Boss. He bought his mother a house, a taxicab for Gustavo and an Italian bicycle for his brother. He donated truckloads of food to the scavengers at the garbage dumps. He took about twenty members of his family to Disney World in Florida, where he went on all of the rides with his son.

When a policeman on Pablo's payroll was moved to another district, he snitched out the operation. The police waited to ambush a convoy of trucks. They would all get rich confiscating so many goods. Pablo had stopped for lunch and told the convoy to continue without him. Thirty-seven trucks were seized. A driver called Pablo who said to tell the other drivers not to speak to the police. With the police after him, he took a bus back to Medellín. Lawyers got the drivers released but were unable to retrieve the merchandise.

Even though his contraband partnership with the kingpin was over, Pablo soon found a more lucrative business opportunity.

CHAPTER 2
TRAFFICKING COCAINE

In Peru, the Cockroach introduced Pablo and Gustavo to suppliers of cocaine paste who were offering it for $60 a kilo at a time when a kilo of cocaine was selling for up to $60,000 in America. The *Narcos* scene with the Cockroach surviving a military firing squad in Chile is false.

In Renault 4s, Pablo smuggled the paste from the Andean mountains, across three countries: Peru, Ecuador and Colombia. He had a separate Renault 4 for each country, with the relevant country's license plate. Sometimes, he raced his cousin, Gustavo – who had penetrating dark eyes, a square face and a tidy moustache similar to Pablo's – to see who could get back to Medellín first. The winner kept all of the proceeds. The paste was hidden in a compartment installed above the passenger's-side wheel, which the checkpoint police never searched.

In a residential neighbourhood, the paste ended up in a house with covered windows, where it was transformed into cocaine. The cooks lived on the second floor. Most of the first floor had been converted into a kitchen. The cocaine was cooked in old refrigerators that Pablo had converted into ovens. Hoping for feedback on his first batch, he gave ten samples away. The majority said they preferred it to weed and requested more. Some said it gave them energy. Others said it calmed them down. Pablo didn't like it. He preferred smoking pot.

With the coca plant growing widely in the jungles and mountains of Peru, cheap paste was readily available. Due to drug laws, the price of cocaine in America was sky high. The US authorities were focused on marijuana and heroin coming in from Mexico, not cocaine. Pablo calculated that he could make more from a single load of cocaine sold in America than he could from a convoy of trucks smuggling normal contraband.

Testing the export business, Pablo discovered that he'd underestimated the demand for cocaine. He could sell any amount to any country, especially to America, the largest consumer of cocaine in the world.

Pablo's smugglers took drugs on flights and returned with large amounts of cash. Trucks replaced the Renault 4s. More workers were hired.

Vulture was one of Pablo's drivers. As he racked up profits from his trips, Vulture started showing off by buying an expensive car, a motorbike and clothes. This did not go unnoticed by one of his relatives in the DAS, the Colombian equivalent to the FBI. Vulture told his relative that he was transporting potatoes.

The DAS stopped one of Pablo's trucks and demanded the driver call his boss to pay a bribe. After Pablo and Gustavo showed up, they were arrested. The next day, Pablo's mugshot was on the front page of the newspaper. His mother sobbed for hours.

After spending eight days in jail, Pablo paid to be transferred to a facility with outdoor recreation, including soccer. He bribed the judge but after two months, it was decided that he would be tried in a military court which was more difficult to corrupt. His lawyer warned that he could get a long sentence. One night, Pablo told a guard that he needed to stretch his legs to reduce his stress. After being allowed onto the soccer field, he escaped.

The prison director called Pablo's mother, begging her to get her son to return, otherwise he'd end up in jail. When Pablo called her, she insisted that he return. Pablo and his mother showed up at the prison, with some x-rays of a sick person. Claiming he'd been ill, Pablo showed them to his military escorts, who were satisfied about his absence. In the end, Pablo bribed the judge. Pablo and Gustavo walked free. Sentenced to five years, the driver ended up in a prison with good facilities. Pablo gave the driver's family a house, a car and money.

Upon his release, Pablo resumed his cocaine enterprise, but

now the police knew about it. He and Gustavo were pulled over by the two DAS agents who'd previously arrested them. They took him and his cousin to a remote area by a garbage dump, tied their hands together and forced them onto their knees. After roughing them up, the agents demanded a million pesos in exchange for their lives. While Gustavo went to get the money, Pablo offered more cash for the name of the person who'd arranged for them to kidnap him. He was surprised to learn it had been the Cockroach.

Once freed, Pablo plotted revenge that he would carry out himself. Being forced onto his knees at gunpoint was unforgivable. Emboldened by their success, the two DAS agents were about to kidnap one of Pablo's workers. They considered Pablo just another easy drug-trafficker target. Pablo's men kidnapped the agents and took them to a house. Pablo made them get onto their knees. As they begged for their lives, Pablo put a gun to their heads and shot them multiple times. The news reported the discovery of their bodies.

In 1974, Pablo fell in love with Maria Victoria Henao Vellejo, a local beauty. Because of her age, fourteen, and Pablo being twenty-five, Maria's mother was unenthused. He persisted, including showing up outside her home one night accompanied by a guitar player and serenading her. By 1976, she was pregnant, so they married. Three months after the marriage, Juan Pablo was born. It took two years for Maria's mother to warm to Pablo, but she did, accepting that he loved her daughter.

Fabio Restrepo was an early cocaine boss in Medellín. By 1975, Restrepo was exporting up to one hundred kilos of cocaine a week to America, where it sold for roughly $40,000 a kilo in Miami. Pablo asked a childhood friend and future business partner, Jorge Ochoa, to set him up with Restrepo. Jorge met Pablo at a small untidy apartment in Medellín, where he bought fourteen kilos of cocaine from Pablo. Two months later, Pablo had Restrepo murdered and informed the Ochoa brothers that he'd taken over Restrepo's business.

Whether Pablo really had Restrepo killed is in dispute. According to *Kings of Cocaine*, Jorge Ochoa was behind the slaying. In the mid-70s, Jorge was selling cocaine in Miami for the old-time smuggler Restrepo. In 1977, Restrepo made the mistake of telling a DEA (Drug Enforcement Administration) informant that he was smuggling up to a hundred kilos a week into America. On October 12, he gave the informant twenty-seven kilos to transport to Jorge in Miami.

A sting operation to capture Jorge was set up at the Dadeland Twin Theaters, a cinema opposite a liquor store. As the deal went down in the parking lot, armed agents surrounded the vehicles and arrested nine Colombians, including Jorge's sister and brother-in-law. Racing away on a motorbike, Jorge slipped through the sting and fled the country.

After Jorge returned to Medellín, Restrepo was murdered. On July 31, 1978, DEA correspondence reported:

Jorge Ochoa is currently residing in Medellín, although he keeps a home in Barranquilla, and it has been learned that Ochoa has inherited the trafficking organization of the departed Restrepo. It is speculated that Ochoa ordered the murder of Restrepo to install himself as the undisputed head of the organization. Several sources of information have related that Ochoa has become one of the most powerful traffickers in Medellín and the northern coast of Colombia, and is continuing to introduce between one hundred and two hundred kilos of cocaine into the US by several unknown methods.

The Ochoa brothers – Jorge, Juan David and Fabio – had grown up with money from cattle breeding and restaurants. Jorge and Juan David were stocky, but nothing compared to their rotund father, Fabio Sr, an esteemed trainer and breeder of Colombian horses. At home, Fabio Sr occupied a throne-like chair custom-ised for his extraordinary girth. He was the patriarch over a big family of adventurous men and strong women. Although he never got caught with his hands in the trafficking operation, some authors have claimed that Fabio Sr was the true godfather of the Medellín Cartel. Pablo respected him and valued his advice and folk wisdom. In the 2006 documentary film, *Cocaine Cowboys*, the former Medellín Cartel associate Jon Roberts mentioned Fabio Sr: "As many people want to believe that Pablo Escobar was the king of cocaine, they can believe that, but the man that was really the king was Ochoa."

In the mid-1960s, the Ochoa family toiled around the clock at their restaurant, Las Margaritas. Jorge Ochoa later joked that he'd invested in cocaine to prevent the rest of his family from working themselves to death in the restaurant. After Restrepo's murder, Jorge (a.k.a. the Fat Man) assumed leadership of the family's cocaine business.

Jorge was quiet, strong on family values, and didn't participate in drugs other than the occasional glass of wine. As exemplified during the sting at the Dadeland Twin Theaters, he had a knack of avoiding the law that would serve him well for the rest of his life.

While Jorge was forming El Clan Ochoa, with an established distribution network in America, Pablo was building his own gang, Los Pablos, with a fearsome reputation on the streets of Medellín. His organisation absorbed people who'd previously been rivals. When a war broke out between two cocaine traffickers in Medellín, resulting in workers and their family members getting killed, Pablo brokered a deal whereby they entered a partnership under him.

Initially, shipping cocaine to America was easy for Pablo and far more profitable than smuggling bulky marijuana. Up to forty kilos could be packed into used airplane tires, which pilots would discard at Miami. They were taken to a dump, followed by one of Pablo's workers who would retrieve them. The cocaine was distributed through a network of Latinos in Miami.

Pablo no longer smuggled drugs himself. He paid others to do it. On the phone, he used code words such as emeralds and diamonds to frustrate the efforts of drug agencies and to avoid providing any verbal evidence that could be used against him.

To stay ahead of the DEA, he continuously changed his smuggling methods. He stopped using airplane tires and had Colombian and US citizens board planes with cocaine in their suitcases or in specially made clothes. Holding up to five kilos, the suitcases had double walls. They were paid $1,000 and their flight tickets. Some wore shoes with hollowed-out bottoms. The shoes had been manufactured with the cocaine sewn inside. As well as passengers, Pablo recruited crew members, including stewardesses, pilots and co-pilots, who breezed through airports without getting searched. People in wheelchairs could smuggle up to $1 million worth of cocaine in the frames. Some smugglers dressed as nuns. Others posed as blind people with canes packed with cocaine. Some swallowed cocaine in condoms. If the condom opened, they died. Newspapers reported such tragedies.

With the authorities obsessed with eradicating the drug that had been demonised for decades in America – marijuana – cocaine slipped into the US unnoticed. The federal government had classified marijuana as a Schedule 1 substance, more harmful than cocaine, and equally as harmful as heroin, where it remains to this day.

Over time, instead of sending people with suitcases, Pablo just sent the suitcases. They were checked onto a flight and picked up at the other end. Airport officials were bribed with hundreds of thousands of dollars to look the other way. An official on a meagre salary ended up getting arrested with $27 million in his bank accounts.

To keep expanding, Pablo paid bigger bribes. To enable the police on his payroll to get promotions and pay increases, Pablo allowed them to confiscate massive amounts of cocaine. The media recorded the busts and reported them on the news. The government was delighted as such seizures enabled them to get more money from America to fight the War on Drugs. The confiscated cocaine was reported as destroyed, returned to Pablo and exported to the US. Corrupt governments all over the world still run this scam on US taxpayers.

Due to the smells released from making cocaine, Pablo moved his kitchens from residential areas to the jungle.

He moved into El Poblado, one of Medellín's wealthiest neighbourhoods with lots of white stucco houses, heavy on marble, glass and armed guards. The locals ate at fancy restaurants with views of the city lights and shopped at expensive boutiques. His brother urged him to stop and focus on real-estate investments, but Pablo was addicted to the power, money and lifestyle.

By offering high rates of return, Pablo attracted investors. An investment of $50,000 would be repaid with $75,000 in two weeks. If the drugs were busted, investors received half of their money back. To obtain investment capital, people sold their cars and houses or cashed in their savings.

Pablo set up a form of insurance whereby businessmen could invest a few thousand dollars for a share in a shipment of cocaine. After it was sold in America, the profits would be distributed. Pablo guaranteed their original investment even if the shipment was seized. For providing this insurance premium, he took ten percent of the American value of the cocaine. He even offered businessmen loans to invest.

Pablo was making millions, but things were still relatively small. For him to become a billionaire, it would take the ideas of a man who worshipped both John Lennon and Adolf Hitler: Carlos Lehder, the character in *Narcos* with a swastika on his arm.

CHAPTER 3
CARLOS LEHDER AND
GEORGE JUNG

Carlos Lehder's dream was to make millions from cocaine and to use the proceeds for revolutionary goals, including the destabilisation of imperialistic America. Of German-Colombian descent, twenty-four-year-old Lehder was arrested in Miami in 1973 for smuggling marijuana, and sentenced to four years. In minimum-security federal prison in Danbury, Connecticut, he rubbed shoulders with a more polished type of prisoner: white-collar criminals, Vietnam War protesters... Unlike the typical Colombian smuggler, Lehder spoke fluent English, enabling him to absorb knowledge from the eclectic mix of prisoners, which he filed away for future use.

Lehder was born in Armenia, Colombia. His father, Wilhelm Lehder, a tall German, was considered a dangerous Nazi by the Colombian police, who suspected him of running a fascist spy ring out of the hotel he owned with forty rooms and hidden transmitters. Wilhelm hated Jews and the American government, and longed for the installation of a totalitarian regime in Colombia. He had a vegetable-oil factory and imported canned goods and wine for his hotel, which his German common-law wife ran. His Colombian beauty-queen wife gave birth to Carlos Lehder.

The youngest of four children, Lehder moved to America with his mother at age fifteen. Considerably shorter than his father, he was handsome, intelligent and ambitious. But every time he turned to crime, he got arrested, commencing with the interstate transportation of stolen cars in America.

His arrest for marijuana brought him into contact with a

cellmate called George Jung – whose life story was portrayed in the movie *Blow*, starring Johnny Depp. It was a meeting that changed their lives forever.

Born in Boston in 1942, Jung was a high-school football star and a natural leader. At the University of Southern Mississippi, he studied advertising, but dropped out to lead a life of smoking and dealing marijuana. Mesmerised by West Coast culture, he became a hippy, embracing LSD and free love. Noticing a discrepancy in the price of weed in South Los Angeles – $60 a kilo – versus on the East Coast – $300 a kilo – Jung started to bulk buy weed from the owner of a hairdressing salon. Demand far exceeded the amounts smuggled by the airline stewardesses he'd hired as mules – including his girlfriend – so he invested in motorhomes.

Soon he had hundreds of thousands of dollars. He bought a plane to fly weed from Mexico that cost $8-$10 a kilo. Only twenty-six, he hired a team of pilots. In 1974, he was busted smuggling 660 pounds of marijuana to Chicago. He bonded out and went on the run. When he visited his parents, they called the police. His sentence was reduced after he argued with the judge.

In 1974, serving a four-year sentence, Jung was bracing to receive a new cellmate in his seven-by-nine-foot room with a view of the countryside. When Carlos Lehder walked in, Jung was relieved by the presence of such a polite young man.

After exchanging pleasantries, Lehder said, "What are you in for?"

"Flying pot out of Mexico," Jung said. For an hour, they discussed their experiences in the marijuana trade.

Standing in the line for the chow hall, Carlos said, "You must know a lot about airplanes and have a lot of people in the US who buy drugs. Do you know anything about cocaine?"

"No," Jung said. "Tell me about it."

"It sells in the US for $40-$50,000 a kilo."

"How much do you get it for, Carlos?"

"Like $2-$5,000."

"Tell me everything you know about cocaine, Carlos. Everything."

For sixteen months, the cellmates ironed out the logistics for distributing cocaine across America. Lehder told Jung that he could obtain unlimited amounts of it from two cousins: Gustavo Gaviria and Pablo Escobar. Aiming to make millions from air transportation, they obtained maps from the prison library, and plotted trafficking routes. Banker inmates taught them about money laundering and offshore accounts. After a doctor incarcerated for Medicare fraud mentioned Belize, which lacked an extradition treaty, Lehder contemplated setting up a regional haven for traffickers.

Jung wanted to transport cocaine to America in light aircraft, just like he'd done with weed. A pilot advised them that a small plane couldn't carry enough fuel for such a long trip. The plane would have to stop somewhere to refuel. If a plane were to fly from Miami to the Bahamas, as if taking its occupants on a vacation, it could continue to Colombia, get the cocaine, and return to the Bahamas. If the plane returned with the end-of-the-week traffic, it would be invisible to the authorities.

Lehder affectionately referred to incarceration as his college days because he was learning so much. He obtained a high-school diploma. Due to his excellent grades, he ended up teaching Hispanic inmates. He never stopped reading. Jung introduced him to Machiavelli, Plato, Nietzsche, Carl Jung, Hermann Hesse and Hemingway.

In 1975, Jung was released to his parents. In 1976, he received a telex from Colombia: "Weather beautiful. Please come down. Your friend, Carlos."

Unwilling to violate parole, Jung sent a friend to Lehder in Medellín on a fact-finding mission. They arranged a fifteen-kilo transaction.

In April 1976, Lehder called Jung with instructions to send two female mules to Antigua with baggage. "Don't tell them anything. We'll explain everything when they get there."

Jung approached his girlfriend and her friend at a schoolyard where they were watching a softball game. "Would you be interested in a free Caribbean vacation?"

"When?"

"Now."

The women took hard-shell Samsonite cases and spending money. They had a blast with the charming Lehder. Jung's girlfriend slept with one of Lehder's friends. They returned home with different cases.

Jung took the new cases home and removed the aluminium lips protecting the fibreglass false bottoms. Snorting the product, Jung thought it was wonderful. It was the beginning of a monstrous drug habit. Carlos paid Jung five kilos to distribute the cocaine. He sold four kilos for $180,000. He paid his female smugglers in cocaine. More trips were organised.

A setback occurred on October 19, 1976, when Lehder was arrested for smuggling Chevrolet wagons into Colombia. Through bribery, Lehder arranged to serve his time in a special terrace in Bella Vista, a new prison in Medellín. While most of the prisoners slept on a filthy floor and ate rotten-horsemeat soup, Lehder had his own bed and ordered food from restaurants.

Lehder buddied-up with an American incarcerated for smuggling weed. He told the smuggler that he wanted to form "a conglomerate of small-time cocaine producers, and to put all their merchandise together into one shipment, so it would pay for the equipment necessary to get into the United States." He aimed to use cocaine to conquer the world like Adolf Hitler.

After two months inside, Lehder was released in time for Christmas. Jung sent Lehder $30,000 and business resumed.

In February 1977, Jung received fifty kilos in Miami, which he transported to Boston to meet Lehder, who was a no-show. Unbeknown to Jung, Lehder had run into difficulty crossing the Canadian border and was on the run. Jung gave the cocaine to his former weed dealer, the Hollywood hairdresser. Two weeks later, it had been sold for over $2 million.

Lehder showed up at Jung's parents, concerned about the fate of the cocaine and that Jung may have ripped him off. Many Colombians had lost cocaine by trusting Americans. When he saw his share of the cash – $1.8 million – Lehder was so delighted that he bought a new BMW. Soon, Jung was making $500,000 a week. Hidden in cars, millions were smuggled back to Medellín by Lehder.

By 1977, a plane was needed to move the cocaine, so Jung hired a Learjet. But constantly smuggling and using cocaine was wearing Jung out.

Lehder was such a strict disciplinarian that he put everybody he knew to work. An exhausted Jung asked Lehder to find someone to bring cocaine to California.

"I'll call you as soon as I have that person in transit," Lehder said. The next day he called Jung. "I have someone. They're on the plane now."

"Who is it?"

"It'll be a surprise."

The next day, Jung heard knocking on the door of his Holiday Inn room. Opening it revealed a little grey-haired lady: Lehder's mother. When Jung objected, Lehder said that everybody had to work, and she had wanted a free trip to Disneyland.

As the business grew, the former cellmates fell out. Lehder viewed Jung's cocaine habit as detrimental to work performance. Jung was snorting a gram at a time, earning him the nickname I-95 because his long lines of white powder reminded the Colombians of that Interstate Highway. Attempting to squeeze Jung out of the picture, Lehder demanded to know the name of the Hollywood hairdresser.

In August 1977, a pilot tested the Bahamas route – the plan hatched in prison – with 250 kilos picked up from one of Pablo's farms outside Medellín. The plane refuelled in Nassau, the capital city of the Bahamas, on its eleventh largest island. It landed in the Carolinas, and the cocaine was transported to Florida. The cocaine sold within days. The profit was $1 million, which Jung and Lehder split. Lehder wanted to move the base of their operations to the Bahamas, but Jung argued against it.

"Look, Carlos, the only way to do this business is to hit-and-run. Keep changing our smuggling routes. Never stay in one place. Then we don't have to be under anybody's thumbs. We make ourselves a hundred million apiece, or whatever. You go your way. I go mine."

Lehder wanted rapid expansion to help him achieve his revolutionary goals, whereas Jung favoured slow and steady progress. For cocaine supply, Jung had stepped on Lehder's toes by marrying a Colombian whose brother was a supplier. Lehder obtained the contact details for the Hollywood hairdresser, so he didn't need Jung as an intermediary anymore. Jung accused Lehder of going behind his back.

Lehder obtained a boat, and searched for an island in the Bahamas. He settled on Norman's Cay, a fishhook-shaped landmass surrounded by some of the clearest blue water on earth, teeming with marine life. The central curvature harboured yachts. At the top of the island, a dozen beach cottages sat on a rocky coast. At the tip of the fishhook was a 3,000-foot airstrip adjacent to four miles of sparkling white sand, forming a beach that curved around water known as Smugglers Cove. On a hill by the airstrip was a yacht club with a four-stool bar, a restaurant and the only telephone on Norman's Cay. Amid hundreds of islands, it was paradise.

Lehder paid $190,000 cash for Beckwith House on the north-eastern bend. He deposited millions in a trust company, which he used to buy up property on the island.

With Jung out of the way – or so Lehder thought – Lehder got down to the business of running all of the wealthy inhabitants off the island, so that he could turn it into a smuggling hub. He started out politely. He showed up at cottages with a suitcase full of cash and told the owners to name their price. Flashing large sums of money, and introducing himself as Joe Lehder, he came off as polite and intriguing.

"Joe, how much money are you worth?" a neighbour asked on Lehder's thirtieth birthday.

"Oh, about $25 million."

He bought the rights to the guesthouse, the bar and the airstrip. He closed the airstrip down for general use by painting a giant yellow X on it, which prevented other residents from flying in and out. He closed the yacht club, the diving school and stopped the hotel from taking reservations.

The remaining residents were starting to wonder what was going on, but Lehder was only just getting started. He decided that the homeowners who'd refused his cash had to go. To pressure them into moving, he filled the island with intimidating characters, including bodyguards and traffickers.

"In case I didn't make myself clear," Lehder told one resident, "if you're not off this island today, your wife and children will die."

A college professor who ran a diving business was told that diving must stop. When he returned for his gear, his plane was surrounded, and he was prevented from leaving. After shooting the plane's radio, Lehder's bodyguards instructed him to fly away and never return. In the air, he noticed that the plane lacked fuel. It had been siphoned. The plane had to emergency-land on a nearby island's beach.

The police did nothing about the complaints from the residents. Lehder had paid everybody off. A Bahamian immigration officer initiated deportation proceedings against a remaining resident.

Emulating his hero, Adolf Hitler, in a way that would have made his father proud, Lehder hired forty German bodyguards, who arrived in the Aryan tradition with Doberman pinchers, automatic weapons and blonde hair. Toting black satchels, they patrolled in Toyota jeeps and Volkswagen vans. Any yachts that approached with tourists, sightseers or remaining residents were shadowed along the perimeter of the island by vehicles full of armed neo-Nazis and dogs capable of tearing limbs off. If they got too close to the shore, a helicopter would hover over them.

The famous TV anchor-man for *CBS Evening News*, Walter Cronkite, travelled by yacht to Norman's Cay on a Christmas vacation. Finding the harbour empty, he dropped his anchor.

"You can't dock here and you can't anchor out there!" yelled a man on the pier.

Cronkite continued to the next island, where he was told that it was common knowledge that the people who'd taken over Norman's Cay didn't want any visitors.

The last resident to leave was Floyd, a handyman who'd built his own house on the island. Lehder had hired him to assemble a couple of prefabricated hangars to store planes and cocaine. While working on a hangar, Floyd watched a plane land, men with rifles jump out, and a truck arrive, from which suitcases were loaded onto the plane. When his work was done, Floyd was ordered to leave the island, but he refused. He told the superintendent that he wasn't interested in selling the house he'd built.

"He [Lehder] doesn't have to buy it. He's just going to take it."

A foreman warned Floyd, "Look, he's [Lehder's] coming by and he has some pretty rough men there, and they probably won't kill you, but they could certainly knife you up pretty bad." After that, Floyd fled.

Planes landed every day. Lehder's associates lived in several of the houses. Out of his twenty-two cars, Lehder preferred driving a 1932 Ford Replica, a classic car with a rectangular elongated body with two round lights at the front.

Even though he'd warned Jung about the detrimental effects of cocaine on business judgement, Lehder started to use cocaine heavily. His associates joined in, and they all became paranoid. To calm them down, planes full of women were flown in. Wild parties ensued with Beatles and Rolling Stones' music. Cocaine-crazed neo-Nazis hauled a houseboat to the top of the island's only hill, and left it there to be used as a lookout. Luxury properties were destroyed and vandalised. Laden with cocaine, a DC-3 crashed in the lagoon and was left to rot. Like his other hero, Che Guevara,

Lehder started dressing in army fatigues and waving guns around. His alter ego continued to assert itself.

Meanwhile, Jung had been reduced to the man who had launched Lehder. In a confrontational mood, he flew to Norman's Cay. Making only $500,000 a year, he coveted Lehder's tens of millions.

"It's over," Lehder said, flanked by two armed Germans. "You have your brother-in-law... You can do your own operation, but this is my island. I own it."

"I'm not going to let you get away with this," Jung said. "There's only one way this will end."

For five years, pilots brought anywhere from 300 to 5,000 kilos. The 5,000 kilos were worth $150 million wholesale at the time. They arrived in a plane with twenty-eight-year-old Jorge Ochoa. The packages were marked with the letters CIA. Larger planes meant bigger cargoes. At Norman's Cay, big loads were divided among smaller planes destined for Florida, creating a Federal Express-type method of delivery. Bales of cocaine were offloaded at remote airstrips or dropped into the water, where high-speed motorboats were waiting.

Lehder charged fees for other traffickers to use his airstrip. They brought marijuana, amphetamines and Quaaludes. Years later in court, Lehder was alleged to have made $300 million from 1979 to 1980. Never had more drugs destined for America come from such a tiny place.

Unlike Jung, Pablo was delighted with the amount of cocaine going through Norman's Cay. Every week in the late 1970s, Pablo made millions, distributing cocaine to states as far away as Colorado for $72,000 a kilo, California for $60,000 and Texas $50,000. Depending upon the sizes of the loads, his pilots made up to $1 million per flight. The word among the pilots of that time was that Pablo's organisation was the most efficient to work for. The merchandise was always on time.

Sometimes, pilots didn't make it due to the combined weight of the cocaine and the fuel. Bad weather, such as a thunderstorm, could cause a heavy plane to stall. Pablo was making so much money that losing a plane was insignificant. Pilots who were arrested in Florida had usually performed dozens of trips. Already multimillionaires, they could hire the best lawyers.

Anything he fancied, Pablo bought, including planes and helicopters. Before he was thirty, he invested over $50 million in the construction of a 7,500-acre luxury ranch-style resort with the Magdalena River running through it. It had a landing strip, artificial lakes, a road system and swimming pools, all protected by mortar emplacements. On top of the cement entry way to Hacienda Nápoles, he'd mounted a lucky charm that had helped to start his fortune: the Piper airplane (tail number HK-617-P) which had transported his first shipment of cocaine to America. The plane welcomed his visitors, who had to drive through the entrance way. His private roads were lined with palm trees.

The suites sometimes housed over 100 guests. Seven-hundred servants attended their needs and kept things running. The guests enjoyed billiard tables, pinball machines, bars, jukeboxes, a bull-fighting ring, tennis courts, outdoor dining areas, a games room and horse stables. If they liked Jet Skis, they could race them on the lakes. With the river so close, they enjoyed boats and hovercraft. Pablo hosted parties. Attendees ranged from politicians, business owners and artists to actors, models and beauty queens.

Pablo hired a professional cameraman to shoot home movies. The cameraman filmed Pablo, Gustavo and their gang on motorbikes in front of another of his proudest possessions: an early 1930s Cadillac that looked like the one driven by Al Capone. To make it seem as if Capone had actually owned it, Pablo allegedly had strafed it with gunfire.

Pablo's zoo – with over 200 exotic animals roaming around – was open for free. "Nápoles zoo belongs to the Colombian people," Pablo told a journalist. "We built it so that children and adults, rich and poor, can enjoy it, and owners cannot pay for what is already theirs." It received 60,000 visitors in 1983; they drove through the grounds to watch animals such as antelope, elephants, gazelles, zebras, exotic birds, giraffes, hippopotami, ostriches, a soccer-playing kangaroo and an elephant that stole food from people's cars. The zoo also had five life-size cement dinosaurs for children to climb. A lover of birds, Pablo owned a parrot that recited the names of Colombian soccer players. Unfortunately, she fell asleep after drinking some whiskey and was eaten by a cat. After that, Pablo banned all cats from Hacienda Nápoles, including lions and tigers.

The main property was protected by armed guards. Only people he had preapproved of were allowed in after their invitations were double-checked by Pablo, who received them by fax from his sentries.

The main house included a theatre, a disco and Jacuzzis. The kitchen had its own menu. Eating with his family, guests and bodyguards, Pablo enjoyed reciting poetry and singing tango music. He always sang in the shower. He enjoyed writing poems to his kids. Pablo and Gustavo lived on the second floor. The rest of the family had the first floor.

Pablo loved spending time with his family. If his son or daughter needed his attention, he'd halt business meetings. The police recorded a conversation between Pablo and his wife. While they discussed family matters, someone being tortured started to scream in the background. Pablo told the torturer to please keep the victim quiet because he was talking to his family on the phone.

With the business needing constant attention, Pablo, Roberto and Gustavo worked different shifts. Gustavo and Roberto were early birds, whereas Pablo didn't usually wake up until noon. He was an obsessive tooth-brusher, who put on a brand-new shirt every day. After wearing each shirt once, he donated it. He also kept emergency supplies of clothes in safe houses. His favourite breakfast was a corn patty with scrambled eggs, chopped onions and tomatoes, accompanied by coffee.

Pablo despised the Colombian elites who scorned the masses, and politicians who promised to help the poor but didn't follow through. He now had the means to realise his childhood dream of ameliorating the lives of the impoverished – something he knew would create powerful enemies for him.

In 1979, he started the social program *Civics on the March*. Poor neighbourhoods adopted trees in response to the United Nations having warned that industry was causing irreversible damage. Giving speeches, he encouraged people to join the efforts to preserve the environment. He extolled the value of planting trees and preserving green areas to improve the health of the community.

Pablo offered young people an alternative to crime by way of sports. He built public areas with volleyball and basketball courts and soccer fields. He installed electric lights in forty pitches in the poorest neighbourhoods, so that kids could keep playing at night. His investment in the professional soccer team, Atlético Nacional, raised their status internationally, which drew many young people into the game.

Pablo met people who lived in shacks at the garbage dumps. They attempted to make a living by sifting through the trash and finding items that could be recycled. A few weeks after his visit, one of the neighbourhoods caught fire. The shacks were destroyed. No one seemed to care except for Pablo, who commissioned the building of houses for the homeless. He invested millions in churches, streetlights, road improvements and recreation centres. He sent doctors into neighbourhoods to heal the sick. Street kids received 5,000 toys every Christmas.

"When we build schools," Pablo said, "it seems that we re-encounter the nation that we long for. We have looked with pain upon children sitting on adobes, in ramshackle locales and upon teachers living without protection before the indifference of the State. We love Colombia and now are capable of giving back some of what this beautiful nation has given us. We are doing it."

Even though they knew that Pablo was a criminal, the poor preferred him to a government they viewed as tyrannical for protecting the interests of the wealthy while allowing people to die of starvation and children to live at garbage dumps. Until Pablo, no one had dared to stand up to the criminals in power and attempt to give dignity back to the poor. Being good or evil in Colombia depended upon the perspective of who was viewing it.

CHAPTER 4
HISTORY OF COCAINE

To understand how Pablo flourished as a trafficker, it's necessary to look at the history of cocaine. For thousands of years, the indigenous people of South America have chewed coca leaves, just like the British enjoy drinking tea. A coca leaf in the mouth combined with a small amount of an alkaline substance is sucked for up to forty-five minutes. The stimulant effect is similar to a boost of energy from coffee. Ancient Andean tribes cherished the coca leaf as a gift from the gods, reserving its use for royalty and high priests. Over time, the masses discovered that it helped them to suppress appetite, increase stamina and overcome altitude fatigue in the Andes Mountains. It was thought to cure everything from stomach complaints to snow blindness. The Incas used it as an anaesthetic for primitive brain surgery performed on injured warriors.

In the nineteenth century, European chemists focussed on coca leaves in the hope of developing new drugs. Using leaves imported to Germany, Albert Niemann extracted the primary alkaloid in 1859 and named the crystalline substance cocaine. Having stripped the leaf of its moderating substances, he'd unwittingly unleashed an addictive drug.

In 1863, cocaine made its way to America as an anonymous ingredient in Vin Mariani, a tonic wine named after the Corsican chemist behind the concoction. It consisted of ground-up coca leaves with red Bordeaux wine, at the rate of six milligrams of coca per ounce of wine. The label claimed it, "Fortifies Strengthens Stimulates & Refreshes the Body & Brain. Hastens Convalescence especially after Influenza."The recommended dose was two to three glassfuls per day, taken before or after meals, and half of that for children.

Helped along by Vin Mariani's advertising genius, the wine became a worldwide sensation. He had 3,000 physicians endorse it, and countless monarchs, politicians, actors, writers and religious leaders, including Queen Victoria, Thomas Edison, Alexander Dumas, Emile Zola and President William McKinley. It was said that Pope Leo XIII never left the Vatican without a flask of Vin Mariani under his robes, and that he'd awarded Vin Mariani a gold medal. When Ulysses Grant was dying from throat cancer, struggling to write his memoirs, Mark Twain sent him Vin Mariani, which revived him sufficiently for him to pick up his fountain pen.

An American pharmacist, John Pemberton, made a non-alcoholic health drink, a mineral-water beverage laced with cocaine, which softened his morphine addiction. It became so popular that Pemberton received an offer of $2,300 from Asa Candler for the rights and recipe. Thirty-eight years later, Candler's $2,300 investment was worth $50 million. The name of the health drink was Coca-Cola. It was advertised as a tonic that gave you energy and cured headaches. People would enter a drugstore, sit on a high stool, hand over a couple of pennies and receive a glass of Coca-Cola. Popular amongst members of the temperance movement, it pepped them up to protest against alcohol.

Viewed as a miracle cure, cocaine was widely adopted in self-administered medicines. The Hay Fever Association latched onto cocaine because it constricted blood vessels. Many asthma preparations contained coca or cocaine. By 1890, it was everywhere, with quacks claiming it cured everything from impotence to baldness and dandruff. As it boosted work performance, it was used by all sections of society, ranging from baseball players to dockworkers. White business owners doled it out to black employees, to squeeze more work out of them. An anti-opium crusader, Dr Hamilton Wright, advocated its distribution to black dockworkers and labourers to increase their productivity.

In literature, it was heralded by Sherlock Holmes, who eagerly injected it every day, as described in *The Sign of the Four* by Arthur Conan Doyle:

Sherlock Holmes took his bottle from the corner of the mantelpiece, and his hypodermic syringe from its neat morocco case. With his long white fingers he adjusted the delicate needle and rolled back his shirt cuff. For some little time his eyes rested thoughtfully upon the sinewy forearm and wrist all dotted and scarred with innumerable puncture marks. Finally he thrust the sharp point home, pressed down the tiny piston, and sank back into the velvet-lined armchair with a long sigh of satisfaction.

"Which is it today," I asked, "morphine or cocaine?"

He raised his eyes languidly from the old black-letter volume which he had opened.

"It is cocaine," he said, "a seven-per-cent solution. Would you care to try it?"

Cocaine was used to treat Civil War veterans addicted to morphine and alcohol. This did not go unnoticed by an Austrian neurologist called Sigmund Freud.

Born in 1856 in the Moravian town of Příbor – now a historic town in the Czech Republic – Freud developed an unnatural interest in reading at an early age. He stacked his bedroom with books, where he remained cloistered even during mealtimes. In 1873, he joined the medical faculty at the University of Vienna, where his studies included physiology, philosophy and zoology. He dissected hundreds of male eels in a quest to find their genitals. In 1882, he started work at the Vienna General Hospital, where his research included cerebral anatomy. He also fell in love with Martha, a petite and intelligent friend of his sisters. Two months later they were engaged. Her family responded by sending her to live near Hamburg. On April 21, 1884, Freud wrote to Martha:

I have been reading about cocaine, the essential constituent of coca leaves which some Indian tribes chew to
enable them to resist privations and hardships. A German
has been employing it with soldiers and has reported that
it increases their energy and capacity to endure. I am
procuring some myself and will try it with cases of heart
disease and also of nervous exhaustion, particularly in the
miserable condition after the withdrawal of morphium...
Perhaps others are working at it; perhaps nothing will come
of it. But I shall certainly try it, and you know that when one
perseveres, sooner or later one succeeds. We do not need
more than one such lucky hit to be able to think of setting up
house. But don't be too sure that it must succeed this time.
You know, the temperament of an investigator needs two
fundamental qualities: he must be sanguine in the attempt,
and critical in the work.

Hoping to make a breakthrough in medicine to generate the
resources to marry Martha, Freud purchased a gram of cocaine
from a pharmacy, supplied by Merck of Germany. He tried one
twentieth himself. With his mood elevated and appetite sup-
pressed, he wondered about its application for depression and
stomach problems. His enthusiasm for cocaine increased after it
provided relief for a patient suffering from gastritis. Freud ordered
more, which he shared with his friends, associates and Martha,
"to make her strong and give her cheeks a red colour." Using it
throughout the day, he documented its effects, including his shifts
in emotion, body temperature and muscular strength. Pining for
Martha, who he hadn't seen in over a year, Freud experienced
depression, which he increasingly self-medicated with cocaine.
High on the substance, he wrote to Martha in the summer of
1884:

Woe to you, my princess, when I come. I will kiss you quite
red and feed you till you are plump. And if you are forward

you shall see who is the stronger, a little girl who doesn't eat enough or a big strong man with cocaine in his body. In my last serious depression I took cocaine again and a small dose lifted me to the heights in a wonderful fashion. I am just now collecting the literature for a song of praise to this magical substance.

The first medical article Freud published was "Über Coca" in 1885, which lauded the use of cocaine in depression and morphine addiction, while also commenting on its anaesthetic qualities. Pleased with his progress, Freud took time off to visit Martha. When he returned in September, cocaine was causing a stir, but not because of his paper. Karl Koller, a colleague Freud had conducted experiments with, had made a breakthrough with cocaine and become an instant celebrity. He'd developed it as a local anaesthetic for eye surgery. Although Freud had touched on cocaine's anaesthetic properties, Koller had identified its tissue-numbing capabilities. As it would have enabled him to marry Martha, Freud envied Koller's success. In later life, he claimed that it was Martha's fault that he was not already famous at an early age.

While Koller was at his house, Freud received a visit from his father, who had an eye complaint. After diagnosing glaucoma, they operated on him the next day, using cocaine as an anaesthetic. His father's eyesight was saved. The medical community scrambled to use it as an anaesthetic in a variety of procedures ranging from tooth extraction to haemorrhoid surgery. It was soon heralded as a cure for hay fever, asthma, opium and morphine addiction and for every complaint imaginable ranging from ingrowing toenails to nymphomania. It was sold in lozenges, cigarettes, cough medicines and cold cures. Bars offered shots of whiskey with cocaine. In America, its price jumped from $2.50 to $13 a gram. The lead producer, Merck, ramped-up production from fifty grams in 1879 to thirty kilos in 1885.

Even though medical professionals had certified cocaine as

being completely safe, by 1885, its side-effects were becoming apparent, especially among those who'd used it first: physicians, chemists, pharmacists, doctors, dentists and their wives, some of whom ended up in the madhouse.

To a friend, Freud had recommended cocaine for morphine addiction. The friend ended up hooked on cocaine and morphine. Freud spent "the most frightful night" of his life babysitting his friend, who, suffering from cocaine psychosis, kept picking at imaginary insects and snakes crawling beneath his skin.

It was determined that cocaine did not cure morphine addiction. It just substituted one addiction for another and sometimes left people addicted to both. One doctor predicted it would be the third great scourge of the human race after alcohol and opium. A Russian doctor gave twenty-three grains of cocaine to a girl he was about to operate on. She died and he committed suicide. Perhaps the last straw for Freud occurred when he fatally overdosed a patient on it.

Dr Albrecht Hirschmüller of the University of Tübingen traced Freud's error back to work Freud had originally read concerning cocaine's use for morphine addiction in a journal called the *Therapeutic Gazette*, which Freud had discovered in the index catalogue of the Surgeon General's Office. Seven papers he had quoted in "Über Coca" were from the *Therapeutic Gazette*, which, unknown to Freud, was owned by the Parke, Davis pharmaceutical company of Detroit, the American manufacturer of cocaine. It was an early instance of Big Pharma co-opting a doctor: Freud had accepted $24 from Park, Davis to vouch for their cocaine, which he had claimed was as good as Merck's.

Flak rained down on Freud for his claims in "Über Coca." Even though he'd finally managed to marry Martha in 1886, Freud described 1887 as "the least successful and darkest year" of his life. He never published any more papers on cocaine. He buried the theories and went on to found psychoanalysis. With the zeal of enemy combatants, researchers still argue over whether cocaine gave Freud the inspiration and vivid dreams that contributed to the development of his later theories.

Although most of its supposed medical benefits were debunked, cocaine use in America climbed as people became addicted to patent medicines. But that was all about to stop, at least for black people.

At the turn of the nineteenth century, agricultural depression and labour struggles increased tension among the whites, some of whom channelled their discontent into the despicable act of lynching black people. Gangs of vigilantes grabbed innocent blacks and hung them from the nearest tree. When the blacks dared to fight back, the whites got it into their heads that the number one cause of such retaliation was cocaine.

For decades, the whites had felt threatened by the customs of the blacks. After the Civil War, the blacks in southern states were banned from drinking alcohol on the grounds that when intoxicated they became dangerous to whites. The majority of politicians believed that the whites were able to behave themselves while intoxicated, whereas black people lacked such restraint.

In 1901, Henry Cabot Lodge spearheaded a law that banned the sale of liquor and opiates to "uncivilized races," including blacks, aborigines, Eskimos, Hawaiians and immigrant railroad workers. Cocaine dodged inclusion until a decade later when headlines courtesy of William Randolph Hearst reported on the new southern menace: cocaine. The same reasoning that had outlawed alcohol and opium to black people now spread to cocaine.

Thus was born the myth of the cocaine-crazed Negro with superhuman strength who you could shoot, but wouldn't die. One newspaper stated, "In attempting to arrest a hitherto peaceful negro who had become crazed by cocaine, a police officer in self-defence drew his revolver, placed the muzzle over the negro's heart, and fired. And yet, this bullet did not even stagger the crazed negro, and neither did a second."

The police were so spooked that they demanded higher-calibre bullets to shoot blacks under the influence of cocaine because anything less would be repelled by their superhuman strength. Calibres .25 and .32 were replaced by .38, which decades later were replaced by Glocks when the Reagan-Bush administration propagandised black crack use to terrify the nation into tightening drug laws, and to spend hundreds of millions of taxpayers' dollars to hunt down Pablo Escobar.

In the early 1900s, according to politicians and the tabloids, cocaine not only made blacks bullet-proof, but it also turned them into something much worse: sexual deviants out to rape every white woman in sight. As with opium smoking in San Francisco fifty years earlier, the idea that a drug was being used to seduce white women was the final straw. Southern states banned cocaine, but illegality did not stymie its availability. The first cocaine dealers were newspaper boys and shoe-shiners offering a sniff of powder for ten cents or a day's supply in a pillbox for twenty-five cents. Cocaine prohibition created a black market that would grow exponentially around the time of Pablo Escobar.

These first drug laws were enacted at the local level. There were no federal laws. While local laws prohibited cocaine from the uncivilised races, the whites still devoured cocaine-based medicines. It was considered legitimate to take a drug if you were sick, but a no-no if you were feeling good. With cocaine tonics having been around for four decades, most addiction was medicine-based. By 1900, it was estimated that five percent of the American public was addicted to cocaine-based drugs. Hardest hit were middle-class white women living in rural areas.

While making grandiose advertising claims, patent-medicine manufacturers refused to label their ingredients, so men, women and children were unknowingly dosing themselves on cocaine. An article in *Collier's* magazine by Samuel Hopkins Adams caught the attention of Congress. It commenced with:

GULLIBLE America will spend this year some seventy-five millions of dollars in the purchase of patent medicines. In consideration of this sum it will swallow huge quantities of alcohol, an appalling amount of opiates and narcotics, a wide assortment of varied drugs ranging from powerful and dangerous heart depressants to insidious liver stimulants; and, in excess of all other ingredients, undiluted fraud. For fraud, exploited by the skilfulest of advertising bunco men, is the basis of the trade. Should the newspapers, the magazines and the medical journals refuse their pages to this class of advertisement, the patent medicine business in five years would be as scandalously historic as the South Sea Bubble, and the nation would be the richer not only in lives and money, but in drunkards and drug-fiends saved.

Adams' exposé included false advertising claims and stories of addiction, abuse and death caused by patent medicines. It motivated Congress to pass the 1906 Food and Drug Act, which required habit-forming medications to be labelled with the contents. It didn't ban drugs. Cocaine, heroin, morphine, opium and marijuana were legal and readily available. But it put most patent medicines out of business. Even Coca-Cola dropped the hard stuff, though it retained the name.

Research by Professor Paul Gootenberg revealed the more sinister role of corporate interests. Making cocaine illegal eliminated the competition for the two producers in America: Merck and Maywood. Before shipping to Coca-Cola, Maywood removed the cocaine from its coca to minimise the risk of Coca-Cola staining its wholesome image. Coca-Cola and Maywood kept the drug czar, Harry Anslinger – a racist who believed that marijuana and jazz music were the work of the devil – informed about events in Peru, where their plantations grew, and in return, he protected Coca-Cola by putting loopholes in international legislation that allowed Coca-Cola the right to import leaves. The wrath of Anslinger would come down on any potential competitors to Coca-Cola, who wanted to import leaves, guaranteeing Coca-Cola's monopoly. If the Peruvian government didn't keep its prices down, Anslinger threatened that Coca-Cola would take their business to Bolivia. Anslinger and Coca-Cola were always on the lookout for the results of any new studies on the coca plant. If it were declared safe, Anslinger would have difficulty maintaining his ban on importation, and the Coca-Cola monopoly would be eliminated by copycats. At the same time, Coca-Cola didn't want coca to be deemed too dangerous because minus its cocaine, it was still a main ingredient, which carried a constant risk of a scandal erupting. Outside of helping Coca-Cola, Peru was discouraged from producing coca, which, according to Gootenberg, boosted the black market, which fed the rise in demand for cocaine from the 1960s onwards. With no legal outlet for coca due to United Nations laws put forward by Anslinger, the Peruvian farmers exported coca paste to traffickers – Pablo Escobar's progenitors – or as Gootenberg put it, "There was a continual rise in cocaine production throughout Peru in the 1950s and 60s. The United States created the cocaine problem itself."

When the Harrison Narcotics Tax Act was proposed, southern legislators seized upon the opportunity to include cocaine. They backed up their demand with stories about black men murdering and raping entire families. Now not only did cocaine give black men superhuman strength, but it also improved their pistol aim. This federal law was passed in 1914. It included cocaine, opium, morphine and heroin. It required anyone handling those drugs – doctors, druggists, pharmacists, distributors, importers – to pay an annual tax, to keep strict records, and to prescribe it only "in the due course of medical treatment." Except for licensed handlers, possession of cocaine was illegal. Over-the-counter medicines were not allowed a scintilla of cocaine, bankrupting the producers of patent medicines who had survived the 1906 Food and Drug Act.

In 1919, the Supreme Court ruled that addiction was not a disease, preventing doctors from prescribing drugs for addicts, criminalising addicts and causing the closure of drug-maintenance clinics. By 1928, one-third of the federal prison population was made up of violators of the Harrison Act, including numerous doctors. To avoid prison, addicts switched from cocaine to drugs outside of the Harrison Act such as amphetamines, which, just like cocaine decades earlier, were being touted as completely safe wonder drugs. Methamphetamines were sold in patent medicines and nasal decongestants, recommended for heroin addiction, and disseminated to troops to improve their performance. The police and prohibitionists hailed the drop in cocaine use as a success, demanded even more severe punishments and cited the large number of addicts in prison as proof that drugs made people commit crimes; after all only criminals ended up in jail. With cocaine users scarce in the face of an expanding anti-drugs bureaucracy, the authorities moved onto potheads, where their focus remained for decades, which allowed Pablo to get cocaine into America unnoticed.

In the following decades, the most famous cocaine abuser was Adolf Hitler. After a failed assassination attempt, he was treated by Dr Erwin Giesing, who prescribed cocaine in ten percent solutions for Hitler's sore throat. After his throat was cured, Hitler demanded more cocaine from his reluctant doctor. Towards the end of the war, Hitler was receiving multiple injections a day of drug cocktails and popping pep tablets such as Pervitin, an early version of crystal meth. Unable to sleep on Pervitin, he took sedatives.

As Hitler intensified his evil treatment of the Jews, Freud escaped to London in 1938, but four of his sisters were killed in concentration camps. In September 1939, in agony with mouth cancer from smoking, Freud was given enough morphine to end his life. With his decision-making processes scrambled by drugs, Hitler shot himself in the head in 1945 to avoid capture by the Russians.

Making cocaine illegal created a black market that would remain small at first and wither during the Great Depression and World Wars, only to accelerate in the latter half of the century to generate enough mayhem to make the authors of the early drug laws squirm in their graves, including hundreds of thousands of murders in Colombia and Mexico as rival cartels fought for control. It was a market that would rain dollars down on exporters of coca paste in Peru and Bolivia and generate even bigger profits for their customers in Colombia such as Pablo.

Prior to 1973, Chile was a centre of cocaine production. Using Peruvian coca leaves and paste, refiners made cocaine in Chilean labs, which was shipped to wealthy US customers. The refiners often hired Colombian smugglers, which is how the Colombians learned the early routes.

As shown in *Narcos*, the good times for the Chilean producers ended abruptly due to regime change. As General Pinochet was a sworn enemy of Communism, the CIA backed his coup in 1973. Once in power, he had the army execute thousands of his own citizens, including traffickers. He shut down dozens of cocaine labs and arrested hundreds of people associated with trafficking. This wasn't to stop the cocaine business. It was a takeover.

Narcos left out that Pinochet and his son organised a production and distribution network, which supplied Europe and America. Pinochet had the army build a lab in Talagante, a rural town twenty-four miles from Santiago. Chemists mixed cocaine with other chemicals to make black cocaine, which could be smuggled more easily than the obvious white stuff – a trick that Pablo would employ. Pinochet earned millions from cocaine production.

In Colombia, three cities set about competing for cocaine business: Bogotá, Medellín and Cali. On November 22, 1975, a plane was busted in Cali with 600 kilos on board. This sparked a cocaine war. In one weekend, over forty people were murdered. But not in Cali. They'd died in the city dominating the cocaine business: Medellín. The authorities started to watch the slum neighbourhoods, where young people armed to the teeth hustled to stay alive and dreamt of raising themselves out of the barrio through fast cash from cocaine.

Pablo had started in the cocaine business a hundred years after the previous boom in American use, when it had been touted as a cure-all by pharmacists and was an original ingredient in Coca-Cola. The scourge of what followed – addiction, insanity, deaths – had long been forgotten. Cocaine was not a problem in America because it was consumed discreetly by the upper class. The rest of society was receptive to this cool new drug that they were told they couldn't get addicted to. Even the DEA issued a report that stated, "it is not physically addictive… and does not usually result in serious consequences, such as crime, hospital emergency room admissions or both." There was talk of decriminalising it. Pablo compared the illegality of cocaine to the prohibition of alcohol in America, from which the Kennedy family had prospered. Through the legalisation of cocaine, Pablo hoped that his business would be legitimised, and his story would become a legend similar to that of the Kennedys.

The black market in cocaine became so big that the US government viewed it as a threat to national security. Post-World War II, the priority of the US government was fighting Communism. Policymakers feared that Communist movements in South America would use cocaine proceeds to obtain arms, topple right-wing dictators favourable to US corporate interests and end up threatening to invade America. Rather than let that happen, the US government through the CIA encouraged right-wingers such as General Pinochet to use cocaine proceeds to arm themselves – with weapons manufactured in America, of course – against Communists, which often resulted in CIA-trained death squads assassinating student protesters, schoolteachers and labourers for the crime of demanding pay rises and better working conditions. Drug laws and the DEA were used to wipe out the cocaine competition, i.e. anyone not working with the CIA. When honest DEA agents tried to indict cocaine kingpins who were contributing to the US anti-Communism crusade, the CIA stepped in and blocked the indictments in the name of national security.

One DEA whistle-blower, deep undercover agent Mike Levine, was prevented from arresting the big fish so many times that he classified the CIA as the world's biggest Mafia. Mike and many other insiders discovered that the CIA-approved traffickers were sending their cocaine to America on planes provided by the CIA – the CIA even had two airlines for this purpose: Air America and Southern Air Transport. On the return journeys, these planes supplied arms to groups fighting Communism. While attempting to justify this trafficking in cocaine as an act of patriotism, big money was being made by pilots, politicians and weapons manufacturers. It also put the American government in the odd situation of simultaneously fighting a War on Drugs, while facilitating their importation.

The Mafia is all about money flowing to the top. If Mike Levine was correct about the CIA being the biggest Mafia, then lesser Mafias would have to pay the CIA to play. There is evidence to suggest that Pablo and his associates made such payments to the CIA. Milian Rodriguez, a money manager for the Medellín Cartel, testified that from 1982 to 1985, he funnelled nearly $10 million to Nicaraguan rebels through former CIA operative, Felix Rodriguez, a friend of George HW Bush. The Nicaraguan rebels were a pet project of the Reagan-Bush administration. After Congress cut funding off and banned the provision of arms to the Nicaraguan rebels, the Reagan-Bush administration continued to provide arms illegally through the CIA. Cocaine worth billions was imported on the return journeys, some of which sparked the crack epidemic – as exposed by the journalist Gary Webb, who was demonised and committed suicide by shooting himself in the head – twice.

When asked whether the CIA knew the source of the money, Milian Rodriguez said, "But the men who made the contact with me did. I was under indictment at the time. But a tremendous patriot like Felix Rodriguez, all of a sudden he finds his troops are running out of money, for food, for medicine, for supplies. I think for Felix it was something he did out of desperation. He was willing to get it from any source to continue his war... The cartel figured it was buying a little friendship. What the hell is ten million bucks? They thought they were going to buy some good will and take a little heat off of them... They figured [that] maybe the CIA or DEA will not screw around so much."

In return for paying off the CIA, numerous investigations into the Medellín Cartel were squashed in the early 1980s and Pablo had access to America weapons, including the MAC 10, much favoured by his hit men. With cocaine becoming the world's most profitable drug, the Medellín Cartel was able to generate annual sales in the billions. The CIA has a history of arming and putting people in power, only to wipe them out later on when it suits its interest. Pablo would be no exception.

CHAPTER 5
DEATH TO KIDNAPPERS

In Colombia, kidnapping was a business strategy. A trafficker owed money might kidnap the child or wife of his debtor. Sometimes family members or business associates were deposited with creditors as collateral. If a deal fell through, depending upon the rationality of the creditor, more time might be allowed for the transaction to be concluded and the collateral released, or the collateral might be killed to set an example to other debtors.

Kidnappers targeted a future founder of the Medellín Cartel, Carlos Lehder. With millions to spend, Lehder decided to invest in his Colombian hometown, Armenia, population 180,000 – where he was remembered as a lively young person willing to share his lunch with fellow high-school students. At first, he donated – by way of a German with blonde hair, who didn't speak any Spanish – a Piper Navajo plane to his community, but they didn't know what to do with it. Adorned with fancy jewellery, clothes, cars and friends, he swaggered around the town, opening businesses and making pronouncements. He triggered a bubble in real estate that tripled prices. He gathered a following of young fans and lovers, several of whom ended up pregnant. Hailing him as Don Carlos, teenagers copied his haircut: tousled with a centre parting. When asked about the source of his wealth, he replied, "I worked in restaurants in New York. Then I sold cars. Later I sold airplanes in the United States."

Lehder should have known better than to travel without his neo-Nazi friends. In November 1981, he got into a chauffeur-driven car and set off for a ranch twenty miles away, towards Cali. After eight miles, he spotted a car in the middle of the road with its hood up, the driver examining the engine. The chauffeur stopped, left his gun on the front seat and both men got out.

Two men with guns appeared, dragged the chauffeur away and deposited him at the side of the road. They tied Lehder's hands behind his back and threw him into the car. They dropped the hood and sped off.

Due to his knowledge of karate, Lehder convinced himself that he could escape. He wriggled his bound hands free, opened the door and dived out. After rolling down a grassy slope, he ended up in a park. While he sprinted away, bullets whizzed by him. Hit in the back, he fell, but managed to spring up again and run so far that the kidnappers quit.

Citizens were outraged by the assault on the German-Colombian investor. A hunt proceeded for the kidnappers. For two weeks, Lehder was convalescing in a clinic, with his entourage all over the place, hanging onto every update on his health.

His hit men tracked the kidnappers down to the April 19 Movement or the M-19, a 2,500-member guerrilla army engaged in a war with the Colombian army in the Valley of Cauca. Just a year earlier, Lehder had boasted to Jung about his alliance with these fellow revolutionaries.

In the 1980s, the M-19 was a popular political movement, but *Narcos* portrayed them as a clownish urban cell willing to do anything for Pablo. Sometimes the M-19 worked with the traffickers, other times they kidnapped them, depending upon whatever was more profitable. After all, the traffickers were wealthy and they couldn't run to the police. They were supposed to be easy targets.

On November 12, 1981, the M-19 snatched Martha Ochoa, the Ochoa brothers' youngest sister, from the campus of the University of Antioquia in Medellín, and demanded millions of dollars from the Ochoas. In response, Jorge Ochoa – seconded by Pablo – hosted a meeting, where he proposed the formation of an army, Muerta a Secuestradores, MAS, translated as Death to Kidnappers. Recovering from his gunshot wound, Lehder also played a key role in the meeting.

Also present was another co-founder of the Medellín Cartel,

Rodríguez Gacha a.k.a. the Mexican because of his love of mariachi music and all things Mexican. Due to his affection for wearing straw fedoras, his other name was Big Hat. Short stubby Gacha named his ranches after Mexican cities. He was born in a small town, Pacho, north of Bogotá, to a poor family of pig farmers. As a young man, he developed a lethal reputation as a hired killer. One of his early alliances was with a cocaine queen who had earned her status by murdering her competition. He rose up in the emerald business, which had an even more violent reputation than cocaine. Killing anyone who got in his way, Gacha pioneered trafficking routes through Mexico and into the US.

Gacha entered *Narcos* with a dramatic scene, whereby he gate-crashed a party and shot all of the guests, including one of his business partners. Although Gacha had sanctioned such a hit, he wasn't present when it had happened in 1989, a decade after its portrayal in *Narcos*. The hit had occurred in the mansion of Gacha's associate, Gilberto Molina, killing eighteen.

Two hundred and twenty-three businessmen based all over Colombia attended the meeting and approved Death to Kidnappers. They included traffickers, smugglers and pilots. Each donated two million pesos and ten hit men.

After the MAS meeting and the drafting of a communiqué, the participants attended a picnic at a ranch outside of Medellín, where they discovered that they had lots in common. Never before had they gathered like this to form public policy.

The relationships cemented that day gave birth to the Medellín Cartel, whose leaders were Pablo Escobar, the Ochoa brothers, Carlos Lehder and Gacha. The term Medellín Cartel came from American prosecutors looking to simplify their cases and obtain longer sentences. A Medellín lawyer, Gustavo Salazar, said that the cartels never existed. They were collections of traffickers who collaborated sometimes.

Copies of the MAS communiqué were loaded onto a plane, which flew towards a Cali soccer stadium on a Sunday afternoon, just prior to a match between Medellín and Cali. After the referee blew the starting whistle, leaflets descended from the sky onto the pitch. They described a general assembly, whose members would no longer tolerate kidnappings by guerrillas seeking to finance revolutions "through the sacrifices of people, who, like ourselves, have brought progress and employment to the country... The basic objective will be the public and immediate execution of all those involved in kidnappings, beginning from the date of this communiqué."

It offered twenty million pesos for information leading to the capture of a kidnapper and guaranteed immediate retribution. The guilty parties "will be hung from the trees in public parks or shot and marked with the sign of our group – MAS." Kidnappers in jail would be murdered. If that was impossible then "our retribution will fall on their comrades in jail and on their closest family members."

Pablo told a journalist, "If there was not an immediate and strong response, the M-19 were going to continue screwing our own families... We paid law enforcement eighty million pesos for the information they had at that moment and the next day, they began to fall. My soldiers took them to our secret houses, our secret ranches, and people from law enforcement went there and hung them up and began to bust them up."

With hit men roaming the countryside, many of the M-19 and anyone suspected of being involved in the kidnapping of Martha were murdered in the tradition of The Violence in which Pablo had grown up, including the Colombian Necktie and the Flower Vase Cut. Within six weeks, over one-hundred of the M-19 had been dealt with, putting the Colombian army to shame as they hadn't apprehended that many since the M-19 had started in 1974.

On December 30, 1981, a terrified woman was discovered chained to a steel gate, with a sign around her neck declaring that she was the wife of the M-19 boss who'd kidnapped Martha Ochoa. Her kidnapped daughter had been returned to relatives because the MAS Constitution prohibited harming innocent children.

On February 6, 1982, the MAS issued a statement about their patience wearing thin. On February 17, Martha Ochoa was released unharmed.

The MAS treated informants the same as kidnappers. According to Brian Freemantle in *The Fix*, the informant who told the DEA about the first MAS meeting didn't fare well. His hands were tied behind his back with barbed wire, and his tongue cut out before they killed him.

The success against the M-19 demonstrated what unity could achieve. The different groups started to see the benefits of not competing against each other. If they pooled their resources to ship cocaine to America, they'd all make more money. Independent operators put aside their differences and started cooperating in the manufacturing, distribution and marketing of cocaine, while continuing to run their own enterprises.

In future meetings, trafficking methods were streamlined. They offered government officials "plata o plomo" – silver or lead – meaning they could either accept a generous bribe or be killed. Their network had access to anyone in Colombia, so officials knew they couldn't avoid the death penalty. With the M-19 under control and the relevant officials accepting bribes, the cocaine business flourished out of Medellín. If the cartel leaders called a meeting, traffickers from across Colombia showed up. The American market was divided up between the Medellín and Cali Cartels. Cali had New York. Medellín had Miami. Los Angeles was split between the two.

As sending death squads in to fight Communism was a beloved strategy of the CIA, the creation of the MAS allied the interests of the traffickers with US foreign policy. After all, the M-19 ideology included revolutionary socialism and populism. In Puerto Boyacá, the MAS model was adopted by local Liberal and Conservative party leaders, businessmen, ranchers and representatives from the Texas Petroleum Company, with the goal of cleansing the region of subversives and anyone who opposed the MAS. They killed a council member, a politician, an activist and a doctor for being members of the progressive wing of the Liberal Party.

The MAS are commonly portrayed as a horde of hit men working for the traffickers, but a government investigation concluded in 1983 that out of 163 individuals found to have links to the MAS, 59 were active duty police and military officers, including the commanders of the Bárbula and Bomboná Battalions. The Americans provided key MAS members with support and training such as a course in Combined Strategic Intelligence in Washington, DC. They also provided arms. On American soil, politicians were obtaining votes by purporting to take a hard line against cocaine, while the US government supplied weapons to the MAS, a death squad allied to Pablo. As usual, these weapons ended up killing mostly civilians. In 1989, the Colombian president stated that the majority of the victims of paramilitaries such as the MAS were not guerrillas, but men, women and children who hadn't taken up arms against institutions.

In his hometown, Lehder bragged about his leadership role in the MAS and his contributions to the Liberal Party. He wanted to be a senator in order "to represent the kidnappables and extraditables of Colombia. I want to represent unions, and I want to represent the poorest of the poor." He drove around with an armed convoy of twenty-five ex-policemen. In private, Pablo started to refer to Lehder as Big Mouth. He disliked Lehder's cocaine habit and viewed Lehder's openness about their activity as a liability.

Inspired by Pablo's Hacienda Nápoles, Lehder set about constructing Posada Alemana, a giant convention centre nestled into green hills fifteen miles north of Armenia, with clubhouses, restaurants, discos, exotic-bird aviaries, beautiful gardens, gazebos and stucco bungalows with thatched roofs. By the entrance was a nude statue of John Lennon, holding a guitar, with a bullet hole in his chest and back, and a dedication: "To the Greatest Musician of the Century."

With the goal of getting rid of Colombia's extradition treaty with America, Lehder started the National Latin Movement Party, with green and white colours and its own brand of Hitler youth called Woodchoppers, consisting of young people toting clubs who policed his Saturday afternoon rallies. The podium included a twelve-foot poster of Lehder speaking. He claimed that Adolf Hitler – whom he referred to as Adolfo – had been misunderstood, and that international Zionism was the root of terrorism in Central America.

The Ochoas lived slightly lower key at La Loma, a hilltop property south of Medellín, where friendly pet ponies ate out of visitors' hands, and also at Hacienda Veracruz, where they bred horses and had their own zoo. They regularly attended horse shows, and Jorge collected vintage Harley Davidsons.

With business forever expanding, new methods of outsmarting the authorities were required. Massive cocaine labs were built in the most inaccessible parts of the jungle. They grew into towns with their own housing, schools, dining facilities and satellite TV. Houses on wheels were used to disguise jungle runways. Cocaine was shipped in refrigerators and TVs with hollow insides. Electrical industrial transformers weighing more than 8,000 pounds were gutted and filled with up to 4,000 kilos. A 23,000 kilo shipment was mixed with dried fish. European and American chemists blended cocaine into items made out of plastic, metals or liquid, and other chemists separated the cocaine out at the destination. Cocaine was mixed with fruit pulp, flowers, cocoa and wine. Liquid cocaine ended up in all kinds of drinks. It was soaked into lumber and clothes such as jeans. Cocaine was turned black and mixed into black paint. It was chemically blended into PVC, religious statues and the fibreglass shells of boats. All of these methods were tested by drug-sniffing dogs.

Pablo bought planes to transport cocaine and cash, including DC-3s – fixed-wing propeller-driven airliners. He decided to invest in submarines. As buying a sub would have attracted attention, he commissioned his brother to build two, with the help of Russian and English engineers. The manufacturing was done in a quiet shipyard. The subs carried around 1,000 kilos. Unable to come close to the shore, they were met by divers who loaded the cocaine onto boats.

By 1982, Pablo was making $500,000 a day, rising to $1 million a day by the mid-80s. Millions were buried underground, but each year ten percent was lost due to rats eating it and water damage. He paid people to live in houses and apartments with up to $5 million stored in the walls, protected by Styrofoam. Using wooden cases wrapped in Styrofoam, millions were stashed below swimming pools in storage chests. Accountants in ten separate offices kept track of the money, some of which was invested in property worldwide, famous paintings and antique cars. Never forgetting the poor, he continued to build houses, schools, hospitals and to give away truckloads of food. He paid for college tuition and built soccer fields.

Refrigerators containing $7 million intended for Colombia were accidentally shipped to Panama. The money disappeared. Pablo calmly responded that sometimes he won, sometimes he lost. A plane with $15 million crashed in the jungle and exploded, turning the money into a bonfire. Workers who lost drugs or cash were given more drugs to make up for the loss. If they messed up again, they were killed.

In Medellín, plenty of killers were available to Pablo, whose reputation for extreme violence enabled his business to grow. According to Gustavo de Grieff, a former Colombian Attorney General, Pablo had sanctioned the use of a hot spoon to remove victims' eyeballs while they were still alive. Another approved method was to drive a heated spike or nail into a victim's skull, which was fatal when it reached the brain. One victim was tied to a tree with barbed wire, given a phone to explain his situation to his family, and tortured to death while they listened.

CHAPTER 6
LARA BONILLA

Hoping to achieve his childhood dream of becoming the president, Pablo ran for political office. While vowing to help the poor, he aimed to gain exemption from laws that would have allowed him to be extradited to America.

With so many of them on his payroll, Pablo was no stranger to politicians. Cartel members competed to own the most powerful ones, just like they outdid each other with luxury cars, homes and zoos. Politicians were approached by cartel lawyers with brown envelopes full of cash. If they declined the bribe, they'd receive a call asking if they'd prefer to be killed. With so many of their colleagues taking money, and the cocaine business bringing so much prosperity to Colombia, it was easy to say yes. Many of them felt that cocaine was America's problem because that was where it was mostly consumed. If they didn't want it, Colombia wouldn't produce it. Due to America's history in Central and South America – supporting right-wing death squads, assassinating democratically elected left-wing leaders, a blood-lust for foreign resources – the US was viewed dimly by many Colombians. Some saw cocaine as the lesser-developed world's atomic bomb against the US, and believed that imperialism would be destroyed from within by its own excesses.

Having created a power base for himself in the barrios of Medellín, Pablo was elected as an alternate to Congress in March 1982, which rendered him immune from prosecution under Colombian law.

Giving speeches as a politician, Pablo wore chino trousers, polo shirts and a gold Rolex. He spoke politely and softly at the openings of soccer pitches, roller-skating rinks, hospitals and schools he had invested in. He started a radio show, *Civics on the March*, and a program called *Medellín Without Slums*. One project, Barrio Pablo Escobar, consisted of five hundred two-bedroomed houses built over a garbage dump, complete with truckloads of free food. It was in north Medellín, a tough area where Pablo was extremely popular – a recruiting ground for young hit men and enforcers. While Pablo did the rounds, he was accompanied by two Catholic priests who were board members of *Medellín Without Slums*. The priests introduced him at public events, accompanied him in the slums and blessed a charity art auction he hosted at the Intercontinental Hotel, which was called Paintbrush of Stars.

Pablo hired publicists and journalists to boost his man-of-the-poor image. A column in his own newspaper, *Medellín Cívico*, lavished him with praise: "Yes, I remember him… his hands, almost priest-like, growing parabolas of friendship and generosity in the air. Yes, I know him, his eyes weeping because there is not enough bread for all of the nation's dinner tables. I have watched his tortured feelings when he sees street children – angels without toys, without a present, without a future."

In April 1983, a popular magazine, *Semana*, branded Pablo as "A Paisa Robin Hood." Pablo told *Semana*, "When I was sixteen, I owned a bicycle-rental business… then I started buying and selling automobiles, and finally I got involved in real estate… I didn't have any money, but as a community action member in my barrio, I promoted the construction of a school and the creation of a fund for indigent students."

The same month that Pablo was elected, March 1982, a new president came to power. His main goals included making peace with the guerrillas and improving housing and education. Drugs seemed to be off his agenda. With the majority of politicians taking donations from the traffickers, why ruffle any feathers? Besides, many previous presidents had taken drug money. Those who hadn't didn't stay in office for long. When the president announced that he was philosophically opposed to the extradition of Colombian nationals, the traffickers were delighted as they all dreaded the prospect of serving life sentences in America.

But the Reagan-Bush administration had other ideas. In 1982, Reagan announced, "My very reason for being here this afternoon is not to announce another short-term government offensive, but to call instead for a national crusade against drugs, a sustained relentless effort to rid America of this scourge by mobilizing every segment of our society against drug abuse."

Ramping up the War on Drugs, the Reagan-Bush administration tried to link the FARC guerrillas with marijuana trafficking, hoping to stir up war by labelling the 5,000-strong pro-Communist army as narco-guerrillas. The Colombians saw through the propaganda. The new Colombian president was upset because the outside interference had disturbed the peace negotiations with the guerrillas. The Americans changed their strategy. The Reagan-Bush administration had their emissaries search for a Colombian politician amenable to their goals. They settled on Rodrigo Lara Bonilla.

After studying law at the Externado University of Colombia, Lara was elected as the mayor of his hometown at age twenty-three. In August 1983, Lara – a member of the New Liberalism Party that he'd helped to create – became the minister of justice. His campaign against corruption upset his bribe-dependent contemporaries and attracted the interest of the DEA in Colombia, who egged him on to go after the traffickers by offering help and support.

On August 16, 1983, Pablo and his bodyguards arrived for the first time at Congress, which was packed with spectators, reporters and photographers. Even the hallways were crowded with people abuzz about a confrontation brewing between Lara and the traffickers. Dressed in a cream suit, Pablo was stopped at the door for not wearing a tie. Someone handed him one with a floral design, and he was allowed inside. People watched closely as he sat near the back. The house president requested the removal of his bodyguards. Pablo gave a nod and they left.

Pablo's ally, Jairo Ortega, started to address allegations of taking hot money from the traffickers. He asked Lara if he knew Evaristo Porras Ardila.

"No," Lara said, shaking his head.

Ortega said that Evaristo Porras – a resident of the Amazon border town of Leticia – had been incarcerated in Peru for trafficking drugs. In April, Porras had written a cheque for one million pesos to Lara as a campaign contribution. Holding up the cheque, he showed it to the ministers present for the debate. Copies of the cheque had been circulated. He added that Lara had thanked Porras for the cheque in a phone call. Ortega produced a tape recorder and played an unintelligible conversation.

"Let the Congress analyse the minister's conduct with this person who offered him a million pesos. Mr Porras is a recognised international drug trafficker, according to Peruvian police. But far be it from me to try to detain the minister of justice's brilliant political career. I only want him to tell us what kind of morality he is going to require of the rest of us. Relax, Minister. Just let the country know that your morality can't be any different from that of Jairo Ortega and the rest of us."

Cheering erupted in the gallery from Carlos Lehder, which others tried to hush. Sat quietly in a swivel leather chair, Pablo watched, while occasionally picking his teeth or forcing an uncomfortable smile.

Thirty-five-year-old Lara stood to respond in a business suit and tie, his thick dark hair swept aside, his charming face clean shaved. Not in the habit of scrutinising the origin of incoming donations, he'd never heard of Mr Porras, nor could he recall any such telephone conversation.

"My life is an open book." Lara said that he was and always had been blameless, rendering him impervious to his enemies' claims. He would resign any moment that suspicion fell upon him "knowing that I will not be followed by complacent ministers affected by the blackmail and the extortion being perpetrated against Colombia's political class." He damned the act of casting suspicion on the alleged recipients of the money as opposed to the senders of it, including "those, who, yes, have to explain here or anywhere else in this country where their fortunes have come from... Morality is one thing, but there are levels: one thing is the cheques... that they use to throw mud at politicians. But it's another thing when somebody runs a campaign exclusively with these funds." Lara pointed an accusatory finger.

"[We have] a congressman [Pablo] who was born in a very poor area, himself very, very poor, and afterwards, through astute business deals in bicycles and other things, appears with a gigantic fortune, with nine planes, three hangars at the Medellín airport, and creates the movement Death to Kidnappers, while on the other hand, he creates charitable organisations with which he tries to bribe a needy and unprotected people. And there are investigations going on in the US, of which I cannot inform you here tonight in the House, on the criminal conduct of Mr Ortega's alternate."

Some of the respondents defended Pablo. They said that all of them were guilty of receiving tainted contributions. Pablo had been attacked, so that Lara might gain political capital.

"It was only when Representative Escobar joined our movement that all kinds of suspicion were thrown on the sources of his wealth," a congressman said. "I, as a politician, lack the ability to investigate the origin of any assets... Representative Escobar has no need to rely on others to defend his personal conduct, which, on the other hand, and as far as I know, has not been subjected to any action by the law or the government."

Simmering with anger, Pablo didn't respond. Re-joining his bodyguards, he left the chamber and walked into a swarm of reporters, whom he tried to dodge.

The next day, Lara received notification that he had a day to back up his claims with evidence, or else be sued. While Lara set about gathering evidence, he issued statements criticising drug-trafficking, which necessitated "a frontal fight, clear, open, without fear or retreat, running all the necessary risks." He classified the allegations of the cheque he'd received from Porras as a smokescreen. "My accusers could not forgive the clarity of my denunciation of Pablo Escobar, who through clever business deals has manufactured an enormous fortune… This is an economic power concentrated in a few hands and in criminal minds. What they cannot obtain by blackmail, they get by murder."

The media contacted Porras, who acknowledged donating a million pesos to Lara and admitted that he had been indicted by the Peruvian police for trafficking, which he put down to a youthful indiscretion. Working in the coca-leaf business for Pablo, Porras claimed that his wealth had originated from winning the lottery three times. Faced with Porras' testimony, Lara admitted receiving the cheque, which he said had been for a family debt. At Pablo's behest, a judge initiated an investigation into the cheque, which went nowhere.

Lara received help from a newspaper, *El Espectador*, which ran a story about Pablo's arrest for cocaine in 1976, including mugshots of Pablo and Gustavo. Pablo ordered his men to buy every copy of the newspaper, which only increased sales and encouraged the newspaper to publish daily stories about him. It described how he'd played the system by having his case transferred to various courts and judges, and how all of his criminal records had disappeared. The exposure led to an investigation into the murders of the policemen who'd arrested him. A new arrest warrant was issued for Pablo, but the judge who'd granted it was murdered in his car.

Lara obtained a recording of a DEA-assisted ABC News documentary about Colombia's biggest traffickers, including Pablo – who they claimed was worth $2 billion – and played it in Congress. While casting Lara a death stare, Pablo demanded proof of the allegations.

Rebutting Lara's accusations in an interview, Pablo said his money came from construction. While denying that he was a trafficker, he extolled the benefits that trafficking had brought Colombia such as creating jobs and providing capital for numerous projects that had contributed to economic growth. Insisting that the allegations of trafficking were untrue, Pablo showed a visa he'd recently obtained from the US embassy. Within days, the embassy cancelled the visa. Pablo lambasted Lara for becoming an instrument of US foreign policy.

Lara held his ground. He exposed how the traffickers had financed Colombia's main soccer teams. He tried to cancel the licenses for 300 small planes they owned. He attempted to confiscate Pablo's zoo animals and named thirty politicians he believed had taken drug money.

On September 2, 1983, an arrest warrant for Carlos Lehder was issued after the Supreme Court ruled in favour of America. Having already disappeared, Lehder claimed he'd seen it coming, "because my friends in the Ministry of Justice alerted me regarding Lara Bonilla's intentions." He told reporters that the only way he would be extradited was over his dead body.

On September 10, Pablo was asked by a senator to quit politics, give up his parliamentary immunity and answer the charges against him. On September 11, Pablo refused, stating that he'd entered politics because, "only inside the government could a man best serve the community."

Within two weeks, a judge issued an arrest warrant for Pablo for conspiracy to murder the DAS agents who'd arrested him in 1976. Two had been executed in 1977. In 1981, hit men on motorbikes had assassinated the officer in charge.

In October, the Supreme Court ruled in favour of the extradition of two marijuana traffickers. Lara signed off on it, but the president refused to do so. He referred it to the Colombian courts. Lehder's extradition order remained unsigned.

Lara demanded that Congress remove Pablo's immunity from extradition. The newspapers reported Pablo's 1974 car-theft indictment, while championing Lara. The biggest newspaper asked, "How is democracy going to continue in Colombia if it is managed and manipulated by these criminals?"

On November 17, 1983, Pablo was fined 450,000 pesos for the illegal importation of eighty-five animals, including camels, elephants, elk and a large Amazonian rodent called a capybara.

The evidence against Pablo was so overwhelming that there was nothing he could do to salvage his political career. He was forced out of the Columbian Liberal Party. He quit Congress in January 1984 and issued a statement: "The attitude of politicians is very far from the people's opinions and aspirations."

His presidential plan had backfired so badly that the media was exposing his cocaine business and the police were trying to muscle in on it. Fighting back in the courts, he managed to get his extradition warrant withdrawn on February 13, 1984.

After a politician pushing for Pablo's extradition was murdered, Lara made an announcement that upset the traffickers: "The more I learn, the more I know of the damage that the *narcos* are causing this country. I will never again refuse the extradition of one of these dogs. So long as Colombian judges fear drug traffickers, the *narcos* will only fear judges in the US."

Lara suspected that Pablo's guys were shadowing him. When he answered his phone, his own conversations were played back. He rebuffed offers of large sums of money. Death threats against him increased.

He hit back by busting cocaine labs across the country. With the help of the DEA, the Colombian authorities located a giant jungle lab called the Land of Tranquillity, which was mostly owned by the cartel leader, Gacha. Over two years, it had produced cocaine worth $12 billion. Almost 200 people lived there. The authorities knew about it, but had been reluctant or unable to find it, lying some 250 miles from the nearest road.

The DEA had discovered that a Colombian working for Pablo was trying to make a $400,000 purchase of ether, an ingredient in the traditional method for processing coca paste to coca-hydrochloride. The two sellers recommended to him were undercover agents. Before the first seventy-six barrels of ether left for Colombia, DEA technicians cut two open and concealed battery-powered transponders inside. Pablo had no idea that when the ether left the plant it could be traced all the way to Colombia.

Signals from the transponders were picked up by a spy satellite as the ether moved south through New Orleans and Panama to Colombia. The signals indicated a spot near the Yari River, deep in the densest part of the jungle, where Gacha and his partners had built the Land of Tranquillity.

Tipped off by the DEA, the anti-narcotics unit of the Colombian National Police was on standby to raid the location with a lone DEA agent. Out of fear that Pablo would receive inside information about the raid, the men in green military garb didn't know the nature of the operation until they were airborne.

On March 10, 1984, helicopters took off from Bogotá at 6 am. An hour later, they started monitoring the transceiver, homing in on the tones. By noon, they were skimming jungle treetops and almost out of fuel when they spotted an airstrip and smoke rising from the trees. The helicopter attempted to land, with a second helicopter giving it cover. Armed with submachine guns, the troops getting off the first helicopter came under sniper fire. After the shooting stopped, they were attacked by tiny gnats and mosquitoes.

Putting up no resistance, dozens of impoverished workers waited to be arrested. Some fled into the jungle. The troops found a giant jungle complex of nineteen labs and eight airstrips. Worried about retaliation, they called for immediate reinforcements. The next day, they filmed more airstrips and labs. It was the biggest cocaine manufacturing plant in world history.

Colombia's head of anti-narcotics, Colonel Ramirez – an early nemesis of Pablo – arrived. Feisty and proud of his country, he was clean shaved with a square solid face and thick lips. Men from Medellín showed up at his brother's house with a message for the colonel: if he would cease all operations in the Land of Tranquillity area and withdraw his forces, he'd receive a multi-million-dollar payment.

Colonel Ramirez responded by ordering gallons of ether to be thrown into each room, many of which contained chemical barrels. When the soldiers lit the ether, it exploded, almost setting them on fire and burning the trees. Multiple explosions through-out the Land of Tranquillity sent thick black plumes up through the jungle trees and into the sky.

The cartel lost 12,000 drums of chemicals and all of the cocaine that was being processed. The colonel's integrity endangered his family. His kids guarded their house with submachine guns.

Paperwork found at the site – waybills, receipts and accounts – helped the authorities piece together information about the cartel. It revealed that the biggest players were combining their raw materials. Some of the evidence alerted them to Gacha's importance. Prior to the raid, the authorities had believed that Gacha worked under Pablo. On a jungle airstrip, they found a crashed plane registered to Gacha's brother. Sources told them that out of all of the investors in the Land of Tranquillity, Gacha had suffered the biggest loss, from which they inferred that Gacha was a senior partner.

Pablo issued a statement to the US ambassador denying any role in the Land of Tranquillity: "I can only characterise your statements as tendentious, irresponsible and malintentioned without any basis in reality; they denigrate the good faith of public opinion. My conscience is clear." He accused Lara of being "the representative of your government in the Colombian cabinet."

After the raid on the Land of Tranquillity, the Medellín Cartel decided that it was time for Lara to go. The $500,000 contract went to Los Quesitos, a gang controlled by Pablo. Three of the gang's field commanders took a green Renault, loaded with guns, grenades and bullet-proof vests from Medellín to Bogotá. After settling into a four-star hotel, they discussed the hit over food in the company of the Snore, a Medellín hitman with lots of kills under his belt who was ready to serve as backup if the others failed. The hit would be performed on a motorbike, with Iván, a thirty-one-year-old drifter, as the shooter. Iván had a history of murder, robbery and assault. The driver would be a teenager called Byron, who was looking to earn a reputation among the big boys. Teenagers like these – poor and with nothing to lose – were easily recruited to perform hits. Unemployed or working jobs that paid $1 a week, they could earn thousands for each murder. For several days, the team waited, made calls back to Medellín and dined out.

The US emissaries encouraging Lara to extradite Pablo showed up with a bullet-proof vest. "You should be more concerned. You should take more precautions." Lara declined the vest, but they left it with him.

Aware of the threat, not just to him but to his wife and three little children, Lara beefed up security. "I am a dangerous minister for those who act outside the law," Lara said. "I only hope that they don't take me by surprise." Despite the tough talk, Lara called the US embassy and excitedly revealed that he was getting transferred out of the country to work as the ambassador to Czechoslovakia.

"You'll be safe there," the US Ambassador said. "All the terrorists are in the government."

As the transfer would take thirty days, Lara said he needed a place for him and his family to hide at because he felt that the Colombian government couldn't protect him anymore. The US embassy offered to put him in a Texas safe house owned by a rich businessman for as long as he needed it.

On April 30, 1984, Lara thanked a journalist friend for publishing an article about his work. "I am going to be killed today, but that article can be my will for the Justice Department." After playing his friend some samples of the fifty death threats that he'd received that morning, Lara said, "If I don't answer this phone, it will be because I am dead."

In the afternoon, Iván and Byron visited the shrine of Santa María Auxiliadora, near Medellín, to say a prayer. For good luck, Byron put a picture of the Virgin Mary into his underwear. At 7 pm, they got on a Yamaha motorbike and headed to Bogotá, armed with grenades and a MAC-10.

Sat on a back seat, Lara was stuck in traffic with his bullet-proof vest next to him.

Iván and Byron stopped at an address they'd been given earlier that day. They were told people were talking about them in

Medellín, which was code for "Find Lara and kill him." On the hunt for a white Mercedes-Benz limo, they found the roads still jammed. It was around dusk when they spotted Lara. Weaving around cars, they homed in from the rear and slowed down.

After extracting the MAC-10 from his jacket, Iván took aim at the figure in the back of the limo. Within seconds, the MAC-10 emptied its magazine, shattering the rear window, hitting Lara fatally seven times in the head, chest, arm and neck. Lara's escort limo pursued the assailants. A bullet hit the Yamaha's gas tank, setting it on fire. The motorbike crashed into a curb. Machine-gun fire exploded Iván's head. Next to the Yamaha, he dropped dead. Hit in the arm, Byron was arrested.

The president and his cabinet stayed up until 3 am, discussing what to do. No cabinet minister had ever been assassinated in Colombia. Perhaps cocaine wasn't just an American problem after all. Trafficking was ruining Colombia's reputation in the eyes of the world. With the justice minister gone, it would appear that the president had lost control of the country. Lara's death swung them in favour of extradition. In an emergency radio broadcast, the president declared war on the traffickers and said that drugs were "the most serious problem that Colombia has had in its history."

In the Rotunda of the Capitol Building, thousands visited Lara's closed coffin, which military guards took to the National Cathedral. Outside, mourners from all sections of society were crying and chanting that they loved Lara. In the cathedral, emotions ran high. Amid the top brass from the military and the government, the president appeared tense.

A plane transported Lara to his home city, where he was buried. At the funeral, the president said, "We have reached a point where we must reflect on what is our nation. What does the word citizen mean? Stop! Enemies of humanity! Colombia will hand over criminals wanted in other countries, so that they may be punished as an example." His eulogy received a standing ovation.

On May 8, 1984, the president signed an extradition order for Carlos Lehder. Traffickers would be tried in military courts and denied access to bail. Prison sentences would be increased, with limited possibility of parole. Suspected traffickers would have their gun permits cancelled.

Immediately, hundreds were arrested and jailed, including the Ochoa brothers' father, Fabio Sr. Property was seized. Helicopters landed at Hacienda Nápoles. With rifles and search dogs, troops in green battle fatigues stormed inside, provoking raucous cawing from Pablo's exotic birds. Seizing weapons and evidence, the troops trashed the property and handcuffed low-level workers, whom they lined up by a swimming pool. After the raid, they left the zoo animals to starve. Upon receiving complaints about the animals, the government reopened the zoo.

With Lehder on the run in the jungle, his property deteriorated. Lacking an expensive diet of fresh horsemeat, his tigers withered. The Humane Society stepped in. As the property crumbled from fire and rain damage, only one thing survived: the naked statue of John Lennon.

In response, the traffickers declared war on Colombia. All-out mayhem ensued: bombings, kidnappings, mass murders and death squads. The judge investigating Lara's death was killed.

Hoping to weaken the cartel, the authorities targeted Lehder, as his extradition treaty had been signed. If they arrested him, they could swiftly send him to his fate in America. On his trail, they missed him by four days, a hundred miles south-east of Bogotá. But this raised their hopes. Moving around with twenty-three aliases and three passports, including a German one, Lehder was unfazed. He called radio stations to rant and penned open letters, criticising American imperialism. Raiding a possible Lehder hideout in November 1984, the police found 230 kilos of cocaine. Sources gave more information about his whereabouts, but he remained elusive.

In February 1985, Lehder authorised a Spanish TV crew to interview him at a hideout. In army fatigues, a black vest and sporting a beard, he announced the formation of a 500,000-man army to defend national sovereignty. "The extradition problem has grown to become a problem of national liberation. It was the people who shot Lara Bonilla before he could – with imperialism's help – send more than 300 Colombians en masse to be processed in the US." When asked whether it was wise to find inspiration in Hitler – who'd killed six million Jews – he replied, "That is misinformation. We know that there were never more than one million Jews in Germany. Half of the blood running through my body is German, right? In other words, if there is someone who can talk about Germany, it is not the Jew, it is the German! If one can talk about Colombia, it is the Colombian. It shall not be a Brazilian or a Czechoslovakian. Am I right?

"I say with all honesty that Adolfo, along with six million soldiers, eliminated twenty-one million Communists, right? And he eliminated ten million Allied enemies. In other words, he, Adolfo, is and shall be – right? – until someone surpasses him, he shall be the greatest warrior the world has ever seen." Despite his ramblings, his eyes were open to the aims of the US, which he described as being "guided by a military industry that forces the US to open fronts of war and fronts for the sale of arms, and one of the newest and most novel excuses [to open such fronts] is the struggle against drug trafficking."

US weapons-manufacturer profiteering was even worse than Lehder had described. Not only were they profiting from fighting traffickers, but through the CIA, they were accepting drug money as one of the biggest forms of payment for arms. In public, the US government was raising Pablo up the charts of enemy status in the War on Drugs, while in secret, the CIA was facilitating cocaine smuggling to finance a war in Nicaragua, cocaine that was flooding America. General Pinochet wasn't the only one fighting a War on Drugs so that he could profit from it personally. It had corrupted governments all over the world. Such covert activity needed constant smokescreens, and a mass murderer such as Pablo was ideal. In the US media, his crimes allowed him to become the personification of the cocaine scourge, but journalists rarely mentioned that his empire existed because of a black market in cocaine worth billions that had been created by US drug laws; or that his weapons came from America. It was a no-lose situation for the Reagan-Bush administration. Even though they knew from America's earlier experiences with the prohibition of alcohol that taking down Pablo wouldn't alter the flow of drugs, fighting traffickers not only justified the military expenditure Lehder ranted about, but it enabled the US to extend its influence into Colombia, a country whose oil and other resources US corporations and bankers, perched like vultures, were eager to plunder.

CHAPTER 7
BARRY SEAL

For a while, Pablo hid out in the jungle, until the Ochoa brothers, Lehder and Gacha fled to Panama to live in a large house by a golf club under the protection of Manuel Noriega, a military dictator and CIA informant whose hospitality had cost them millions. With a down payment of $2 million, Pablo had authorised the deal a few months before Noriega had come to power.

Known as Pineapple Face due to his pockmarks, Noriega had ended up ruling Panama by having a bomb – provided by the CIA – planted in the plane of his predecessor, whose leftist stance – he had believed in democracy and the rights of poor people – whiffed of Communism. A master of playing every side, Noriega had profitable relationships with the CIA and the Colombian traffickers, who were working together in the fight against Communism by supporting the Nicaraguan rebels. In an expectation of CIA protection, the cartel had contributed to the Nicaraguan cause. For America, Noriega provided security for the Panama Canal, with its American bases housing over 10,000 military personnel. His contributions to America's anti-Communism crusade included money laundering and hosting guns-for-drugs flights for the Nicaraguan rebels.

In 1982, Pablo had set up a deal with Noriega, whereby Panama was used as a trans-shipment point for cocaine heading to America, with Noriega collecting six-figure fees per load. Noriega also collected fees on the billions that the drug cartels – and intelligence agencies such as the CIA – laundered through Panama. It is alleged that Jeb Bush tapped into some of this hot money by establishing banking relationships between the CIA and the Medellín and Cali Cartels. Working in Venezuela for his

CIA director father, Jeb supposedly disguised the drug money as oil industry revenues from front companies such as Texas Commerce Bank, a cartel favourite.

Protected by bodyguards assigned by Noriega, the cartel leaders entertained themselves by playing soccer on the golf course, working out at the gym and swimming. Eventually, they rented their own homes. It was around this time in Panama that Pablo and Jorge Ochoa had discussions with Barry Seal, who'd flown cocaine worth billions into America. Even though they'd never met face-to-face, Barry was considered highly reliable. From Baton Rouge, Louisiana, Barry was an overweight ace pilot with flamboyant mutton-chop sideburns, who was addicted to living on the edge. The Colombians called him the Fat Man.

Pablo recruited Barry to fly 600 kilos to America, but the drugs were seized by the DEA in Florida. Unbeknown to Pablo, Barry was a CIA pilot and DEA informant, operating under a fake name: Ellis MacKenzie. Barry had been sent on a mission by George HW Bush, who wanted to trick Pablo into doing a cocaine deal with the Communist Nicaraguan government, which Bush hoped to use as an excuse to continue to arm the Nicaraguan rebels and stir up a war from which his associates were profiting.

Even though the Medellín Cartel had contributed to the Nicaraguan rebels, its members had become far more useful to Bush as enemies to justify his War on Drugs, which was about military expenditure, advancing corporate interests overseas and providing cover for CIA drug-trafficking, which was Barry Seal's main occupation (as detailed in my book, *American Made: Who Killed Barry Seal? Pablo Escobar or George HW Bush*). Barry was portrayed in *Narcos* as a former CIA pilot turned drug smuggler, which is false. The DEA, on the other hand, had a different objective for the cartel leaders: they wanted Barry to entice them onto US soil, so that they could be arrested and incarcerated for life.

To Panama, Barry brought Pablo large amounts of cash, daily reports from one of Pablo's business administrators in Florida and items from a list of goods Pablo wanted purchased in America. Pablo asked Barry to fly 1,500 kilos of cocaine, but Barry said that he needed to inspect the airstrip in Nicaragua first.

Pablo told Barry that the cartel hadn't ordered the assassination of the justice minister, Lara Bonilla. He claimed that it was a CIA plot designed to make the Colombian government want to extradite traffickers. He said that their cocaine labs had been dismantled and cocaine supplies moved to the mountains. He urged Barry to transport the 1,500 kilos as soon as possible. They would instruct him from their new headquarters in Panama.

On May 20, 1984, Barry met the cartel again in Panama, in the basement of a white stucco house. Barry later told his DEA handlers – whom he was trying to impress – that the cartel introduced him to Federico Vaughan, a Nicaraguan government official. With slicked-back grey hair, Vaughan was sharply dressed in a silver business suit, tie, an expensive watch, sunglasses and cufflinks. Vaughan would accompany Barry to the Nicaraguan airfield, so he could inspect it. To avoid any harm in Nicaragua, Barry was to follow Vaughan's instructions. Vaughan introduced himself to Barry as the interior minister of the Nicaraguan Sandinista government, which was ready to process cocaine paste for the Medellín Cartel with ether from Germany.

Barry, his Honduran co-pilot and Vaughan took a commercial plane to Managua, Nicaragua, sitting separately, so as not to be associated with each other. At the airport, Vaughan got them through immigration without having their passports stamped. Vaughan's wife transported them to their house, where they stayed overnight.

Driving to the airfield the next day, Vaughan told them not to be worried about the guards and checkpoints, which were a mere formality. Five miles outside of Managua in a rural setting, they stopped at a large oil refinery.

"This is the country's only refinery. Never fly near or over it." Vaughan pointed at anti-aircraft batteries on the perimeter. "Any aircraft that flies over the refinery, friend or foe, will be shot down immediately." He took them to a massive sunken lake, a volcanic crater full of clear blue water. "This is the purest water in the country. The only unpolluted drinking water for Managua. In its own way, it's as vital as the oil refinery. If you fly near it, you will be shot down."

They travelled around a mountain, across a railroad track and onto a military airfield called Los Brasiles, with a lone paved runway. At roadblocks and checkpoints, Vaughan was waved through by guards wielding AK-47s. He took them to a hangar designated for their mission. Inside was a Piper Cheyenne owned by Pablo.

Barry asked about the length of the airstrip and its foundation and texture. Vaughan escorted them along the 3,500-foot runway.

When Barry and his co-pilot walked onto the grass to examine a drainage ditch, Vaughan yelled, "Stop! It's mined with landmines. If you have any problem landing your aircraft, don't veer to the western side, or you'll be killed."

Afterwards, they ate at a steakhouse. Vaughan produced a map of Nicaragua and drew arrows to indicate the smuggling mission's entry and exit routes. "You need a code for entering Nicaraguan airspace. You are to call the Sandino tower on a certain VHF frequency and identify yourselves as Yankee November Whisky X-ray Yankee. Then the tower will reroute you to Los Brasiles. All approaches to the city of Managua are covered by anti-aircraft guns to protect against night attacks by the Contra rebels."

On the map, Barry drew circles around the gun emplacements, the oil refinery, Vaughan's house and the Sandinista People's Army headquarters.

Back in Panama City, Barry told Pablo that the runway was ideal, but the hangar was too small for the plane he had in mind. Pablo said that Barry's mission had changed. Instead of picking up a second shipment in Nicaragua of 2,000 kilos, Barry needed to go to Bolivia for 6,000 kilos of cocaine base for their new labs in Nicaragua.

After returning to America, Barry showed up for a routine

court appearance and ended up in jail. The DEA got him out, eager for him to set up a sting operation on Pablo and the other members of the cartel.

Fresh out of jail, Barry immediately called his Honduran co-pilot, who asked where Barry had been. Barry said he'd been busy. With the 1,500 kilos scheduled to be transported the next day, they had no time to waste.

Paranoid after free-basing cocaine, the co-pilot was convinced that his wife had become a government informant. "She was busted for coke while we were in Panama, but when I got home, she'd been released. She'd come with me on trips to Panama. She may have talked. Unless she comes with us, I'm not going. I need to keep an eye on her."

Barry tried to talk him out of bringing his wife, but it was no use. For two days in Louisiana, Barry waited for the co-pilot, who kept promising to get on the next flight, but never showed up. In the end, Barry asked his trusted friend, Emile Camp, to step in.

On May 28, 1984, they flew a Learstar from Arkansas to Medellín over the Colombian jungle.

"That strip looks mighty wet!" Barry yelled.

"So," Emile said. "You gonna try it?"

"I didn't fly all this way to turn around."

"That mountain's awful close, and that river's pretty high. Do not enter that banana grove. It'll take the wings off. That grass is too wet. You're gonna pay hell getting out of there, I'll tell you that."

"Anything else?" Barry asked.

"It's a piece of cake."

With its propellers roaring, the plane swerved to land. Water and mud splashed off the wheels as it skidded on the landing strip.

Barry was talking to the ground crew when a long-haired man galloped towards the plane on a white Arabian stallion, brandishing a machine gun and barking orders.

"Who the hell are you?" Barry asked.

"Carlos Lehder!" he yelled. Barry had heard stories about Lehder and Norman's Cay. "Now you will do what I say! Immediately! Before someone sees your plane from the air!"

A tractor appeared, pulling over a ton of cocaine.

"Holy shit!" Emile said. "They expect us to fly out of this swamp with all of that shit."

"No, of course not," Barry said.

"We can't get up with that much weight."

"Don't you worry. I'm gonna reason with the man." Barry laughed. "Hey, lifting off this muddy strip with all of that weight is impossible."

Barry's attempt at reasoning ended up with him pinned against the tractor and Lehder shoving a gun in his chin. "I don't care what you say. You'll fly every last gram of it out of here, just like you contracted to do. And if you refuse, I'll kill you right now, and your co-pilot will do it. We're going to load this plane and you're going to get out of here. You start loading fuel."

With a defeated expression, Barry complied. In fifteen minutes, 1,500 kilos of cocaine in duffel bags and burlap sacks were loaded.

Barry manned the plane. "You ready?"

"No," Emile said.

"I knew I could count on you."

As it picked up speed on the muddy runway, the plane rumbled and bounced, but failed to gain height.

"C'mon, baby," Emile said.

Lehder gallop alongside, shooting into the earth, his workers lined up at the periphery of the jungle, yelling for the plane to rise. It lifted to cheering, but fell and skidded. The right wheel sank into the mud and was ripped from its undercarriage. Barry lost control. The plane crashed with a crunch of mechanical destruction.

"Get out, man! The fuel's gonna blow!" Barry said, scrambling to exit.

Lehder appeared, bursting off more gunfire. "Gringos! Maricones!"

Anticipating an explosion, Barry and Emile dived into the jungle.

Lehder ordered his workers to rescue the cocaine from the burning plane.

"That crazy bastard's making them go to the plane," Emile said, clutching a tree. "They'll be barbecued."

Barry and Emile leapt from the jungle and tried to stop the two dozen workers charging towards the plane.

"Help them now!" Lehder yelled, shooting his gun at the dirt around their feet.

Barry and Emile joined the men grabbing huge packages of cocaine from the plane. As they charged away, the plane exploded, knocking the men over. Flames shot dozens of feet in all directions. Two workers were burnt. The tractor transported the cocaine back to its storage facility, where it was inventoried.

"Cabrones, we have another plane!" Lehder yelled.

"I don't give a damn what kind of plane you've got," Barry said, his face muddy. "We can't take off with that load. We've gotta wait for this field to dry."

Barry and Emile were flown to Medellín. After showering in a cartel member's mansion, they were shown around the grounds. They admired a waterfall, a tropical garden, a swimming pool and an Olympic-sized cycling track.

A replacement plane was found: a Titan 404. "Certainly you're not going to be able to carry the full 1,500 kilos that you tried to carry with the larger plane. Can you carry half of it?" the cartel man asked.

"No, sir," Barry said, worried about the plane going down in the Gulf of Mexico. "Because then I wouldn't be able to add any fuel."

"And with a stop in Nicaragua? How much can you take?"

"Well, with a stop in Nicaragua, we can probably take 700, 750 kilos." The crash had played into Barry's hands because the sooner he could get to Nicaragua, the more the Reagan-Bush administration would be satisfied by the drugs link and the more predisposed they would be to helping his legal situation.

At the Hotel Intercontinental in Medellín, Barry called the DEA to appraise them about the new flight schedule. In Gulfport, DEA agents were waiting for the cocaine with a recreational vehicle. Such a large seizure would make their careers.

The next day, Barry and Emile returned to the jungle airstrip. Each got on top of the burned remains of the Learstar while the other snapped photos. In the jungle, they spent three days with Lehder, who was guarding the cocaine. Lehder showed them 3,000 kilos and claimed that 6,000 kilos of cocaine base in Bolivia were heading for Nicaragua.

On June 2, 1984, Barry told the DEA that he was flying to Nicaragua the next day. On June 3, at 10:30 pm, the DEA received a call in Miami from one of Barry's associates, stating that a radio transmission had been received and Barry was returning to Nicaragua after experiencing engine trouble. Three hours later, the DEA heard that Barry had landed in Nicaragua and might have some legal problems. No more contact was received.

Three days later, Barry appeared in the US without any cocaine. At a debriefing, he told the DEA that on June 3, he'd flown the Titan 404 from Colombia with 700 kilos of cocaine aboard. Stopping for fuel in Los Brasiles, Nicaragua, had taken longer than expected. After taking off in darkness, Barry had flown without any lights over a mountainous region. North of Managua, the plane was illuminated by anti-aircraft tracers. His left engine was hit. The plane started to descend fast. To avoid crashing, Barry had returned to Los Brasiles. Unable to land at the dark airfield, he scrambled to radio Vaughan, but he'd gone home.

With no options left, Barry radioed an emergency broadcast to Sandino International Airport in Managua, using a code provided by Vaughan. Upon landing, the plane was surrounded by soldiers. Barry insisted on talking to Vaughan and was granted a phone call. Vaughan was still not home.

A sergeant who knew Vaughan had the cocaine unloaded from Barry's plane. He told Barry and Emile to keep quiet and to play along with whatever happened. "Everything will be fine."

Barry and Emile were incarcerated overnight in The Bunker, a military compound in downtown Managua. The next day, they were released to Vaughan and transported to a large landed estate. Pablo greeted them. He'd moved there to supervise the cocaine-processing operation.

A few days later, Vaughan showed up with a newspaper, *El Nuevo Diario*. "This is the reason we wanted you to keep your mouth shut at the airport, because we had to keep this entire incident very quiet in the newspapers. We don't control all the newspapers here." He showed Barry a two-paragraph article that stated anti-aircraft gunners at Sandino Airport had shot at an Agrarian Reform Air Transport Company plane because the plane was unable to signal its location:

"The DAA [Anti-Aircraft Defense] had to signal and fire warning shots to induce it to land at the airport – which happened without untoward consequences."

Vaughan said that the accident had happened because he hadn't prepared for a smuggling flight in the darkness. The gunners hadn't seen Barry. They'd heard him and shot at the noise. Better communication was required for the next time. Upset that he hadn't been able to reach Vaughan from the plane, Barry said they should buy walkie-talkies.

Pablo said that the new cocaine lab was at a ranch south of Managua. It would be ready for full production in two weeks. Lehder had almost fifteen tons of cocaine base, which would produce approximately one-fifth of the cocaine consumed in America annually.

"Well, that's going to take a real large plane," Barry said. "You should buy a military cargo plane like those I've seen advertised in the aviation-trade magazines."

Pablo wanted Barry to obtain such a plane and to pick up the first 700 kilos.

"Is that cocaine safe?" Barry said.

"We haven't lost one single gram," Vaughan said.

In Escobar's Piper Cheyenne, which required maintenance in America, Barry and Emile flew home with Pablo's latest shopping list, which included night-vision goggles and a dozen high-frequency radios that cost $12,000 each.

The CIA provided Barry with a Fairchild C-123K Provider, a massive camouflage-green twin-engine military cargo plane from the Vietnam War. He nicknamed it the Fat Lady. On June 18, 1984, Barry flew the Fat Lady to Rickenbacker Air Force Base near Columbus, Ohio. Repairing and retrofitting the plane, Air Force employees worked around the clock. The military made repairs worth $40,000 at the taxpayers' expense.

Barry was instructed to take pictures of Nicaraguan officials associated with cocaine. He told the CIA, "Let me explain something to you, mister. There's gonna be a lot of men with guns down there. Nervous men, who aren't gonna exactly say cheese to some gringo pilot with a camera."

Five days later, the plane was at Homestead Air Force Base near Miami. A transponder was installed to allow the DEA to track its flight. The CIA added a hidden 35-mm camera in the nosecone and another was put inside of a fake electronics box in the rear cargo hold, facing the doors. A pinhole lens in the box allowed the camera to film the cocaine coming into the back of the plane. Barry was given a radio-controlled trigger for the cameras, with a long wire antenna attached to it.

"What! Where in the hell do you expect me to hide that? Stick it up my ass?" Barry said, referring to the antenna.

"You can put it in your pocket."

"All five feet of it?"

"Put it in your pocket and let the antenna slide down your leg."

Barry did so and pressed the remote control. Enraged by the loud noise the camera made, he cursed the CIA men in suits. "I'm tired of wasting my time with you assholes. I'll get your fucking photographs. Autographed! But what are you gonna do for me?"

"We have a deal, Mr Seal."

"The judge. Say it, dammit!"

"We'll speak to the judge on your behalf."

In a Miami hotel room, Barry called Vaughan, recording the call for the DEA. "I was going to see my grandmother at noon on Saturday," Barry said, using code for the cocaine shipment. Referring to the Fat Lady, Barry said, "It's a big Cadillac... Very big, big car... I just wanted to make sure that my grandmother was going to tell the landlord that the car was very big, so that the landlord wouldn't be excited when they saw it." Worried about getting shot down again, Barry wanted the Nicaraguan government to stay calm when they saw the Fat Lady.

"No, no, no," Vaughan said. "Everything is OK about that."

On June 24, 1984, Barry told Vaughan about a party tomorrow at his grandmother's, meaning the cocaine was coming the next day. "I mean, everybody is coming to the party, and you've notified those boys in green." Barry was still concerned about getting shot down.

"Right," Vaughan said.

"Everybody is notified?" Barry said.

"Yes," Vaughan said.

"Excellent. OK. I just want to make sure. I don't want any problems."

"Yes, everybody is going to be there."

"OK, good. And is Pedro coming? Because I have that liquor for him," Barry said, referring to Pablo and the items on his shopping list.

"Yes, yes, he's coming," Vaughan said.

"I'm leaving for the party at midnight. Has it been raining on the yard where we park the cars at the party?" Barry said.

"It's dry and hard and only a little bit muddy in one small area."

"I can't stay at the party long. I have to try to leave as soon as possible," Barry said, hoping for a fast refuelling.

"Yeah, we're going to be ready for that."

"OK. Now remember this motorhome is very big, and it's a funny, funny colour, so don't let anybody get excited."

Vaughan laughed. "No, that's perfect."

At 1 pm on June 25, 1984, Barry landed at Los Brasiles near Managua and dropped open the back of the plane. He'd brought $454,000 for Pablo. He later claimed that on the ground were Vaughan, Pablo, Gacha and a group of soldiers. "How do you like the plane?" Barry yelled over the engine noise. "I call her the Fat Lady."

Soldiers started loading duffel bags of cocaine into the cargo hold. Every time Barry pressed the remote control to take a picture, the camera clicked so loudly that it could be heard outside the Fat Lady. To drown out the noise, Barry switched on the plane's generators. An American spy plane above took high-resolution pictures.

"Shut down your engines!" Pablo yelled.

"I can't. We gotta keep them hot," Barry said, maintaining the sound to disguise the camera noise.

An overweight bodyguard with a gun entered the plane and started looking around as if he could hear the camera noise. Emile revved the propellers to camouflage the sound. The bodyguard checked around and finally left. After being loaded with 700 kilos of cocaine and 2,000 gallons of fuel – which took about an hour – the plane took off.

The following morning, the Fat Lady landed at Homestead Air Force Base near Miami. The DEA seized the cocaine and the CIA took the camera film. The mission had been a success. The photos showed Barry, Pablo, Vaughan and Gacha loading twenty-five-kilo duffel bags.

With Barry's mission complete, George HW Bush had him assassinated through the CIA, which used Colombian hit men, so the blame could be put squarely on the Medellín

Cartel – documented in my book, *American Made*. Following his successful mission to Nicaragua, Barry had felt so let down by George HW Bush that he'd threatened to blow the whistle on the cocaine he'd been transporting to Mena, Arkansas for the CIA, and he'd also boasted that he had videotape evidence of Jeb and George W Bush getting caught in a DEA sting operation.

On March 16, 1986, one month after Barry's death, Ronald Reagan went on TV with Barry's photos. "I know every American parent concerned about the drug problem will be outraged to learn that top Nicaraguan government officials are deeply involved in drug trafficking. This picture, secretly taken at a military airfield outside Managua, shows Federico Vaughan, a top aide to one of the nine commandants who rule Nicaragua, loading an aircraft with illegal narcotics bound for the United States." Reagan was attempting to drum up support for the provision of weapons and training for Nicaraguan rebels on the basis that the Nicaraguan government was involved in trafficking cocaine, which was killing young people in America. Even though they didn't know that the opposite was true – that the Nicaraguan rebels were trafficking cocaine with the help of the CIA – the public wasn't swayed.

The DEA knew that Reagan had lied. Furious over the death of Barry Seal – who'd been one of their key operatives and was on the verge of helping them take down the Medellín Cartel, which would have been the biggest drug arrests in history – the DEA stated that it had no information implicating "the Minister of the Interior or other Nicaraguan officials." It seems that Barry had embellished the Nicaraguan government's involvement in cocaine to try to curry favour with George HW Bush. After Reagan showed the grainy photographs on TV of Pablo in Nicaragua loading drugs onto Barry's plane, Pablo told his brother that he couldn't possibly have been in that photo because he never loaded drugs onto planes. Maybe the CIA had doctored the photos.

With the Reagan-Bush administration hyping-up the crack epidemic for political gain, the US authorities increased their efforts to extradite Pablo. Eight different agencies were pursuing him, including the DEA, US Customs, the Coast Guard, federal police, state police and the military, none of which put a dent in the supply of cocaine to America, which tumbled in price from $40,000 a kilo to $9,000.

In April 1986, Reagan signed National Security Decision Directive 221, which classified drug-trafficking as a threat to national security. In retaliation, traffickers targeted the staff at the American embassy in Bogotá, and a $350,000 contract was put out on the head of the DEA. Car-bombers repeatedly attacked the buildings occupied by Americans. Family members of diplomats and DEA agents fled Colombia.

Pablo had wanted to make Panama a temporary hub, but Noriega hadn't embraced the idea. The agreement had been to make Panama a transportation point, not an operations centre. Pablo got word from a Panamanian Colonel that Noriega was making overtures to the DEA. For the benefit of the cartel, Noriega had authorised the construction of a cocaine lab in Panama, but his military seized 16,000 barrels of ether destined for the new lab and arrested twenty-three Colombian workers. The angry cartel leaders demanded an explanation, but were told that Noriega was in Europe.

Through President Fidel Castro, a meeting was arranged for the Colombians and Noriega in Cuba. Before Noriega arrived, the cartel attended a preliminary conference with the Panamanian government. After the meeting, Noriega released the Colombian prisoners and returned $3 million in cash and lab equipment to the cartel.

Growing homesick and distrustful of Noriega, the cartel tried to reach an agreement with the Colombian government, whom they asked to consider the possibility of their re-incorporation into Colombian society in the near future. They denied any responsibility for the assassination of Lara Bonilla. Their memorandum offered a history of drug trafficking in Colombia and asserted that their organisations "today control between 70 and 80 percent of

Colombia's drug traffic," which equated to "an annual income of around $2 billion." Pablo offered to move billions from overseas accounts into the Colombian banking system and to dismantle the cocaine empire, but the deal was refused.

On June 15, 1984, the cartel lost 1.2 metric tons of cocaine packed in freezers and perfume cartons to US Customs agents in Miami. A Panamanian charter company owned the cargo jet transporting the cocaine. The next week, Panamanian authorities confiscated 6,159 drums of ether.

Pablo advised his fellow Colombians to leave Panama. Private planes and helicopters arrived. The Colombians dispersed to Medellín, Brazil and Spain. According to Roberto, Pablo and his brother went to Nicaragua. Pablo took 1,100 kilos of cocaine with him, aiming to convert it into cash.

Even though extraditions to America had begun, things had settled down a bit in Colombia since the aftermath of Lara's death. The majority of those who'd been arrested in the raids following Lara's death, including Fabio Ochoa Sr, had been released due to a lack of evidence and the usual corruption.

Giving an interview from abroad, Pablo said, "People who know me understand very well that I am involved in industry, construction and ranching... the fact that I attack extradition does not make me extraditable."

Lehder had managed to evade capture, and was still issuing statements: "I am a symbol of those men who battle imperialism. In this struggle, the end justifies the means." In 1984, his political party, Carlos Lehder's National Latin Movement, won two seats and four city council seats.

The pressure on the authorities from the traffickers had never relented. They had obtained the president's private telephone number – which had spooked the president – and were issuing threats.

Outside a courthouse, a man approached the judge who'd indicted the cartel for Lara's murder and requested a temporary dismissal. "Ask for whatever you want, and they'll put it wherever you want it, in Colombia or outside the country... Then you can relax. Neither your life, nor the lives of your family members will be in danger." The judge refused. Climbing into a taxi, he was shot dead by five men in a Mazda.

Armoured vehicles transported US embassy staff. Their children went to school on a bus protected by army jeeps with machine guns. On the roads, the staff kept their eyes peeled for motorbike assassins. Some kept their windows down, so they could listen for the distinct sound of a motorbike approaching. In their guarded living quarters they heard guns fired every night. An empty car aimed at the embassy rolled down a hill, hit a curb and exploded, sending flames three hundred feet into the air. Embassy staff was reduced to a bare minimum.

Any locals working with the Americans were killed in grotesque ways. One had pins inserted under his fingernails, before being shot in the head and left on the street with a sign around his neck: "Killed for Being a DEA Informant." After the DEA got word that a guerrilla hit team had been contracted by Pablo to kidnap key members, they closed their Medellín location.

In the latter half of 1984, Pablo thought it was safe to return home. He convened a meeting of seventy important people, ranging from traffickers to priests, who arrived with 200 bodyguards. Extradition was discussed. Pablo proposed that Medellín should have a united group of bodyguards divided into zones. Among the big four founders of the Medellín Cartel, Gacha's power was rising, while Lehder's was falling. Lehder was assigned to oversee jungle operations and to maintain relations with the guerrillas guarding the labs.

A little after midnight on the night of the meeting, a Mercedes arrived at the farmhouse. A well-dressed woman emerged. She knocked on the door and claimed to have flowers for Dr Hernandez. Roberto told her that she was at the wrong address. He warned his brother that he'd never seen anyone in the flower-delivery business arrive in a Mercedes-Benz. Pablo dismissed it as nothing. Roberto instructed the bodyguards to start shooting in the air if any strangers showed up.

Around 2 am, shots were fired. Pablo and his brother ran out of the back of the farmhouse. A shot grazed Roberto's leg and pieces of brick hit him in the face, causing lots of bleeding. They came across one of their bodyguards returning in a car. They escaped in it along with Gustavo.

A trafficker from the city of Cali, which had a history of rivalry with Medellín, had attended the meeting at the farmhouse and subsequently snitched Pablo out, hoping for a government guarantee against extradition.

The colonel in charge of the raid had been paid $50,000 a month by Pablo. Pablo sent him a message, "Now you are against me and you know what I think about that."

On the same night as the raid, Jorge Ochoa got into trouble in Spain, where he'd emigrated with the boss of the Cali Cartel and settled in an 8,000-square-foot mansion, complete with a swimming pool, tennis courts, a disco and four Mercedes-Benz. An informant told Spain's Special Prosecutor for the Prevention and Repression of Drug Trafficking that Ochoa was in Madrid under a fake name: Moisés Moreno Miranda.

Surveillance showed Ochoa living a life of luxury, frequenting restaurants and concerts, and his wife depositing hundreds of thousands of dollars in local banks, which the police concluded was hot money. The Spanish authorities tipped off the DEA, who notified Washington: "Intelligence… has indicated that suspected Colombian trafficking group intends to create investment company with unlimited funding and is in the process of purchasing several extremely expensive residences, indicating intent to remain in Spain."

For almost three months, the Spanish authorities monitored the two drug bosses. After Ochoa asked about buying 10,000 acres in southern Spain, the police feared that he was about to set up a global cocaine hub.

On November 15, 1984, the two Colombian bosses and their

wives were arrested. Attempting to capitalise on the windfall, the Americans made overtures to the Spanish in the hope of getting the Colombians extradited. The stage was set for a lengthy legal battle.

In volatile Colombia, even forming an army called Death to Kidnappers didn't always serve as a deterrent. In 1985, Pablo's father was kidnapped by policemen. On his way to visit one of Pablo's farms, he was pulled over by six men in a jeep. After tying up the workers accompanying him, they drove him away. They wanted $50 million.

After she found out, Pablo's mother spent hours yelling and crying and praying. Pablo put out the word that if his father ended up with a single bruise the ransom money they got wouldn't be enough to pay for their own burials.

Remaining composed, Pablo formed a plan to capture the kidnappers. His father needed medicine for open-heart surgery. Many of the two-hundred drugstores in Medellín had security cameras. He installed cameras in those that didn't. He offered a reward for photos of anyone buying the heart medicine his father needed. Two kidnappers were identified. As the kidnappers used payphones, Pablo gave hundreds of radio transmitters to people with instructions to listen to a certain radio station. Whenever the kidnappers called Pablo's mother, the station announced a song dedicated to Luz Marina. After hearing this, the people with the transmitters rushed out to the nearest payphones.

Over eighteen days, Pablo's brother negotiated the ransom down to $1 million. The money was delivered in duffel bags with electronic tracking devices, which the kidnappers took to a farm. The house was surrounded and assaulted from every direction. Three of the kidnappers were captured and sentenced to death by Pablo. His father was released unharmed.

Perhaps things weren't as safe in Colombia as Pablo thought. He went everywhere with bodyguards, moved around a lot and took extra precautions.

CHAPTER 8
THE EXTRADITABLES

After the MAS had started to annihilate the guerrillas responsible for kidnapping Martha Ochoa, Pablo had met their leader, Ivan Marino Ospina. Not only did each side agree not to attack the other, but as a show of good faith, Ospina gave Pablo the famous sword of the liberator Simón Bolívar, a Venezuelan military leader who'd helped Colombia gain independence from Spain in 1810. The founder of the M-19, Jaime Bateman, had stolen the sword – a symbol of unfulfilled liberation – from a museum in 1974 and announced that it would not be returned until the government agreed to peace with the M-19. Initially, Pablo hung it on a wall. Eventually, he gave it to a nephew to hide. The chronology of these events was condensed in *Narcos*, which showed a sad and incompetent member of the M-19 and his glamorous lover breaking into a museum to steal the sword, only to have their leader hand it to Pablo in the next episode.

Relations between the guerrilla groups and the cartel were generally in a state of flux; however, since the handing over of the sword, the friendship between Pablo and the M-19 leader, Ivan, had lasted. With the M-19 known for committing spectacular attacks against the government, they came to mind when Pablo thought of targeting the government's files on extradition, which were housed in the Palace of Justice in Bogotá. If Pablo could destroy or intimidate the Colombian judiciary system in a sensational way, then maybe he could take over the entire country. He would do the unthinkable: go after the Supreme Court.

By September 1985, six Colombians out of 105 on the US list had been extradited, and nine were in jail. Pablo formed a group called the Extraditables with the motto: "Better a grave in

Colombia than a jail cell in the US." The cartel leaders made a blood pact that they would commit suicide rather than rot away in an American prison. Their preferred method was to shoot themselves behind the ear, which allowed a bullet easy access to the brain by circumventing the skull.

Since his early arrests, Pablo had refined his intimidation tactics against judges. A judge assigned to a narcotics case would be visited by a bright young well-dressed lawyer, carrying a briefcase. On the judge's desk, he'd put a brown envelope.

The lawyer would say something like, "You have a choice. You can have lead, bullet in your head, or silver, some money as a payoff. It's your call." If the judge prevaricated, the lawyer would reach inside his briefcase and take out a photo album containing pictures of the closest family members and friends of the judge: their children leaving home in the morning, going to school, playing in the playground, talking to friends... The threat of their entire family being wiped out persuaded most judges.

Pablo was about to refine his tactics again. The Extraditables sent letters to the Supreme Court justices, demanding that they declare the extradition treaty illegal. The letters were designed not to give any evidence to the police. Block letters were used. They were signed by the Extraditables or a first name such as Manuel. When Pablo wasn't writing on behalf of the Extraditables and he wanted people to know that he'd authored a letter, he wrote in his own handwriting, signed his name and added his thumbprint. Some people wondered whether Pablo was the Extraditables, whereas others thought that he was a front for them.

The Extraditables obtained the justices' private phone numbers and threatened them. With a ruling due on extradition, the justices were afraid. More letters came for the justices stating that the Extraditables knew everything going on in their lives.

"We declare war against you. We declare war against the members of your family. As you may suppose, we know exactly where they are – we will do away with your entire family. We have no compassion whatsoever – we are capable of anything, absolutely anything."

Some letters included taped recordings of private conversations they'd had. A voice on a tape recorder warned a justice called Alfonso that his wife wouldn't be alive to make an upcoming trip.

"I'm having a little trouble," Alfonso told his wife. "You should change your travel routes during the day. Don't talk to me over the phone about your plans, and, really, be very careful."

After Alfonso reported the intimidation tactics, he was assigned four DAS bodyguards, and his wife got one.

Alfonso learned that all of the justices were suffering the same treatment. One had taken his daughter to a hospital for an operation and was about to leave her there when he was paged to the reception. A nurse handed him a phone. A voice said, "We know where she is."

A judge with a heart condition received a miniature coffin with his name on it, which caused him panic attacks.

Even though Alfonso had four bodyguards, the pressure from the cartel increased. Numerous letters arrived on one day, including one for his wife: "You must convince your husband to abrogate the treaty. Remember, we are the same people who dealt with Rodrigo Lara Bonilla. Your bodyguards won't save you, no matter how many you have." An accompanying cassette contained recordings of his wife on the phone in her office in the Foreign Ministry.

The couple stopped taking walks and going out at night. They gave relatives numbers to decode to ascertain their whereabouts. Alfonso insisted that they no longer drive to work together. "That way, you'll save yourself."

The night before the decision about extradition, the couple couldn't sleep. Before leaving for work, Alfonso kissed his wife. Heading for the Palace of Justice on November 6, 1985, he had a bad feeling in his stomach.

Due to visiting foreign dignitaries, pomp and circumstance was in full swing in the Protocol Salon of the National Palace.

National anthems were being played. Armed grenadiers were marching in the courtyard. At first, the gunfire was difficult to hear over the noise, but the sound of marching boots made people question what was going on.

At 11:40 am, dozens of guerrillas with rifles, machine guns and grenades jumped from a truck and stormed the Palace. They blasted at security guards and joined their comrades who'd entered the night before in civilian clothes. In no time, they had almost 300 hostages, including Alfonso and most of the justices. Other hostages included lawyers, secretaries, shopkeepers and shoeshine people. The guerrillas blocked stairwells with furniture and mounted machine guns on top. They issued a demand for the highest court in the nation to put the president on trial for failing to keep his promise to establish peace.

The police on the scene rescued some hostages, but were repelled with gunfire. The army showed up with tanks, grenade launchers, helicopters and hundreds of troops with hard helmets and rifles, who positioned themselves in rows against various walls for cover. They blasted rockets at the massive building with its masonry façade, making holes in the walls. Debris littered the sidewalk. Tank fire and rockets pounded the entrance door. Helicopters landed on the roof, and troops alighted to sniper fire coming through the skylights. Troops who managed to get inside couldn't get past the blocked stairwells and received machine-gun fire. A day went by with the guerrillas in control of the building.

Alfonso was trapped on the fourth floor with his bodyguards. With no guerrillas there, they felt relatively safe until a secretary screamed, "They're coming through the wall!" When the guerrillas arrived, they put up no resistance.

Alfonso's phone rang. A guerrilla commander angrily told Alfonso's son to tell the police and soldiers to stop shooting. He gave the phone to Alfonso.

"I'm all right," Alfonso said, "but see if the DAS and the police will stop shooting."

With the sound of shooting in the background, the guerrilla

commander got back on the phone. "If they don't stop shooting in fifteen minutes, we're all going to die!"

When Alfonso's son called back, the distraught guerrilla commander was prophesying doom because the government was refusing to negotiate. A goal of the guerrillas was to draw attention to the systematic aerial bombardment of their forces in the wake of a negotiated peace agreement with the president.

"The shooting must stop," Alfonso told his son, who was so frustrated that he gave a radio station his father's telephone number.

With the televised attack shocking the nation – Pablo was watching, too – Radio Caracol called Alfonso. Across the country, Colombians heard Alfonso request a ceasefire and negotiations. An hour later, he spoke to his son. "The guerrillas want to negotiate." Shortly after 5 pm, the line cut out.

Around 7 pm, smoke started filtering through the building. Burning files ignited a fire, which spread to the wooden building dividers. Gagging and coughing, some of the people hiding on the top floor went downstairs, where the guerrillas captured them. They were thrown on top of sixty hostages compressed into a bathroom, who were traumatised by the likelihood of imminent death. Some were bleeding. Others had stopped breathing. The room stank of sweat and bodily fluids.

The next afternoon, troops braced to go inside. Instead of complying with the guerrillas' demand for negotiations, the president had authorised a military assault. After a tank rammed the front door, troops charged in. The guerrillas sifted through the corpses to find the living, whom they ordered to get up. Hostages shoved out of the door were annihilated by the army. Grenades toppled some of them, leaving them injured and bleeding or dead. Guerrillas threw corpses down the stairwell, including one of the justices who looked dead but was still alive, his artificial leg shattered by a bullet. After the guerrillas left that area, the injured justice crawled to the cellar and up a flight of stairs. Mustering energy, he raised himself and his arms. "Don't shoot!"

Approximately one hundred died in the bloodbath. Alfonso didn't make it. He was one of the eleven justices – half of the Supreme Court – shot dead. All of the guerrillas died, as well as eleven police and soldiers. Some of the survivors disappeared immediately afterwards, with the government suspected of killing them.

At first, the cartel's role wasn't obvious. Many people blamed the guerrillas and the government's overreaction. Controversy remains to this day, with some researchers claiming that the fire that torched the extradition files was due to the army's response. Roberto Escobar stated that the Extraditables had financed the operation for the destruction of the records – not mass murder – and the traffickers had offered to double the fee to the guerrillas if the government negotiations had worked out.

Survivors, including the justice who'd been thrown down the stairs with the corpses, criticised the government for not negotiating. When the president eulogised in a church for the dead justices, the survivors didn't attend.

Afterwards, some people quit working for Pablo, others for the government, including many judges.

The violence increased into 1986, with journalists, prosecutors and judges getting killed by hit men on motorbikes.

CHAPTER 9
COLONEL RAMIREZ
AND CANO

In late January, 1986, an informant told the police that Pablo had issued a contract worth $150,000 on a police colonel, which had gone to the Medellín chapter of the Ricardo Franco Brigade, a guerrilla group that had recently butchered a few hundred of its own members suspected of being police infiltrators. The Brigade had delegated the hit to its chief of executions, Foxy, who'd taken a $12,000 down payment from Pablo, which had been spent on a MAC-10, four pistols and a revolver. The weapons were outside one of Pablo's safe houses in North Bogotá, stashed in a Renault 18, with one hit man overseeing it.

The informant said that Pablo had accumulated a file of information on the colonel, which he'd shared with Foxy. Pablo had paid $30,000 for the information to a lieutenant trusted by the colonel. They were aware that the colonel was starting a course at generals' school, and they had details of his going-away party. They knew where he lived, his mother's address, the car he owned and that he drove an armoured Mercedes-Benz on loan from the DEA – the informant gave all of the specific details.

A hit scheduled for outside of a club had been called off due to the colonel's large escort. A hit at his mother's house had also fallen through as too many relatives had accompanied the colonel, and Pablo wanted a clean kill without numerous casualties. The hit team had picked three potential locations: his mother's house, a highway overpass by a police academy and across the street from a bakery. In regular contact with Foxy, the informant pledged to give further information for the right price.

Police intelligence pegged Colonel Ramirez as the target and assigned surveillance to the safe house with the weapons in the car outside. Neighbours spotted the undercover agents taking photos and called the police.

With Colonel Ramirez on leave – he'd been relieved of duty at the end of 1985 – it was decided not to tell him about the hit until they knew for sure.

Ramirez returned to work in February in high spirits. He'd survived his tenure as Anti-Narcotics Unit police chief, during which his men had managed to make almost 8,000 arrests and confiscate more than half of the cocaine seized in the world in 1985, as well as countless vehicles, boats and planes. Also in 1985, he'd overseen the destruction of ninety percent of the marijuana crop, which had been poisoned by crop dusters with herbicide provided by the DEA. He'd won awards, was ready for a promotion to general and his advice on drug eradication was being sought around the world.

Ramirez had cost the cartel so much money that other members had bought shares in the hit: Gacha wanted revenge for the Land of Tranquillity; Lehder because the colonel had hounded him for more than a year, almost arrested him twice, had incarcerated the mother of his three-year-old daughter, had decimated his trafficking operation and reduced his stature in the cartel.

On August 5, 1985, Lehder had only just managed to slip away from Ramirez by fleeing towards a river in his red underwear, carrying a machine gun. The police found a letter from one of his lawyers: "All your problems began when you started with the politics. The trick is to make yourself dead, the phantom – no publicity so the gringos and Colombians forget you... The important thing is not to die rich. The important thing is to live rich – like before."

In February 1986, Ramirez and his family relocated to the General Santander Police Academy in Bogotá, which offered extra protection. He was safe at the base, but he had to drive to the war college daily. He knew the traffickers wanted him dead, but would they dare go after him? No evidence had come about from surveying the safe house with the Renault parked outside.

Ramirez grew more concerned after questioning the informant, who detailed the two previously planned hits that had been cancelled. The thought of hit men staking out his parents' Christmas Eve party disturbed him. When the interview ended, the informant promised to keep providing information. Ramirez told his family that the informant was truthful.

The threat had come at an awkward time because Ramirez was no longer in command of an armed force that could retaliate against Pablo. Unable to adhere to his motto of constantly kicking the traffickers in the nuts, he started to worry. For eight months, he only left the base to drive to police headquarters in an armoured Ford LTD provided by the DEA, wearing a bullet-proof vest, armed with a revolver and a MAC-10 and protected by a chauffeur with a revolver. Mindful of the details provided by the informant, the driver always varied the route. Before Ramirez set off, the route was checked by police on motorbikes.

The threat made his wife ill. His father dreamt that he was dead. He urged his brother to minimise any descriptions of the danger to his father. His two boys travelled to school in an armoured bus. The family rarely went out to eat, and if they did, they wore bullet-proof vests. One of his sons had become proficient in the use of a MAC-10, which accompanied them on family journeys.

Prior to Easter Sunday, his brother invited him and his family to stay at a cabin. Ramirez was desperate to blow off steam. "I've always been the pursuer, and now they're pursuing me. I'm the one who puts people against the wall, not the other way around."

The information coming from the informant suddenly stopped after he revealed that the hit team had acquired nine vehicles, explosives and rocket-propelled grenades and launchers. Security around Ramirez was increased. Investigators were unable to find any new leads or the identity of the lieutenant alleged to have been providing information to the cartel.

Due to his previous successes with traffickers, Captain Ernesto

Mora of the Anti-Narcotics Unit was assigned to infiltrate the cartel and issue reports to Ramirez with any updates on the threat. Ernesto ascertained that the contract with Foxy was still active and that other cartel leaders had shares in the contract. New information had come to light that Pablo was considering cancelling the contract, but this needed further confirmation.

Pablo's overtures to Ramirez – requesting a meeting to talk things over – were declined by Ramirez, who believed that the proposal was a trap. Not necessarily that he would be killed, but secret photos would be taken of him with Pablo, and his career ruined. Ernesto delivered a message from Ramirez: Pablo would be treated fairly if he turned himself in.

In May 1986, four strangers – who'd arrived in a red Renault – were noticed lurking around the ranch belonging to Ramirez in Granada. Their leader had curly hair and a solid build. For a few days, they walked around, staking out the house. The caretaker took a bus to Ramirez. At the police academy, the caretaker identified the leader of the strangers from a photo.

In August, Ramirez and his classmates went to Europe for a month, where they visited other law enforcement and did workshops. With his luggage crammed with tons of information and reports, Ramirez returned excited to apply the knowledge in the hope of enhancing and modernising the police force.

While awaiting his new career, scheduled for the end of the year, Ramirez did jobs at police headquarters and also worked as a consultant with foreign governments fighting the War on Drugs. In Bolivia, as part of the DEA's Operation Blast Furnace, Ramirez was finally able to strike back at Pablo by helping to find some of Pablo's labs, which the authorities burned down. Returning to the thick of the action lifted his spirits, but the threat from Pablo – particularly to his family – gnawed at him.

On October 21, 1986, Foxy was killed in a gunfight in Medellín. In light of this development, Ernesto told Ramirez that Pablo had probably cancelled the contract, and that it was unlikely that anyone would attempt to kill Ramirez in the wake of Foxy's death as a new hit team would have to start from scratch, gathering information and staking out locations. The safe house with the Renault outside had been raided many times. The raids had produced no leads. No further sightings of the strangers led by the curly-haired man had occurred.

Feeling safer, Ramirez gave up his bodyguards. On a daily basis, he spoke to Ernesto. Each day, there were no new developments, so he relaxed more.

On Thursday, November 13, 1986, Ramirez was invited to a family dinner scheduled for Monday. Even though the thirty-mile drive seemed comparatively risk-free, Ramirez said that he would have to give it more thought.

On Friday, he received a ten-minute call from Ernesto. After hanging up, he turned to his wife. With his face transformed into a relaxed state that had been absent for a long time, he said, "They've suspended the contract."

With the threat gone, the family looked forward to the upcoming get-together. It was the kind of occasion that they'd learned to appreciate after everything they'd been through. Finally, things were back to normal.

On Sunday afternoon, they left the armoured vehicle in the garage and set off in a Toyota minivan with a MAC-10 on the floor by one of Ramirez's sons. With so much holiday traffic, it would be difficult for any pursuers to set a trap. After stopping to eat at a ranch near Bogotá, they drove for another hour to a friend's house, where they stayed overnight.

At 10 am on Monday, they set off in high spirits for the ranch belonging to the brother of Ramirez. The four family members hadn't taken a trip together like this in a long time. The ranch was packed with family members in a celebratory mood, anticipating a feast.

In-between eating pigs' knuckles, Ramirez told stories to everybody sat around outside on the lawn. He was proud of his imminent promotion. It now looked like he was going to become the police's chief of personnel. Excitedly, he described how he was going to employ many of his former men in his new department, and encourage everyone to keep fighting the traffickers. It would be like old times.

After 4 pm, Ramirez said it was a good time to leave in order to beat the holiday traffic returning to Bogotá. As they set off, multiple cars – that had been parked in the area for hours – followed the minivan.

At 5:43 pm, the minivan encountered heavy traffic on a highway bridge. Failing to notice their pursuers, they crept along in the right-hand lane. Ramirez and his wife discussed how they were getting on in years, and how they'd like to spend the rest of their lives together. When they were halfway over the bridge, a red Renault 18 approached their left side as if overtaking the minivan. It slowed. Its occupants were watching Ramirez. One of them raised a MAC-10.

"Get down!"

An explosion of shots ripped into Ramirez, forcing him forwards, where he stayed slumped as if dead.

His two sons had been shot: one in the hand; the other in the thighs, producing lots of blood; nevertheless, the latter son tried to find the MAC-10. Hit in the knee, his wife reached for the steering wheel. Veering towards the side of the bridge, the minivan stopped at a curb.

The Renault halted in front of the van. Three smartly-dressed passengers in their twenties got out, brandishing MAC-10s. While two remained at the Renault, the third approached the van.

Bleeding from the leg, Ramirez's wife was crawling across the bridge, hoping to get to the other side of the van to assist her husband. She looked up at an assassin. "Please don't kill me."

Leaving her unharmed, the hit man opened the driver's door and blasted Ramirez. He got in the Renault, which sped away.

The day after the murder of Ramirez, the US authorities went public with a super indictment of the top traffickers – the Ochoa brothers, Pablo, Lehder and Gacha – charging them with, among other things, producing fifty-eight tons of cocaine from 1978 to 1985:

From as early as 1978 to the date of the return of this indictment there existed an international criminal narcotics enterprise based in Medellín, Colombia, South America, known by various names, including "The Medellín Cartel" (hereinafter "Cartel"), which consisted of controlling members of major international cocaine manufacturing and distributing organizations... Through the Cartel, major cocaine organizations were able to pool resources, including raw materials, clandestine cocaine conversion laboratories, aircraft, vessels, transportation facilities, distribution networks, and cocaine to facilitate international narcotics trafficking.

The indictment made more headlines in Colombia than America, especially with the newspaper *El Espectador*, which published multiple stories. It was the same newspaper that had published Pablo's mugshot, seriously harming his political goals. It employed one of the bravest Colombians still willing to speak out against Pablo and the traffickers. His name was Cano, a highly respected sixty-one-year-old newsman with white hair. He wrote this in a column:

Legalise drug-trafficking? That would be like legalising and justifying all the collateral activities: money laundering, the assassination of Supreme Court justices, of Cabinet ministers, of judges, and of so many other persons who, by doing their duty have fallen victim to the narcotics traffickers and their hired killers.

On December 17, 1986, Cano returned to his office from a lunch break, laden with Christmas gifts. After working late, he left the building in the evening. With the gifts on the backseat, he started his station wagon and joined the traffic. He changed lanes to make a U-turn. While Cano waited for an opening to turn, a young man nearby stepped off a motorbike, placed a case on the ground and took out a MAC-10. He hurried over to Cano's car. The firing began.

El Espectador lost ten staff members, including Cano. Its building was car-bombed twice. The cartel went after investigative reporters, political columnists, editors and anyone else who opposed them. Even a statue of Cano erected in his honour was bombed to bits in Medellín.

In a political debate on trafficking, a voice of reason offered a solution. "The drug business will cease to be profitable for the drug traffickers," said the president of the Council of State, "if it is legalised and if the Colombian state assumes total control not only of its sale, but also of its use." As usual, his proposal was ignored.

CHAPTER 10
ARRESTS

Just like after Lara's assassination, Cano's death provoked demands for retribution and public opinion began to swing against the cartel. People from Cano's profession marched in silence. Speeches were given, praising almost two-dozen journalists killed in recent years. Thousands attended the funeral, including the president, whose car led a convoy past mourners waving Colombian flags.

On top of Cano's death, the president was dealing with the murder of Ramirez and the return of Jorge Ochoa from Spanish jail. To earn his freedom, Ochoa claimed to have paid $6 million to the Spanish judges.

Lara's successor, who'd signed Pablo's arrest warrant and the extradition order for Lehder, ran into trouble in Hungary. Hoping he'd be safe overseas, he'd gone to work in the Colombian Embassy. Death threats started coming in: "You can run, but you can't hide." Pablo's men trailed him for weeks. They knew his routine, including when he drove to the embassy or took the bus.

January 13, 1987 in Budapest commenced with a blizzard. The ambassador left his house in the hills above the capital and examined his car. As the roads were iced over, he decided to walk to the bus stop. Going down a hill, he spotted a man.

"You, Enrique Parejo?" the stranger yelled.

"Yes."

Instantly, a gun was drawn. The first shot entered his neck. With a bullet lodged in his spine, he collapsed. Unable to move, he watched the man stand over him, take aim at his head and shoot him in the mouth, cheek and arms. Miraculously, he survived thanks to doctors who removed the bullets in two operations.

The authorities clamped down with the usual arrests,

destruction of labs and seizures of property, cash, weapons and drugs that hardly disrupted the flow of cocaine. Something more needed to be done.

The government made a secret list of the 128 most wanted traffickers, including 56 on the extradition list, and managed to arrest eight of them. If only they could arrest one of the big four.

Thanks partially to Colonel Ramirez, Lehder's organisation had disintegrated. Stories of Norman's Cay had leaked out and it was no longer being used. The government liquidated his assets. He was almost bankrupt, after once being worth $2 billion. While on the run, he caught a severe jungle fever. Pablo sent a helicopter for him and had him treated in Medellín, where he recovered. They spent time together, travelling across the country, staying at ranches. Rather than keep working as a bodyguard for Pablo, Lehder wanted to remake his fortune.

George Jung – Lehder's old cellmate, who he'd squeezed out of the business – was in federal prison, with revenge festering in his mind. For importing 300 kilos of cocaine, he was serving fifteen years. When the FBI offered to transport Jung to Colombia to entice Lehder into a trap, Jung said yes, not to help the FBI, but to murder Lehder. At night on his bunk, Jung fantasised about the different ways of killing Lehder.

In December 1986, Lemus, the police chief of Rionegro, started to receive information that Lehder was in a safe house in the area, soliciting Pablo to invest in a joint cocaine venture. In the wake of Cano's death, Lemus had been granted special powers to search anywhere, but he'd turned up nothing. His gut told him that Pablo had put Lehder in a mountainside chalet, but he didn't know which area of the vast forest to search.

On February 3, 1987, Lemus was introduced to an informant who had noticed some noisy men at a chalet in the woods. Upset with the mess they were making, the caretaker of the chalet had complained to the informant.

Around 4 pm, Lemus, accompanied by two policemen – who were under the impression that they were searching for guerrillas, not cartel leaders who could have their entire families slaughtered – located a two-storey chalet disguised by vegetation. It had a lawn upfront, an outbuilding at the side and behind it was a canyon with a stream. Three armed bodyguards protected the front and each side. For two hours, the police hid among the trees, observing sixteen occupants go in and out of the yard.

At 6 pm, Lehder emerged with a canvas chair.

Taken aback, Lemus whispered to a colleague, "Do you know that guy?"

"No."

Realising he was about to reveal the nature of the operation, which would have spooked his colleagues, Lemus kept quiet. He sent one of his men for reinforcements.

Thirty-six police arrived, including a special-weapons team. They surrounded the chalet. Lemus stationed a dozen men at the back. Others blocked the escape routes.

Even with his special powers, Lemus couldn't raid the house before 6 am without a warrant. He sent a constable for one, who returned at 4 am by which time cold fog had descended. Unable to find anyone to sign the warrant, the constable had signed it himself.

At 6:30 am, a bodyguard fired at a police sniper. The bodyguard was shot. A gun battle erupted between bodyguards on the second floor and the police behind the chalet in the woods.

Fearful of Lehder escaping, Lemus charged for the front door, clutching his gun with both hands, ready to blast someone in the face. On the other side of the door, Lehder was racing towards it as the assault from the police at the rear had convinced him that the front was the best escape route.

When the door opened, Lehder almost ran into the gun of Lemus. "Little chief, don't shoot me."

"We aren't killers," Lemus said. "Put your hands on your head and get down on the floor."

Lehder complied. As he dropped, he fished a wad out of a pocket and threw it on the floor. "That's a million pesos."

"Pick it up, señor," Lemus said. "You're going to need it for soft drinks."

"Do you want green instead? How much?"

"No, I'm just doing my duty."

"Oh, little chief, what a hot number you are. You're the most famous man in the world. You know those gringo sons of bitches want to hang me by the balls, and now you've got me. Too bad we didn't meet earlier."

In the front room, the captives were searched and lined up. "Gentlemen, I'd like to introduce you to Carlos Lehder." The remark from Lemus was met with silence. Out in the yard, captives were photographed by Lemus. "Where's the soccer ball? We're taking the team picture." Everybody laughed.

At 10 am, vans collected the captives. Taking no chances, Lemus transported Lehder in his car. A dishevelled Lehder chatted with Lemus and women along the road.

At a telephone booth, Lemus called his boss. "We got him!"

"Yes, calm down. You got who?"

"The Virgin has smiled on us. We have captured Carlos Lehder."

While the reporters mobbed the police vans containing the captives, Lemus sneaked Lehder into the police station, where he gave him lunch. The telephone rang continuously and death threats were issued. Lemus was ordered to immediately gather his family and belongings, so that the US embassy could relocate them out of the country.

At 2 pm, an army helicopter landed to take Lehder to the Rionegro airport, where he boarded a military plane to Bogotá. Having been told that they could have Lehder right away if they had a plane available, the US embassy advised the Colombian government that a DEA plane was being rerouted to Bogotá. Lehder was rushed aboard a DEA Aero Commander. On the runway, a camera was filming. Fearing reprisals from the cartel, every soldier had his face covered with a black shroud. On

February 4, 1987, 5:15 pm, the Aero Commander took off. The DEA issued a worldwide alert for cartel retaliation.

"You got me now," Lehder told the DEA agents aboard.

The plane stopped to refuel in Cuba, where the army base was locked-down due to Lehder's high profile. The DEA agents offered Lehder a cigarette.

"No, that's all right. I only smoke marijuana."

On February 5, 1987 at 2 am, the Aero Commander landed at Tampa International Airport, where it was immediately surrounded by agents with shotguns and automatic weapons. Lehder was rushed into a car. A convoy of armed agents escorted Lehder to a federal courthouse. His mugshot was taken.

In the morning, Lehder appeared in court, smiling. "I don't have any money."

"Is the information true?" a magistrate said.

"Yes, Your Honour. Most of my assets were frozen by the government of Colombia."

Facing a maximum sentence of life without parole plus 135 years, Lehder was assigned a public defender. The US Attorney demanded that no bail be set because there had been death threats made against judges.

"That's a lie!" Lehder yelled.

"He has said if he were caught, he'd kill a federal judge a week until he's freed," said the US Assistant Attorney.

At a hearing on February 9, Lehder claimed to have no access to any money.

"Are you aware that your watch is worth approximately $6,000?" the US Attorney said.

"No."

"Your Honour," Lehder's public defender said, "we understand that he [Lehder] was turned into the police by an underworld figure: Pablo Escobar." No evidence was offered to back up her claim.

Lehder was refused bail. On the basis that Lehder had earned

$300 million in 1979 and 1980, the IRS slapped a $70 million lien on him.

In a response mailed to Colombian newspapers, Pablo conceded that he'd had "personal quarrels with Lehder on several occasions, but these would not lead me to perform such a low and cowardly act as to betray him to the authorities." Pablo believed that Lehder's public defender had initiated a "plan to attack my moral and personal integrity."

In Marion, Illinois, Lehder was housed in the highest-security federal prison in the country. Then he was transferred to Talladega, Alabama. Although in isolation, he was disturbed by a neighbour who "spent much of the night and day yelling and emitting unintelligible guttural sounds." His lawyers complained that he "was unable to sleep day or night because of the incessant noise." He ended up in Atlanta on a maximum security floor with empty cells. On the floors below him, 1,800 Cubans from the Mariel Boatlift disturbed his sleep. "Primal screams punctuate the air minute by minute, from time to time the din is so pervasive that one cannot hear himself think."

Eventually, Lehder hired two high-priced lawyers. Without his lawyers' consent, he sent a letter to George HW Bush on which the *Miami Herald* reported: "Accused Colombian Drug Chief's Offer To Cooperate Described As Frivolous."

His lawyers issued a statement: "It is absolutely false beyond any doubt that Carlos Lehder is cooperating. This letter [to George HW Bush] is to some degree the product of his solitary confinement."

Frustrated with Lehder for thwarting his plan to murder him by getting arrested, George Jung was amused by Lehder's letter to George HW Bush. Previously, Jung had refused to cooperate. But with Lehder in custody, Jung couldn't resist the opportunity to get revenge. After contacting the FBI, he wrote a letter about Lehder.

Despite the authorities bracing for a violent response to Lehder's extradition, none came, leading them to wonder what the cartel was up to.

Behind the scenes, cartel lawyers were busy battling the legality of extradition. On June 25, 1987, the Supreme Court ruled that the president had acted unconstitutionally by re-signing the extradition legislation. Without going on a murderous rampage, the cartel had won its battle against extradition. The US authorities were appalled.

In custody, Lehder described the day of extradition reversal as the happiest of his life. He blamed his extradition on "the burial of a Supreme Court that had sold out to imperialist interests." He mistakenly thought that with extradition ruled illegal, he would be returned to Colombia.

On July 22, 1987, three requests for the provisional arrest of Pablo were dismissed as unenforceable. Citing a lack of evidence, a judge withdrew orders for the arrest of Pablo and Gacha for the murder of Cano. Citing improper methods of obtaining evidence, a judge dismissed Pablo's indictment for Lara's murder. Now Pablo's only outstanding cases dated back to the 1970s, and all of the witnesses were dead. With their legal difficulties behind them, the remaining big three factions of the Medellín cartel started to regain their strength.

Thirty-eight-year-old Lehder arrived for trial on November 17, 1987. Wearing a tailored suit and with his hair freshly cut, he grinned at reporters. During the proceedings, he took notes and ate sweets. Three armed US marshals sat behind him.

"This case will take you back in time to 1974," the US Attorney said, "and forward over the course of many years in which Carlos Lehder pursued a singular dream, a singular vision, to be the king of cocaine transportation... He was to cocaine transportation what Henry Ford was to automobiles... He saw America as a decadent society. He saw cocaine as the wave of the future in the US, reeling from Watergate and Vietnam, particularly susceptible to the seductive allure of cocaine."

Lehder's lawyers portrayed him as a Colombian whom American smugglers – now turned informants against him – had preyed on. "Lehder was his own worst enemy. He was a young wealthy brash Colombian, flamboyant, to say the least… He confronted the DEA with his mouth."

Numerous of Lehder's cohorts testified against him. Even the TV personality, Walter Cronkite, described getting threatened at Norman's Cay.

Jung took the stand, a small man with long brown hair. While he detailed his story, his wizened face lit up. He smiled often as if savouring his revenge. The cross-examination was structured to trip Jung up.

"Knowing you to have used people before when it fits your interest, would you be using Mr Lehder in this case in order to lower your prison sentence maybe?"

"Do you really believe that?" Jung said.

"I'm asking the questions."

"Then, no…"

"And when you wrote down that you had been to Pablo Escobar's farm numerous times weren't you trying to sort of puff up your importance in this case, to see if you can get a better deal, better letter from the government, to see if they will reduce your parole and your sentence? Were you trying to do that, knowing Pablo Escobar to be somebody who has been publicised?"

"No. I didn't have to expand my role. I was married into a Colombian family that is tied in to people down there. That was well known. I didn't have to exaggerate my role. I mean, I was arrested in 1985 with 660 pounds of cocaine, and, in essence, they suddenly confiscated more on the airstrip, close to 3,000 pounds of cocaine. I don't believe that I had to exaggerate my role with 3,000 pounds of cocaine."

After the testimonies of 115 witnesses, the jury heard even more damning evidence: recordings from some of Lehder's interviews over the years, in which he described himself as a poor Colombian peasant who had made something of himself.

From June 28, 1983: "This was our obligation, to bring the dollars back to our people however we could. So then, that is it. It can be called Mafia. It can be called syndicate. It can be called a bonanza. It can be called whatever you like, but the truth is that it is a fact, and it is out in the open. In other words, Colombia would not be able to deny that it was the world's foremost producer of marijuana and cocaine." At fault was the US, "where there are forty-million marijuana smokers and twenty-five-million cocaine consumers... What I ask that they do is help the Colombian drug addict that they themselves corrupted."

From another recording: "I have never transported drugs. It is just that my lands, the flexibility afforded by their location being 200 miles from the US, provided the opportunity for the Colombians, who were being trapped like flies over there with little suitcases and with little boxes, of going in there, by means of a different system, a different means, a different platform."

Speaking loudly, one of Lehder's lawyers expressed outrage. "This is a case in which the government brought into this court-room twenty-nine bought witnesses."

Holding up a MAC-10 that had been found on Norman's Cay, the US Attorney attacked Lehder's businessman defence. "You have seen tragedy upon tragedy come into this courtroom. They were at war with society, together with Mr Lehder. He's still at war. He hasn't stopped... A trail of bribery, corruption, violence and personal debasement has been created and fostered by Mr Lehder with the help of those witnesses, and that wreckage exists in Colombia, the Bahamas and the US. That wreckage is the legacy of Mr Lehder's children. That wreckage in Colombia and the Bahamas and the US is an open wound, and that wound will not be healed by vengeance. That wound will only be healed by justice and truth and reconciliation." Holding up a spoon, he said it held one thirtieth of a gram of cocaine, and that Lehder was responsible for bringing in eighteen million grams or one billion snorts.

"Mr Lehder was an opportunity waiting to meet another opportunity: the US demand for drugs... His strength, ladies and gentlemen, was he was able to capitalise on the weakness of others... the disenchanted, the rogues, the crippled. He bought, charmed or pushed aside all obstacles. He's finally come to a situation where he can't do that."

In his final rebuttal to Lehder's lawyers, the US Attorney said, "The striking story in this case is that America, a substantial portion of America, has been an active partner with Mr Lehder. While it is true, as Mr Lehder told you on his own tapes, tragically, that his acts were motivated by hatred and bitterness against the US, it is also true that all of Mr Lehder's money and all of his guns and all of his power could not force American pilots to fly for him, could not force American businessmen to sell property to him, could not force aircraft salesmen to sell planes for cash, could not force victims of Mr Lehder's crimes to inject cocaine into their arms… or to snort it up their noses. The story of this case is the story of an absence of love, an absence of responsibility, a fleeing from responsibility by the witnesses in this case and by Mr Lehder. So your verdict is an act of reconciliation with truth, an act of reconciliation with the past. You have a duty and you have a privilege of returning a true verdict in this case, a duty which you must not shirk and you must not fear. Thank you."

After the jury left to deliberate, Lehder held up a sign to the journalists and other attendees: "Just Say No to Racism."

Over seven days, the jury deliberated for forty-two hours. In the packed courtroom, the anticipation of the verdict was palpable. While three women on the jury cried, the judge announced that Lehder was guilty on all counts. With a blank expression, Lehder gazed at the floor.

Both legal teams made announcements to the press. "Until we take the problem out of the schoolyard," one of Lehder's lawyers said, "you can put all of the Carlos Lehders you want in prison, but the problem is it doesn't work. What have we accomplished? Do we have one gram of drugs less available to us because of this prosecution?"

The US Attorney claimed it was a victory for the good guys and the American people. It "reflects to people in other nations that we are a nation of laws and will not tolerate the violence of drug traffickers." As if challenging Pablo directly, he said that the cartel had "nowhere to run, nowhere to hide… I think their days are numbered."

A journalist asked about the effect on the drug trade.

"The War on Drugs is not measured in terms of the amount of drugs that's seized. It's a war of the human spirit… the real issue is will. The will of the American people versus the will of the cartel." He said that the violent nature of the Medellín Cartel would be its downfall. "The Carlos Lehders of the world are going to have a narrower and narrower opportunity to wreak their crimes on this country."

Lehder had grown a beard by the time of his sentencing hearing on July 20, 1988. He spoke for almost half of an hour. "I feel like an Indian in a white man's court." He said he was a political prisoner, a victim of an overambitious prosecutor, and it had been a case of "twenty-nine confessed criminals against one Latin… Witnesses that never had a second underwear claimed they made millions from Lehder… I was kidnapped from my own country with the complicity of some Colombian police officers… I was flown against my will to this country. It's a far worse crime than any of these allegations. I am also against drug abuse. But I am also against kidnapping and extradition. This trial is illegal."

"The truth of the matter," the judge said, "is your main goal was to make money, and you did so at the expense of others. Your conspiracy burned a path of destruction and despair from the coca fields of South America to the streets and byways of this country. Accordingly, Mr Lehder, the sentence I impose on you today is meant to be a message for drug smugglers who control large organisations and for importers of cocaine and for street pushers. This sentence is a signal that our country will do everything in its power and within the laws to battle the drug problem that threatens the very fabric of our society."

He sentenced Lehder to life plus 135 years without any possibility of parole.

On the afternoon of November 21, 1987, thirty miles east of Cali, a white Porsche worth a quarter of a million dollars slowed down for a tollbooth and was instructed to pull over by two policemen. They approached the driver's side and requested to see ID. After the driver gave an unsatisfactory response, the policemen said that the car, the driver and his female passenger would have to go with them to Palmira. The driver offered $12 for them to let him go, which they refused. He increased his offer. They refused $200 and $48,000 and $400,000. There was no way around it: Jorge Ochoa was going to Palmira police headquarters.

Ochoa had an arrest warrant for a bull-smuggling conviction and for violating parole. Getting booked into the jail, he was hugged by a female lawyer, who promised to sort everything out. Attempting to get an official to sign his release, she made some calls, but was unsuccessful.

From a holding cell, Ochoa was transferred to an army prison, where he spent the night. On Sunday, a military plane took him to Bogotá, where policemen on motorbikes awaited him. By armoured van with a motorbike escort, he was transported to a military complex. There was no way for him to bribe his way out of the maximum-security prison cell they put him in.

The DEA issued a statement: "The president of Colombia could be courageous and greatly assist his country by throwing out Jorge Ochoa. Once Jorge Ochoa arrives in the US, he, like Carlos Lehder, will not be able to bribe, murder or intimidate his way out of police custody."

Many Colombians thought Ochoa would be extradited as swiftly as Lehder, but Ochoa was only being held on bull-smuggling and the Supreme Court had ruled against extradition. The government's strategy was to keep Ochoa incarcerated, while arranging his extradition. The US government sent a legal team to Bogotá to find an extradition mechanism.

Unlike Lehder, whose status in the cartel had slipped, Ochoa was a dominant force and one of Pablo's closest friends. His extradition had to be stopped at all costs.

Shortly after Ochoa arrived at his cell in the military complex, a dozen hit men were dispatched to the house in Medellín of Gomez Martinez, the editor of the city's biggest newspaper. They banged on the door. Peeping out of a window, the editor's son yelled that murderers were outside.

Martinez stopped watching TV, crouched behind a chair, grabbed a gun and started firing. Hit men sprayed the house with gunfire. Attempting to break down a sheet steel garage door, a van reversed into it multiple times, only bending it.

After fifteen minutes of mayhem, a neighbour called the rest of the neighbours to arms. "They're trying to kill Gomez Martinez. Let's do something!"

Under fire from the neighbours, a hit man was shot. His accomplices loaded him into a van and they disappeared.

Having failed to kidnap Gomez Martinez with the goal of having him deliver a message, Pablo issued a communiqué:

Respected Sir,

We have found out that the government is trying by whatever means possible to extradite citizen Jorge Luis Ochoa to the United States. For us, this constitutes the vilest of outrages.

... in case citizen Jorge Luis Ochoa is extradited to the United States, we will declare absolute and total war against this country's political leaders. We will execute out of hand the principal chieftains...

The Extraditables

A week after his arrest, Ochoa's six lawyers, including three former Supreme Court justices, started to demolish the case. They were aided by the departure of the US legal team in mid-December, 1987. By arguing that Ochoa had already served his time for bull-smuggling during his incarceration in Spain, Ochoa was released in time to celebrate New Year's Eve.

CHAPTER 11
WAR

Sensing weakness in its rival, the Cali Cartel started to move against the Medellín Cartel in the late 1980s. Both groups had different organisational structures. The Medellín was an alliance between independent operators, whereas Cali was run by a four-man executive board. Below the board were accountants, engineers and lawyers, and then the workforce. The executives, some of whom had law degrees, considered themselves more sophisticated than the rustic men from Medellín. They were known as the gentlemen of trafficking, whereas Medellín was regarded as thuggish. The head of the New York DEA told journalists, "Cali gangs will kill you if they have to, but they prefer to use a lawyer."

In 1988, the Cali Cartel rebuffed Pablo, who wanted both cartels to join forces against the government. Instead, the Cali Cartel cut a deal with the authorities whereby its business operations would be left alone in exchange for providing information about the Medellín Cartel. The Cali Cartel told the enemies of the Medellín Cartel the whereabouts of Pablo's safe houses and hiding places. These enemies included special units of the Colombian police assigned to find Pablo. The authorities were supposedly after Pablo to stamp out his illegal trafficking, yet were helping the Cali Cartel expand its cocaine business.

A cousin of Pablo's was at a farm with his family on vacation when the police showed up. After stating that he didn't know where Pablo was, he was hung upside down with his eyes covered, tortured by electricity and had needles inserted into his testicles. He died in front of his family. Friends, associates and bodyguards of Pablo received the same treatment. Due to the police torturing and killing so many of his associates, Pablo put a bounty on their heads. Teenage hit men attacked police stations with machine guns and bombs to claim thousands of dollars. In retaliation, police death squads drove through the barrios, machine-gunning young people unlucky enough to be out after dark.

After eating dinner on January 12, 1988, Pablo left his family in Monaco, an eight-storey apartment building, protected by reinforced steel. He hid out at a farm ten miles away. Around 5:30 am, a bomb went off at Monaco that woke people up two miles away. The blast killed two night watchmen, left a crater in the street thirteen feet deep, shattered windows throughout the neighbourhood, broke water mains and cracked the entire face of the building. Within minutes, a Renault arrived to transport Pablo's wife and son to a safe house.

Pablo made a call. "Mom, you'll soon watch some news about a bomb in Monaco. But I just called you, so you'd know nothing happened to me."

By the time Roberto showed up, Pablo said he already knew who was responsible. Half an hour after the explosion, he'd received a call from the Cali Cartel's Gilberto Rodríguez Orejuela, who said he'd heard about the bomb and wanted to know if Pablo and his family were OK. Rumours were circulating that the bomb had been planted by DAS agents, but Pablo suspected Gilberto.

Pablo knew that Gilberto had spent time in prison in Spain with a bomb-maker for the Basque guerrillas. Pablo tracked the bomb-maker down, asked him to train some of his workers and promised him excellent prices on cocaine to sell in Spain. After the bomb-maker agreed, Pablo asked if he'd ever had any experience working in Colombia. The man replied that he'd met someone in jail who'd brought him to Colombia to train some guys to make a bomb to be used against the government. Surrounded by armed bodyguards, Pablo said that the bomb had been used against him. The bomb-maker's face turned white. Pablo told him not to worry and urged him to start to train Pablo's workers.

Gilberto called Pablo, protesting that he hadn't done anything. Pablo told him to stop lying and to get ready to be hit.

A car bomb exploded by Pablo's mother's house. Cut by glass, she was hospitalised. Pablo's pregnant sister had also been asleep on the fourth floor. In hospital, she gave birth to a baby that had to live in an incubator for several weeks. Another sister on the fifth floor was treated for shrapnel wounds.

Regarding the Cali Cartel, Pablo told his mother, "If they broke my heart it was because they placed the first bomb."

The Cali Cartel offered a band of killers from Medellín $5 million to kill Pablo, but he hired the killers himself. Pablo ordered the firebombing of the drugstores through which Cali laundered money.

By 1989, bombs were exploding almost daily, and international mercenaries, including ex-SAS members, had joined the hunt for Pablo.

Pablo's nemesis in the police was the man in charge of the DAS, Miguel Alfredo Maza Márquez, who'd refused Pablo's offers of bribery and pledged to defeat the Medellín traffickers. Pablo and Maza set about trying to kill each other. On May 30, 1989, a remote-detonated car bomb with 350 kilos of dynamite failed to seriously hurt Maza, but killed seven of his bodyguards. Although the underbelly of his armoured car was destroyed, the general opened the door and emerged, holding one of his injured men. "All at once I felt as if I had been tossed into the air by the surf," the general said. Afterwards, a psychiatrist was assigned to help Maza recover.

With a price on his head of $10 million, Pablo went on the run without bodyguards because he believed that amount of money could tempt anyone. For eight months, he stayed at a farm forty miles away from Medellín, in the company of his brother and a couple who lived there. Visitors such as politicians or lawyers were brought to Pablo blindfolded. He stationed lookouts in the neighbouring farms, which he owned. He passed the time swimming in a pool by apple and orange trees, playing dominoes outside with a barbecue cooking or with his dog, Hussein, which had bitten him when he'd bought the farm.

The police arrived one morning. Pablo moved into a secret compartment built into the house. Pretending to be an artist, Roberto answered, wearing a cap and an artist's glasses. In the living room was an unfinished painting of a farm and a small cow. The police said they were searching the neighbourhood because they'd found a head on one side of the road and a body on the other. Roberto said he'd been up painting and was oblivious to the goings-on outside. The police came in, drank some coffee and left. To let Pablo know that the police had gone, Roberto knocked in a special way that only they could decode.

For several months, Pablo stayed at another farm called the Parrot with members of the cartel including Jorge Ochoa and Gacha. It was by a river so clear that all of the fish were visible.

One night, Roberto had a bad feeling, so he made sure their boat had plenty of fuel. A local farmer radioed at 6 am, warning them to flee because trucks and helicopters were on the way. Pablo's usual response to helicopters was to call them mosquitoes and to gesture slapping them away as if they meant nothing, but this time they had to hurry. With bullets whizzing by them, they raced out of the farm and headed for the mules and boats.

Without shoes or a shirt on and abandoning his paperwork in the house, Pablo dashed out with a machine gun. Bullets rained down and tore through the vegetation. The traffickers returned fired at the helicopters. Trying to get to a river, Pablo's brother-in-law came under heavy fire. Shooting at the helicopters, Pablo watched his brother-in-law die. Others trying to escape were cut down by bullets.

They were so surrounded that Jorge Ochoa took his gun out as if contemplating the suicide pact agreed by the Extraditables. Pablo told him that the time wasn't right. If it was, he would do the same. Jorge put his gun away and they escaped into the woods. The police arrested fourteen people, but none of the leaders. When they were safe, Pablo – known for remaining calm under all circumstances – cried for the loss of his brother-in-law.

These close calls lasted for months. The traffickers ended up sleeping in tents disguised by jungle brush. Many of them got sick.

From living luxuriously, Pablo had become a wartime commander. Despite all of the setbacks, the cocaine continued to flow. Pablo was listed as one of the richest men in the world in *Forbes Magazine*, with a net worth of $3 billion.

On the evening of August 18, 1989, a presidential candidate, Luis Carlos Galán, set off in a blue car for a speaking engagement to 10,000 people in a small working-class town. Years earlier, back when Pablo had attended Congress, Galán had helped Lara to expose Pablo's criminal history. Galán was charismatic, admired, fearless and the favourite to win the next election.

His car stopped by a town square. Wearing a bullet-proof vest, he got out. To get Galán to the podium, his bodyguards and assistants had to push their way through the placard-waving crowd. Arriving at a wooden stage on a steel frame, his bodyguards scanned the area for threats and signalled the all-clear.

Carried by aides and besieged by animated supporters who were attempting to touch him and shake his hand, Galán moved briskly past a cluster of pink balloons and arrived at the podium. Back on his feet, he ascended the stairs. On the platform, he was greeted by a councilman. Standing by men in light-coloured suits, Galán lifted his arms – causing his bullet-proof vest to rise – and turned to salute the crowd.

Gunfire erupted from a hit man with a machine gun hidden behind a poster, shooting upwards from the ground at Galán's exposed midsection. To a chorus of screams, the people on the stage fell or scattered. Hoping to shield themselves from gunshots, some pressed themselves to the side of the podium and clutched onto the wooden frame. Blasted in the abdomen, side and groin, Galán collapsed with severe internal bleeding. As shots continued from the killer's accomplices, most of the people in the area remained crouched. Guards in beige suits, one holding a machine gun, dragged a body to a car. The killer rushed to a transit office, put on a grey sports jacket and escaped through the crowd. Around 10 pm, Galán was pronounced dead in hospital.

Under Maza's leadership, the DAS claimed that the Medellín Cartel had put a $500,000 contract out on Galán. Pablo and Gacha were blamed. This was disinformation to hide something more sinister.

On May 13, 2005, a former justice minister and congressman of the Colombian Liberal Party, Alberto Santofimio, was arrested and accused of being the intellectual author of Galán's murder. According to the confession of Escobar's former hit man, Popeye, Santofimio had suggested Galán's murder at a secret meeting in order to eliminate his competition should Galán ever win the election. During the original murder investigation, Santofimio had been mentioned and his involvement was rumoured, but no direct evidence existed. From prison, Popeye told the media that he'd earlier denied Santofimio's participation due to the congressman's political power at the time. On October 11, 2007, Santofimio was sentenced to twenty-four years for the murder. He was released on appeal, but in August 2011 the Supreme Court reinstated the conviction, and he surrendered himself.

With the news reporting Pablo as the murder suspect and the government offering a reward for his capture, Pablo's mother visited him, hoping to get an explanation. "Did you see the news?"

"Yes, Mom," Pablo said, "but don't believe that I did everything they say. I'm not that bad, and the first person I would tell what I do is you. I'm not a saint, but if they forced me to be bad, what can I do?"

In the aftermath of Galán's death, the Colombian president declared a state of siege.

President George HW Bush made a statement: "In such difficult times, democratic nations faced with such common threats to their national security must stand together. Today we stand together with Colombia. The narco-traffickers who again have robbed Colombia of a courageous leader must be defeated. Colombians must know that we stand by its efforts to move aggressively against these criminals who seek to destroy both our societies." When it came to battling traffickers, never had such strong words of support been issued by a US president to the rulers of Colombia. Bush was itching to send troops.

On August 21, 1989, the authorities arrested over 10,000 people. Seizures included 1,000 buildings and ranches, 350 planes, 73 boats and five tons of cocaine. Riveted to the TV, Colombians watched the security forces raid Hacienda Nápoles. Another of Pablo's properties, a two-storey hilltop cabin was seized. Inside, they found thirty-eight Italian shirts and a mirrored ceiling over Pablo's brass bed. The raids on Gacha's property were just as impressive. Outside one of his mansions was a stone bridge over a man-made pond. Inside were porcelain cats, crystal coffee tables, Chinese vases, a pool table, a white marble bathroom with gold plumbing fixtures and Italian toilet paper with prints of naked women on each sheet.

Worst of all for the traffickers: extradition was reinstated with a new set of rules. Traffickers could be extradited to America by executive decree, without being processed through the courts or the government having to utilise the antiquated treaty that had been suspended in 1987. On August 21, 1989, the police arrested a cartel treasurer and started extradition proceedings.

On August 24, the Medellín headquarters of the Liberal and Social Conservative parties received bombs. Some politicians' houses were set on fire.

A new communiqué announced "now the fight is in blood."

We declare total and absolute war against the government, the industrial and political oligarchy, the journalists who have attacked and insulted us, the judges who have sold themselves to the government, the magistrates who want to extradite us, the union leaders, and all those who have pursued and attacked us.

We shall not respect the families of those who have not respected our families. We shall burn and destroy the industries, properties, and mansions of the oligarchy.

From the Extraditables and the Expropriated to the people of Colombia.

Bush sent $65 million to Colombia in emergency aid, which included twenty Huey helicopters, eight A-37 reconnaissance and attack jets, five C-130 transport planes, anti-tank weapons, assault boats, machine guns, grenade launchers… Dozens of US military advisers arrived with the equipment.

"We will provide only material support and training," Bush said. "The United States has complete confidence in the capability of the Colombian police and military to deal with this situation."

Based on information from ninety-three US attorneys, the Americans released a Top 12 Most Wanted list. The top five were Pablo Escobar, Jorge Ochoa, Fabio Ochoa, Juan David Ochoa and Gustavo Gaviria. Gacha was only ninth. According to the US Attorney General, the purpose of the report was to compile "the business structure of drug trafficking… find out once and for all how the deadly game is being played. Demystify it. Drag it out from under the rock where it lives and breeds, so that we can fully educate the American public as to the size and breadth of these illegal and insidious business operations."

According to the report, the Medellín and Cali Cartels "control approximately 70 percent of the cocaine processed in Colombia and supply 80 percent of the cocaine distributed in the United States. These cartels act as true cartels in the classic sense that they attempt, through collusion, to set prices and to eliminate any effective competition."

"Among the cartels, the Medellín Cartel is the most sophisticated organization." It controls "most of the modern office buildings in the city of Medellín and many of the retail establishments. Overseas communications are done by fax. In the US, cartel managers serve on a rotating basis."

"Of the three other major Colombian organizations, the Cali Cartel, founded in the late 1970s or early 1980s, comes closest to rivalling the Medellín Cartel in wealth and influence... A tacit agreement of ten years' standing, giving the bulk of the New York City cocaine trafficking distribution to the Cali Cartel, was breached, and tons of cocaine were shipped directly into that market by the Medellín organization."

On August 25, the Medellín Cartel announced that ten judges would die for every Colombian extradited. Over a hundred judges resigned. Seventeen bombs exploded within a few days, which were all blamed on Pablo. The Ochoas and Gacha tried to make peace with the government, but the president said that he would not rest until the traffickers were destroyed. Over a two-week period, the price of cocaine in Miami rose from $13,000 a kilo to $19,000, indicating that the crackdown had disrupted the short-term supply.

On August 29, old Fabio Ochoa Sr wrote an open letter to the president, identifying himself as the father "of so-called Extraditables, poor fellows, may God protect them," who "prefer a tomb in Colombia to a life term in a cell in the United States – in other words, a living death..." But they "are also human. They have mothers, fathers, children, brothers, relatives and friends. They also have a heart. We are all brothers." He asked the president to "let there be dialogue, let there be peace, let there be forgiveness, let us try wiping the slate clean and starting a new account. Let us forgive as Jesus Christ taught us." The president ignored him.

On September 2 at 6:40 am, a pickup truck at a petrol station by the headquarters of the newspaper *El Espectador*, carrying 220 pounds of dynamite, exploded, injuring 75 people. Windows were shattered and the newspaper's photo lab was destroyed. The damage totalled $2.5 million. The next day, the public bought half a million copies of the Sunday edition to help the newspaper.

On September 5, 1989, President Bush went on TV to deliver a speech:

In Colombia alone, cocaine killers have gunned down a leading statesman, murdered almost 200 judges and seven members of their supreme court. The besieged governments of the drug-producing countries are fighting back, fighting to break the international drug rings. But you and I agree with the courageous President of Colombia, Virgilio Barco, who said that if Americans use cocaine, then Americans are paying for murder. American cocaine users need to understand that our nation has zero tolerance for casual drug use. We have a responsibility not to leave our brave friends in Colombia to fight alone.

The $65 million emergency assistance announced two weeks ago was just our first step in assisting the Andean nations in their fight against the cocaine cartels. Colombia has already arrested suppliers, seized tons of cocaine and confiscated palatial homes of drug lords. But Colombia faces a long uphill battle, so we must be ready to do more. Our strategy allocates more than a quarter of a billion dollars for next year in military and law enforcement assistance for the three Andean nations of Colombia, Bolivia and Peru. This will be the first part of a five-year $2 billion program to counter the producers, the traffickers and the smugglers.

I spoke with President Barco just last week, and we hope to meet with the leaders of affected countries in an unprecedented drug summit, all to coordinate an inter-American strategy against the cartels. We will work with our allies and friends, especially our economic summit partners, to do more in the fight against drugs. I'm also asking the Senate to ratify the United Nations antidrug convention concluded last December.

To stop those drugs on the way to America, I propose that we spend more than a billion and a half dollars on interdiction. Greater interagency cooperation, combined with sophisticated intelligence-gathering and Defense Department technology, can help stop drugs at our borders.

And our message to the drug cartels is this: the rules have changed. We will help any government that wants our help. When requested, we will for the first time make available the appropriate resources of America's Armed Forces. We will intensify our efforts against drug smugglers on the high seas, in international airspace and at our borders. We will stop the flow of chemicals from the United States used to process drugs. We will pursue and enforce international agreements to track drug money to the front men and financiers. And then we will handcuff these money launderers and jail them, just like any street dealer. And for the drug kingpins: the death penalty.

Bush was challenged in an open letter from Milton Friedman, the 1976 Nobel Laureate in Economics:

The path you propose of more police, more jails, use of the military in foreign countries, harsh penalties for drug users and a whole panoply of repressive measures can only make a bad situation worse. The drug war cannot be won by those tactics without undermining the human liberty and individual freedom that you and I cherish.

You are not mistaken in believing that drugs are a scourge that is devastating our society. You are not mistaken in believing that drugs are tearing asunder our social fabric, ruining the lives of many young people and imposing heavy costs on some of the most disadvantaged among us. You are not mistaken in believing that the majority of the public share your concerns. In short, you are not mistaken in the end you seek to achieve.

Your mistake is failing to recognize that the very measures you favor are a major source of the evils you deplore. Of course the problem is demand, but it is not only demand, it is demand that must operate through repressed and illegal channels. Illegality creates obscene profits that finance the murderous tactics of the drug lords; illegality leads to the corruption of law enforcement officials; illegality monopolizes the efforts of honest law forces, so that they are starved for resources to fight the simpler crimes of robbery, theft and assault.

Drugs are a tragedy for addicts. But criminalizing their use converts that tragedy into a disaster for society, for users and non-users alike. Our experience with the prohibition of drugs is a replay of our experience with the prohibition of alcoholic beverages.

I append excerpts from a column that I wrote in 1972 on "Prohibition and Drugs." The major problem then was heroin from Marseilles; today, it is cocaine from Latin America. Today, also, the problem is far more serious than it was 17 years ago: more addicts, more innocent victims; more drug pushers, more law enforcement officials; more money spent to enforce prohibition, more money spent to circumvent prohibition.

Had drugs been decriminalized 17 years ago, "crack" would never have been invented (it was invented because the high cost of illegal drugs made it profitable to provide a cheaper version) and there would today be far fewer addicts. The lives of thousands, perhaps hundreds of thousands of innocent victims would have been saved, and not only in the US. The ghettos of our major cities would not be drug-and-crime-infested no-man's lands. Fewer people would be in jails, and fewer jails would have been built.

Colombia, Bolivia and Peru would not be suffering from narco-terror, and we would not be distorting our foreign policy because of narco-terror. Hell would not, in the words with which Billy Sunday welcomed Prohibition, "be forever for rent," but it would be a lot emptier.

Decriminalizing drugs is even more urgent now than in 1972, but we must recognize that the harm done in the interim cannot be wiped out, certainly not immediately.

Postponing decriminalization will only make matters worse, and make the problem appear even more intractable.

Alcohol and tobacco cause many more deaths in users than do drugs. Decriminalization would not prevent us from treating drugs as we now treat alcohol and tobacco: prohibiting sales of drugs to minors, outlawing the advertising of drugs and similar measures. Such measures could be enforced, while outright prohibition cannot be. Moreover, if even a small fraction of the money we now spend on trying to enforce drug prohibition were devoted to treatment and rehabilitation, in an atmosphere of compassion not punishment, the reduction in drug usage and in the harm done to the users could be dramatic.

This plea comes from the bottom of my heart. Every friend of freedom, and I know you are one, must be as revolted as I am by the prospect of turning the United States into an armed camp, by the vision of jails filled with casual drug users and of an army of enforcers empowered to invade the liberty of citizens on slight evidence. A country in which shooting down unidentified planes "on suspicion" can be seriously considered as a drug-war tactic is not the kind of United States that either you or I want to hand on to future generations.

Milton Friedman's mistake was assuming that Bush was genuinely concerned about the drug problem. Bush was using Pablo and the traffickers to justify transferring billions of taxpayers' money over to weapons manufacturers and prison industries – small change compared to the trillions US taxpayers would spend fighting a War on Drugs that only exacerbated the problem exactly as Milton had predicted. The black market in cocaine was as profitable for those fighting the traffickers as it was for the cartels. Decriminalisation would have wiped out the profit for both sides. Milton was also unaware of the CIA's role in drug trafficking, because anyone who blew the whistle back then was silenced.

On September 17, Pablo responded to Bush in a slightly more aggressive fashion than Milton Friedman. Near the US embassy – which was on a high state of alert – a man was taking a stroll in a park. After scoping out his surroundings for witnesses, he pulled out a rocket-propelled grenade launcher, took aim and fired. The rocket hit the embassy building, but failed to explode. It only damaged the cement facade. Diplomats sent their families home.

On November 27, 1989, a presidential candidate was expected to board Avianca Airlines Flight 203 from Bogotá to Cali. At a meeting with Pablo present, it was decided to eliminate the candidate by putting a bomb – consisting of five kilos of dynamite – on board the plane. A ticket for seat 15F was purchased in a fake name. An unwitting accomplice was given a suitcase he was told contained a recording device, and instructed to use it to record the conversations of the Cali Cartel people scheduled to sit in front of him.

At 7:13 am, the plane took off. It was in the air for five minutes and flying at a speed of 794 kilometres per hour when the accomplice turned a knob on the recording device. At an altitude of 13,000 feet, the bomb blasted a hole in the floor and the side of the plane and ripped the airliner apart. The nose section separated from the tail section, which tumbled down in flames. All 107 people on board were killed, as well as three on the ground from the falling debris.

At the last minute, the presidential candidate had switched to a private flight. Eventually, he became the president.

After the explosion, a Bogotá radio station received a call from a member of the Extraditables, claiming responsibility because the passengers had included five informants. Four years later, the bomb maker confessed to the DAS that he'd been paid a million pesos by a senior Medellín Cartel member.

The death of two Americans on-board Avianca Airlines Flight 203 prompted the Bush administration to classify Pablo as a clear and present danger and to begin Intelligence Support

Activity on him. George HW Bush dispatched the CIA, a secret surveillance unit called Centra Spike and Delta Force, the top counterterrorism unit.

Mostly language experts and technicians, Centra Spike specialised in eavesdropping on electronic communications to find people. By tracking Pablo's phone calls, they mapped out the members of the Medellín Cartel. They forwarded the information to Search Bloc, a group of elite Colombian police and soldiers hunting Pablo.

Pablo announced he would destroy the Search Bloc within eight days. Two car bombs killed twenty-five officers. Instead of disbanding, they received more men and ammunition, turning them into a seven-hundred-strong SWAT team.

In November 1989, Gacha's son was released from jail. Two months earlier, he'd been arrested during a raid on a ranch north of Bogotá, and charged with possessing illegal arms. Hoping he'd lead them to Gacha, the police shadowed him. In December, he joined his father at a small ranch. Having finally pinpointed his location, the government sent more than 1,000 Colombian National Police and Marines.

Colombian military personnel aboard two helicopters opened fire on Gacha, hitting him in the leg. In a gun battle, Gacha, his son and fifteen bodyguards ended up disfigured by bullets. A chunk of Gacha's head had been blown off. Initially, the extent of the damage to his head and the noise of grenades going off led the neighbours to believe that he'd committed suicide by holding a grenade to his head. But this was debunked when it was confirmed that his hands had not been damaged. It is believed that a bullet to the face from a helicopter-mounted machine gun killed him. Even though he'd been a murderous cocaine trafficker, 15,000 people attended his burial, many of whom viewed him as a public benefactor due to his building projects and assistance to the poor.

In December, 1989, Pablo launched his biggest attack on General Maza. A bus brought a 500-pound bomb to the DAS building. Inside the lobby, one of Pablo's workers was waiting for the arrival of Maza and his bodyguards to give the signal. A man outside was supposed to send the bus into the lobby. But Maza arrived through a different entrance, thwarting the original plan. The man in the lobby gave up waiting for Maza and exited the building. Upon seeing him, the men outside detonated the bomb at 7:30 am, almost killing Pablo's man as he walked out.

It was one of the biggest ever explosions in Colombia. The blast opened a crater ten feet deep and demolished a complex of two-story commercial buildings next to the avenue where the bus had been parked. The bus crashed into a car. The entire front of the eleven-story DAS building fell off. Numerous buildings were damaged and windows shattered in a twenty-six-block area. Out of the almost one thousand injured, those who could stand wandered through an area strewn with rubble, destroyed cars, corpses, blood-splatter and body parts.

Despite the devastation and dozens of deaths, Maza emerged without a scratch. "It was like a mini-atom bomb," he told reporters. "The ceiling fell down on top of me." He said that the bomb was positioned to aim shock waves at the upper floors of the building. "Without a doubt, it was aimed at me." He credited his survival to the grace of God and the steel protecting his office. Pablo put a $1.3 million contract on him.

On August 7, 1990, a new president called for a reduction in the demand for cocaine from the consumer countries, which was viewed as a peace offering to the traffickers. But on August 12, Pablo's cousin, Gustavo, was located in a house in Medellín. In what the police claimed was an exchange of gunfire, he was killed by members of the Search Bloc. Any hope of peace was off. Devastated by the loss of his right-hand man, Pablo started to torture and kill people inside his organisation whom he felt were cooperating with the authorities.

According to the Colombian National Police, there were

25,000 murders in Colombia in 1990. They included judges, politicians, three presidential candidates and many of Pablo's associates, friends and family.

CHAPTER 12
GEORGE HW BUSH AND
CIA DRUG TRAFFICKING

Narcos focused on the DEA's quest to capture Pablo, while omitting the CIA's complicity in cocaine trafficking throughout that time. DEA agent Steve Murphy was Pablo's nemesis from episode one, but Murphy only arrived in Colombia in 1991, so his presence in all of the Pablo-related events from 1976 to 1991 is fictional. Murphy was a minion of Pablo's real nemesis: George HW Bush.

Throughout the 1980s, the Reagan-Bush administration launched an expansion of the War on Drugs. The "Just say no" campaign was funded largely by tobacco, alcohol and pharmaceutical companies. The government claimed that the war was necessary to take down the Pablos of this world, but its burden fell mostly on hundreds of thousands of non-violent marijuana users, many of whom were SWAT-team raided and dragged off to jail.

Reagan's wife, Nancy, was a leading spokesperson: "If you're a casual drug user, you're an accomplice to murder." The campaign, in combination with sensational headlines about rabid black crack users murdering white people, prostituting themselves for a pittance and giving birth to malnourished alien-like babies caused public opinion about drugs to swing in favour of the zero-tolerance policies that filled prisons with non-violent drug users from the poorest neighbourhoods. Private prisons and all of the industries that grew up around them became a massive source of profit for the politicians taking contributions from them.

In 1982, Ronald Regan created the South Florida Task Force,

headed by George HW Bush. It combined elements of the FBI, army and Navy to fight traffickers who weren't working with the CIA. The media published images of soldiers, surveillance planes and helicopter gunships off the coast of Florida, waging war with Pablo's smugglers. As drug seizures rose, Reagan and Bush posed for photos amid tons of confiscated cocaine, and proclaimed their success in the War on Drugs. They never mentioned that the price of cocaine in America was falling despite the gunboats, a sure sign that the supply into America was increasing. Even DEA agents complained that the War on Drugs was just a handover of money to the military.

In 1983, a program called Drug Abuse Resistance Education (DARE) started in American schools. Students were encouraged to let the police know about their friends' and families' drug habits, so they could swiftly be incarcerated. The Reagan-Bush administration doubled the federal prison population. Young offenders and non-violent drug users were sent to Special Alternative Incarceration boot camps to have their rebellious attitudes demolished. They often emerged traumatised and more inclined to take drugs.

Simultaneously, the Reagan-Bush administration quietly instructed American universities to destroy all of the research into marijuana undertaken between 1966 and 1976, which could have benefited people with a range of ailments, including cancer patients at risk of death because they couldn't eat, and children born with rare conditions who had hundreds of seizures a week and were at risk of entering comas and dying.

The federal government used planes to illegally spray marijuana fields in Kentucky, Georgia and Tennessee with the toxic weed-killer Paraquat, risking the lives of marijuana smokers. Banned in several European countries, Paraquat is highly toxic to animals and has serious and irreversible delayed effects if absorbed. As little as one teaspoonful of the active ingredient is fatal. Death occurs up to thirty days after ingestion. It's also toxic if absorbed through the skin, and can cause nose bleeding if inhaled. No antidote for poisoning exists although it is recommended that hospitalisation is sought without delay. The government was able to use it by classifying it as having low acute toxicity when sprayed.

Reagan's Drugs Czar, Carlton Turner, said that kids deserved to die as a punishment for smoking poisoned weed, to teach them a lesson. Two years later, he called for the death penalty for all drug users. On one occasion, the DEA had been ordered to spray Paraquat on a marijuana plantation in Georgia, but the Forest Service had miscalculated the location. The Paraquat ended up on a corn crop. Drugs Czar Turner was a co-owner of a patent, along with the University of Mississippi, on a chemical test that detected the presence of Paraquat on crops. Although he stood to earn royalties from the patent, he denied any conflict of interest.

Extending the War on Drugs into Colombia included dropping chemical poisons on peasants and their crops. Many had to leave the little pieces of land they owned, and they were reduced to begging. Their land often ended up in the hands of the wealthy and foreign corporations.

By 1986, officials in Florida acknowledged that the amount of drugs entering the US had skyrocketed. The Government Accounting Office stated that cocaine imports had doubled in one year.

In the summer of 1989, the Commissioner of US Customs resigned because he believed that the only real battles were being fought against minorities and the downtrodden, while those in authority were protecting the government's monopoly in the trade. "The War on Drugs is a war of words," he said.

While the international narcotics trade thrived, Reagan declared the War on Drugs to be one of his best achievements. But in 1989, the Iran-Contra scandal revealed that the US government – via the CIA – had been trafficking in hard drugs for military weapons. During the investigation, the increasingly frail and senile Reagan feigned ignorance and most people believed him. Throughout Reagan's term, ex-CIA-director Bush had really been calling the shots.

President Bush was inaugurated on January 20, 1989. On September 5, 1989, he outlined his strategy for eradicating drug use. He asked Congress for $7.9 billion, 70 percent for law enforcement, including $1.6 billion for prisons. "This scourge will stop." His focus was on reducing demand, meaning arresting more drug users, rather than prevention, education and medical treatment. He increased the repressive measures against marijuana users. "Our nation has zero tolerance for casual drug use… You do drugs, you will be caught, and when you're caught, you will be punished. Some think there won't be room for them in jail. We'll make room."

The story of Keith Jackson illustrates Bush's duplicity in the War on Drugs. On September 5, 1989, President Bush appeared on TV. "This is the first time since taking the oath of office that I've felt an issue was so important, so threatening, that it warranted talking directly with you, the American people. All of us agree that the gravest domestic threat facing our nation today is drugs. Drugs have strained our faith in our system of justice. Our courts, our prisons, our legal system, are stretched to breaking point. The social costs of drugs are mounting. In short, drugs are sapping our strength as a nation. Turn on the evening news or pick up the morning paper and you'll see what some Americans know just by stepping out their front door: Our most serious problem today is cocaine, and in particular, crack…" Reaching to his side, Bush produced a bag labelled EVIDENCE with chalky rocks in it. "This is crack cocaine seized a few days ago by Drug Enforcement agents in a park just across the street from the White House. It could easily have been heroin or PCP. It's as innocent-looking as candy, but it's turning our cities into battle zones and it's murdering our children. Let there be no mistake: this stuff is poison. Some used to call drugs harmless recreation; they're not. Drugs are a real and terribly dangerous threat to our neighbourhoods, our friends and our families…"

Bush's claim aroused suspicion in Michael Isikoff, an NBC correspondent, who doubted that crack was being sold in Lafayette

Square, an urban park north of the White House. Through contacts at the DEA, Isikoff learned the truth. Bush's speech writers had decided that a prop would enhance the president's rhetoric, so they wrote the Lafayette Square crack story into the script before it had happened. After Bush approved the idea, the DEA was told to make a drug purchase near the White House in order to fit the script.

The assignment ended up with Special Agent Sam Gaye, who was asked by his boss, "Can you make a drug buy around 1600 Pennsylvania Avenue? Can you call any defendants you've been buying from?" In court, Gaye testified, "I had twenty-four hours to buy three ounces of crack."

Using informers, Gaye set up a purchase, which fell through after the dealer didn't show up in the park. During the second attempt, the agent's body microphone malfunctioned, and the cameraman about to film the transaction was assaulted by a homeless person.

Finally, an informant contacted an amenable low-level dealer, Keith Jackson, an eighteen-year-old high-school student who lived across town. Gaye asked Keith to meet him in the park.

"Where's Lafayette Park?" Keith said.

"It's across the street from the White House."

"Where the fuck is the White House?" Keith said.

"We had to manipulate him to get him down there," said William McMullan, assistant special agent in charge of the DEA's Washington field office. "It wasn't easy."

When the DEA video tape was played in court, the jury laughed. It showed Gaye waiting on Pennsylvania Avenue with the White House and tourists behind him. Before Jackson and an informant arrived by car, an irate woman sprung up from below the camera's vision, and yelling was heard as an altercation unfolded.

"There was this lady," Gaye said, "who got up off the ground and said, 'Don't take my photo! Don't take my photo!'"

For the White House transaction, as well as three earlier

sales, Keith ended up facing ten years to life without parole even though he had no previous convictions. The first trial was a mistrial, but on retrial he was convicted of three counts with two being dropped, including the Lafayette Park sale. The judge sentenced him to ten years due to the mandatory minimums for selling crack near a school, but suggested that he seek clemency, which was never granted.

A teenager had been sacrificed to improve Bush's ratings.

After the fall of the Berlin Wall in 1989, and with the Soviet Union contracting, the US was rapidly running out of Communists to fight. Bush needed enemies to maintain his popularity at the voting booths and to keep the war machine in business. Pablo was ideal.

In November 1990, Bush signed a bill that coerced the states into suspending the driver's licenses and revoking government permits and benefits (including college loans) of those convicted of drug crimes. He advocated the heavy use of forfeiture or confiscation of property that the government believed to be drug related. It was primarily used to take cars and currency, and the money was recycled back into the state and federal government. These laws operated under presumed guilt, which did not require a trial or even a conviction.

By 1992, there were more people in federal prisons for drug charges than there were for all crimes in 1980, with the burden overwhelmingly falling on black people. Twice as many people were arrested for possession than supplying. Chief Justice of the Supreme Court, William Rehnquist, said there were too many arrests. New York City jails filled to breaking point, and jail boats had to be opened. Bush's policies did nothing to stop people from buying and selling drugs.

That the US government was simultaneously waging a War on Drugs while facilitating their importation via the CIA is hard for some people to swallow. But it must be probed further to understand why Pablo was taken down.

In 1985, Retired US Navy Lieutenant Commander Al Martin

had dinner with George HW Bush, Jeb Bush and a CIA veteran Felix Rodriguez, who'd taken $10 million from the Medellín Cartel for the Nicaraguan rebels (as detailed in Chapter 4). Over food, George HW Bush boasted that he operated on the Big Lie principle, whereby big lies would be believed because the public couldn't conceive that their leader was capable of bending the truth that far, such as a president railing against drugs while overseeing drug trafficking worth billions.

Anyone who tried to blow the whistle on Bush's phoney War on Drugs ended up paying a price. Former DEA agent Cele Castillo wrote *Powderburns: Cocaine, Contras & the Drug War* (1998), in which he detailed a meeting with George HW Bush. Assigned to El Salvador in 1986 to investigate a pilot who stored his plane at the Ilopango airbase, Castillo had discovered that the Nicaraguan rebels were smuggling cocaine to the US, using the same pilots, planes and hangers as the CIA and NSC (National Security Council), under the direction of Bush's frontman Oliver North. At Ilopango, he often saw Bush's buddy, Felix Rodriguez, whom Castillo described as an American terrorist. Bewildered, he told his bosses about the cocaine smuggling. They instructed him to use the word "alleged" in his reports instead of stating things as factual.

Castillo reported that a CIA agent was requesting a US Visa for a Nicaraguan-rebel drug smuggler who was flying cocaine from Costa Rica to anti-Castro Cubans in Miami. The cocaine in Costa Rica was picked up from the ranch of an American, John Hull, who, by the admission of the CIA's station chief in Costa Rica, was working with the CIA on military supply and other operations on behalf of the Nicaraguan rebels, and was being paid $110,000 a month by Oliver North.

After Castillo blew the whistle, Vice President Bush met him briefly during a visit to Guatemala City on January 14, 1986, at a cocktail party at the ambassador's residence. Protected by a retinue of Secret Service agents, Bush was talking to embassy personnel and Guatemalan dignitaries. Bush approached Castillo and read the tag on his lapel, which identified him as a member of the US embassy. Shaking hands, Bush asked what he did.

"I'm a DEA agent assigned to Guatemala."

"Well, what do you do?"

"There's some funny things going on with the Contras in El Salvador."

Without uttering a response, Bush smiled and walked away. Castillo realised that Bush was in on the drug trafficking.

Following the party at the ambassador's house, the US Ambassador to El Salvador sent a back-channel cable to the State Department. A few days later, the DEA closed down Castillo's investigation. The reports he'd filed disappeared into what Castillo called a black hole at DEA headquarters. In February 1987, DEA investigators found "no credible information" to indicate that traffickers were part of any political organisation, including the Nicaraguan rebels and the government of Nicaragua. Castillo received so much harassment that he ended up quitting the DEA in 1990.

Presidential candidate and billionaire, Ross Perot, hired Bo Gritz, a Green Beret who'd earned multiple medals for bravery, to find American POWs imprisoned in Asia decades after the Vietnam War. While on his mission, Gritz came across General Khun Sa, a Burmese drug lord, who offered to identify US government officials he claimed had been trafficking in heroin for over twenty years. Having uncovered CIA drug trafficking in Asia, Perot and Gritz were shocked.

Perot requested a meeting with George HW Bush, so that he could present his evidence. Bush told Perot to go to the proper authorities and refused to help any further.

Here are extracts from a letter Gritz wrote to Bush:

Sir:

Why does it seem that you are saying "YES" to illegal

narcotics in America?

I turned over video tapes to your NSC staff assistant, Tom Harvey, January 1987, wherein General KHUN SA, overlord of Asia's "Golden Triangle" offered to stop 900 tons of heroin/opium from entering the free world in 1987. Harvey told me, "...there is no interest here in doing that."

Unfortunately, Khun Sa knew nothing about US POWs. He did, however, offer to trade his nation's poppy dependence for a legitimate economy.

Instead of receiving an "Atta Boy" for bringing back video tape showing Khun Sa's offer to stop 900 tons of illegal narcotics and expose dirty USG officials, Scott was jailed and I was threatened. I was told that if I didn't "erase and forget" all that we had discovered, I would, "hurt the government." Further, I was promised a prison sentence of "15 years."

I returned to Burma with two other American witnesses, Lance Trimmer, a private detective from San Francisco, and Barry Flynn from Boston. Gen Khun Sa identified some of those in government service he says were dealing in heroin and arms sales. We video-taped this second interview and I turned copies over in June 1987, to the Chairman of the Select Committee on Intelligence; Chairman of the House on Foreign Affairs Task Force on Narcotics Control; Co-Chairman, Senate Narcotics Committee; Senator Harry Reid, NV; Representative James Bilbray, NV; and other Congressional members. Mister Richard Armitage, Assistant Secretary of Defense for International Security Affairs, is one of those USG officials implicated by Khun Sa. Nothing was done with this evidence that indicated that anyone of authority, including yourself, had intended to do anything more than protect Mr Armitage. I was charged with "Misuse of Passport." Seems that it is alright for Oliver North and Robert MacFarlane to go into Iran on Irish Passports to negotiate an illegal arms deal that neither you nor anyone else admits condoning, but I can't use a passport that brings back drug information against your friends.

Lance Trimmer and I submitted a "Citizen Complaint of Wrongdoing by Federal Officers" to Attorney General Edwin Meese, III on 17 September 1987. Continuous private and Legislative inquiries to date indicate that the Attorney General's Office has "lost" the document. Congressional requests to the Government Accounting Office have resulted in additional government snares and stalls.

January 20, 1988, I talked before your Breakfast Club in Houston, Texas. A distinguished group of approximately 125 associates of yours, including the Chief Justice of the Texas Supreme Court, expressed assurance that you are a righteous man. Almost all of them raised their hand when I asked how many of them know you personally. If you are a man with good intent, I pray you will do more than respond to this letter. I ask that you seriously look into the possibility that political appointees close to you are guilty of by-passing our Constitutional process, and for purposes of promoting illegal covert operations, conspired in the trafficking of narcotics and arms.

Please answer why a respected American Citizen like Mister H Ross Perot can bring you a pile of evidence of wrongdoing by Armitage and others, and you, according to *TIME magazine* (May 4, page 18), not only offer him no support, but have your Secretary of Defense, Frank Carlucci tell Mr. Perot to "stop pursuing Mr Armitage." Why Sir, will you not look into affidavits gathered by The Christic Institute (Washington, D.C.), which testify that Armitage not only trafficked in heroin, but did so under the guise of an officer charged with bringing home our POWs. If the charges are true, Armitage, who is still responsible for POW recovery as your Assistant Secretary of Defense ISA, has every reason not to want these heroes returned to us alive. Clearly, follow-on investigations would illuminate the collective crimes of Armitage and others.

...in May 1987, Gen Khun Sa, in his jungle headquarters, named Richard Armitage as a key connection in a ring of heroin trafficking mobsters and USG officials. A US agent I have known for many years stopped by my home last month en route to his next overseas assignment. He remarked that he had worked for those CIA chiefs named by Khun Sa, and that by his own personal knowledge, he knew what Khun Sa said was true. He was surprised it had taken so long to surface.

I am a registered Republican. I voted for you twice. I will not do so again. If you have any love or loyalty in your heart for this nation; if you have not completely sold out, then do something positive to determine the truth of these most serious allegations. You were Director of the CIA in 1975, during a time Khun Sa says Armitage and CIA officials were trafficking in heroin. As Director of Intelligence you were responsible to the American people for the activities of your assistant – even as you should know what some of these same people are doing who are close to you now as our Vice President because I feel these "parallel government" types will only be promoted by you, giving them more reason to bury our POWs.

Parting shot Mr Vice President: On 28 January 1988, General Khun Sa tendered an offer to turn over to me one metric ton (2,200 pounds) of heroin. He says this is a good faith gesture to the American people that he is serious about stopping all drugs coming from the infamous Golden Triangle. If you and Nancy Reagan are really serious about saying "NO" to drugs, why not test Gen Khun Sa? I challenge you to allow me in the company of agents of your choice to arrange to receive this token offer worth over $4 billion on the streets of New York City. It will represent the largest "legal" seizure of heroin on record. You can personally torch it, dump it in the ocean, or turn it into legal medication; as I understand there is a great shortage of legal opiates available to our doctors. I think Gen Khun Sa's offer is most interesting. If you say "YES" then the ever increasing flow of heroin from Southeast Asia (600 tons—'86, 900 tons—'87, 1200 tons—'88) may dry up – not good for business in the parallel government and super CIA circles Oliver North mentioned. If you say "NO" to Khun Sa, you are showing colors not fit for a man who would be President.

Respecting Your Office,

James "Bo" Gritz, Concerned American, Box 472 HCR-31 Sandy Valley, NV 89019, Tel: (702) 723-5266

Further investigation of the CIA drug trafficking led Ross Perot to Mena, Arkansas (a hub of CIA-sponsored trafficking that I detail in my book *American Made*) and Bush's involvement.

"When you look into the [Vietnam POW] cover-up," Perot said, "you find government officials in the drug trade who can't break themselves of the habit. What I have found is a snake pit [CIA drug trafficking] without a bottom. They will do anything to keep this covered up."

Unable to get Bush to acknowledge the trafficking, Perot ran against Bush in the 1992 election. Ex-CIA cocaine-smuggling-pilot Chip Tatum stated that Bush was so terrified of Perot becoming president and prosecuting Bush for drug crimes that Bush made plans to assassinate him. When Perot ran again in 1996, Tatum wrote him a letter:

Dear Mr Perot:

As you prepare your part for the 1996 election, there is a matter of grave importance of which you should be aware.

In 1992, as the commander of a Black Operations Unit called Pegasus, I was ordered to neutralize you. Our unit was directed by President George Bush. It was determined, at some point, that the party you formed was counter to the American system of democracy. In his attempt to justify your neutralization, Mr Bush expressed not only his concerns of the existence of your party and the threat which you posed to free America, but also the positions of other US and world leaders.

I had been associated with Pegasus since its creation in 1985. The original mission of our unit was to align world leaders and financiers with the United States. I was personally responsible for the neutralization of one Mossad agent, an army Chief of Staff of a foreign government, a rebel leader and the president of a foreign government.

However, all of these missions were directed toward enemies of the United States as determined by our President. And because of this, I did not hesitate to successfully neutralize these enemies.

The order to neutralize you, however, went against all that I believed in. It was obvious to me that his order was predicated on a desire to remain as President rather than a matter of enemy alignment. I refused the order. I further advised the President and others that if you or members of your organization or family were threatened or harmed in any way, I would cause information, which includes certain documents, to be disseminated from their six locations in various areas of the world, to various media and political destinations. I walked away from Special Operations that day with the knowledge that you don't just quit! I felt, however, that the time capsules protected my interests.

In September of 1994, I received a telephone call demanding the information "or else!" It was obvious from the day that I walked out of Pegasus that to turn this information over would be terminal. In the spring of 1995, I was arrested by the FBI for wire fraud. Although innocent of the allegations, I found it necessary to plead guilty in an attempt to tarnish my credibility. It was my opinion, as I expressed it to [Felix] Rodriguez when he called and threatened me, that if I were of questionable credibility, the documents, if ever made public, may not stand on their merits.

With this arrest, I seized upon the opportunity to effect this theory. I have since been indicted on a second fraud charge, this time involving my wife. I will not allow this prosecution of my family. I have notified the authorities that I intend to put my case to a jury. While awaiting the trial, I wrote a book involving my first experience in the Special Operations arena. Since then, I have found that the US Marshals have instructed the Hillsborough County jail to hold me, regardless of the outcome of the instant trial charge.

The new charge is treason. For over twenty years I have dedicated my skills, time, and health to my country. I have been shot, tortured, and beaten, fighting to protect our right to form and run our government as determined by the Constitution. I am not aware of an active Pegasus unit. I had assumed it was disbanded with the new President... Someone had to orchestrate this. So, be aware and alert!

Good luck and good fortune in 1996.

In 1996, Perot's strategy to take votes from Bush worked, and Bill Clinton won – a president involving in drug trafficking was replaced by another involved in trafficking as detailed in my book, *American Made.* As Governor of Arkansas, Bill Clinton was paid off by the CIA to allow cocaine to flow through his state.

On YouTube, Chip Tatum stated that Bush had direct knowledge of the drug operation coming out of Central and South America. Tatum saw Bush at a drugs camp, standing by a cocaine press. Thanks to YouTube, the testimonies of numerous US pilots who flew drugs into America for the CIA are available: Google Beau Abbott, Tosh Plumlee or Terry Reed.

In April 1989, Senator John Kerry's Subcommittee on Terrorism Narcotics and International Operations released its report, "Drugs, Law Enforcement and Foreign Policy." It included diary entries from Bush's frontman Oliver North. In July 1984, North wrote that he wanted "aircraft to go to Bolivia to pick up paste, want aircraft to pick up 1,500 kilos." On July 12, 1985, he wrote, "$14 million to finance [arms] Supermarket came from drugs."

While others took the fall for trafficking, the DEA never investigated North. Even though he'd kept his hands clean by not actually flying the drugs himself, he was guilty of conspiracy under statutes passed by Congress in 1953, concerning anyone committing any act, no matter how small, in the furtherance of a crime. The DEA had stood down, even though North had used international traffickers on the DEA's most wanted list.

One example in the Kerry Report was the airline SETCO, described as "the principal company used by the Contras in Honduras to transport supplies and personnel," in 1986. As early as 1983, US Customs had told the DEA that the owner of the airline was Juan Matta Ballesteros, one of the biggest cocaine traffickers in the world. By 1980, the DEA was aware that Matta and his co-conspirators were estimated to be trafficking one-third of the cocaine used in America. Oliver North had obtained funding from the State Department for Matta's SETCO and three other airlines, all established and run by traffickers. The DEA's response was to close their office in Honduras and to have their officials lie to the public. The difficulty of this deceit was compounded after Matta and his accomplices conspired to kidnap, torture and murder a DEA agent in Mexico in 1985. As they'd all been contributing drug money and weapons to the Nicaraguan rebels, Matta wasn't arrested until 1988, as part of a strategy for George HW Bush's run for the presidency.

Born into a CIA family, Mike Ruppert rose up the ranks as an LA police officer. After witnessing huge CIA shipments of cocaine into California, he blew the whistle and was forced to quit amid death threats. After the journalist Gary Webb detailed the CIA cocaine trafficking that Bush had overseen, people were so outraged that the CIA director appeared at a town-hall meeting at a high school in LA – an epicentre of the crack epidemic that CIA cocaine had helped to fuel. Mike Ruppert decided to attend.

A Congresswoman approached the microphone. "It's not up to us to prove the CIA was involved in drug trafficking in South Central Los Angeles. Rather, it's up to them to prove they were not."

As CIA director Deutch got up to speak, the crowd booed and jeered. "I'm going to be brief," he said. "I want to make four points, and only four points. First, the people of the CIA and I understand the tremendous horror that drugs have been to Americans, what drugs do to families and communities, and the way drugs kill babies. We understand how ravaging drugs are in this country. CIA employees and I share your anger at the injustice and lack of compassion that drug victims encounter."

"He sounds just like Clinton!" someone yelled.

"During the past two years," Deutch said, "while I have been director of Central Intelligence, our case officers' intelligence operations have directly worked to capture all of the Cali Cartel drug lords. We have seriously disrupted the flow of coca paste between the growing areas of Peru and Bolivia to the cocaine processing facilities in Colombia. We have seized huge amounts of heroin grown in the poppy fields of Southwest Asia. Our purpose is to stop drugs from coming into the US. So my second point is that the CIA is fighting against drugs." The audience grumbled.

"Our activities are secret. Accordingly, there's not a lot of public understanding of what we do. I understand that people are suspicious of the CIA, and in the course of recruiting agents to break up those groups that bring drugs into the US, our case officers, our men and women deal with bad people, very bad people, sometimes at great risk to their lives. These are criminals with which we must deal, if we are going to stop drugs from coming to the country. They frequently lie about their relationships with us for their own purpose. So it is hard for members of the public to know what is true and what is not true...

"Now we all know that the US government and the CIA

supported the Contras [Nicaraguan rebels] in their efforts to overthrow the Sandinista government in Nicaragua in the mid-80s. It is alleged that the CIA also helped the Contras raise money for arms by introducing crack cocaine into California. It is an appalling charge that goes to the heart of this country. It is a charge that cannot go unanswered," Deutch said, pounding on the table.

"It says that the CIA, an agency of the United States government founded to protect Americans, helped introduce drugs and poison into our children and helped kill their future. No one who heads a government agency – not myself or anyone else – can let such an allegation stand. I will get to the bottom of it and I will let you know the results of what I have found.

"I've ordered an independent investigation of these charges. The third point I want to make to you is to explain the nature of the investigation. I've ordered the CIA Inspector General to undertake a full investigation." The crowd yelled their discontent so loudly that Deutch had to wait a minute before continuing. "Let me tell you why he's the right official to do the job. First, the IG is established by law of Congress to be independent, to carry out activities, to look for fraud and crimes within the CIA. Secondly, the inspector general has access to all CIA records and documents, no matter how secret. Third, the IG has the authority to interview the right people. Fourth, he is able to cooperate with other government departments. For example, the Department of Justice, the DEA, the Department of Defense, all of which had operations on-going in Nicaragua at the time. Finally, the IG has a good track record of being a whistle-blower on past misdeeds of the CIA. For example, just last month he uncovered that some CIA employees were misusing credit cards and they are now in jail."

"What about Guatemala? What about those murders?" a heckler yelled, referring to CIA-sponsored military regimes in Guatemala murdering thousands of civilians.

"Most importantly, when this investigation is complete, I

intend to make the results public, so that any person can judge the adequacy of the investigation. Anyone in the public who has a wish to look at the report will be able to do so. I want to stress that I am not the only person in the CIA who wants any American to believe that the CIA was responsible for this kind of disgusting charge. Finally, I want to say to you that as of today, we have no evidence of conspiracy by the CIA to engage in encouraging drug traffickers in Nicaragua or elsewhere in Latin America during this or any other period."

A question came from a graduate student of the Tuskegee Institute in Alabama: "I'd like to know how this incident differs from what happened at my school, where, for forty years, the government denied inflicting syphilis on African-American men?"

Deutch conceded that what had happened at Tuskegee was terrible. "Let me say something else. There was no one who came forward forty years ago and said they were going to investigate."

"… where I live there are no jobs for the children and our kids are just seen as commodities," a woman said. "They are being cycled through the prisons. They come back to the street and are marked and scarred for the rest of their life. You, the President and everybody else should be highly upset. You should be saying, how did this cancer get here?"

A man stood up. "And now we are supposed to trust the CIA to investigate itself?"

Deutch tried to quell the malcontents by overemphasising the Inspector General's independence, which incensed the crowd.

"Why don't you turn it over to an independent counsel? Someone who has the power to issue subpoenas. It would have more credibility."

Deutch responded that no independent counsel was possible because no criminal complaint had been filed.

It was Mike Ruppert's turn to speak. For years, he'd been waiting for such an opportunity. The rowdy audience hushed as Mike said, "I will tell you, director Deutch, as a former Los Angeles Police narcotics detective, that your agency has dealt drugs throughout this country for a long time."

There was a standing ovation. The audience went wild. It took a few minutes to calm everybody down.

"Director Deutch, I will refer you to three specific agency operations known as Amadeus, Pegasus and Watchtower. I have Watchtower documents heavily redacted by the Agency [CIA]. I was personally exposed to CIA operations and recruited by CIA personnel who attempted to recruit me in the late 70s to become involved in protecting Agency drug operations in this country. I have been trying to get this out for eighteen years, and I have the evidence. My question for you is very specific, sir. If in the course of the IG's [CIA Inspector General's] investigations... you come across evidence of severely criminal activity, and it's classified, will you use that classification to hide the criminal activity or will you tell the American people the truth?"

There was more applause and cheering as Deutch wrung his hands and clasped them together as if praying.

"If you have information," Deutch said, "about CIA illegal activity in drugs, you should immediately bring that information to wherever you want, but let me suggest three places: the Los Angeles Police Department—"

"No! No!" the crowd yelled.

"It is your choice: the Los Angeles Police Department, the Inspector General or the office of one of your congresspersons..."

The audience started chanting, "He told you!"

"If this information turns up wrongdoing," Deutch said, growing exasperated. "We will bring the people to justice and make them accountable."

"For the record..." Mike said, "I did bring this information out eighteen years ago and I got shot at and forced out of LAPD because of it." Mike finished to massive applause.

"My question to you is," a spectator said to Deutch, "if you know all this stuff that the Agency has done historically, then why should we believe you today, when you say certainly this could never happen in Los Angeles, when the CIA's done this stuff all over the world?"

"I didn't come here thinking everyone was going to believe me," Deutch said. "I came here for a much simpler task. I came here to stand up on my legs and tell you I was going to investigate these horrible allegations. All you can do is listen to what I have to say and wait to see the results."

"But how can we know how many documents have been shredded and how can we be certain that more documents won't be shredded?"

"I don't know that anybody has found any lost documents in the operational files," Deutch said. "I know of nobody who has found any gaps in sequences, any missing files, any missing papers for any period of that time. That may come up."

"Hey, do you know Walter Pincus?" a man asked, referring to a journalist who spied on American students abroad for the CIA.

"Yes," Deutch said. "Why?"

"Is he an asset of the CIA?"

As if he'd had enough, Deutch clasped his head and shook it.

The crowd vented on the lady who'd invited Deutch to the meeting. "I don't know why this lady is saluting Deutch's courage for coming here today, when everybody knows this building has got hundreds of pigs in it. There's pigs behind those curtains. There's pigs on the roof. We're not going to get no ghetto justice today." The crowd murmured its approval.

A man stood and pointed at Deutch. "To see you coming in this community today in this way is nothing more than a public-relations move for the white people of this country. So you are going to come into this community today and insult us, and tell us you're going to investigate yourself. You've got to be crazy."

Refusing to take any more questions, Deutch concluded with, "You know, I've learned how important it is for our government and our agency to get on top of this problem and stop it. I came today to try and describe the approach and have left with a better appreciation of what is on your mind."

Immediately, the media tried to spin the meeting in a way

favourable to the CIA. Via satellite, Ted Koppel of *Nightline* interviewed members of the audience, trying to extract a positive testimony, only to find himself rebuffed by questions such as, "You come down here and talk about solutions. We have kids that are dying. We have hospitals for babies born drug addicted. When are you guys going to come down and bring cameras to our neighbourhood?"

"I'm not sure that anybody even thought that was why Director Deutch came there today," Koppel said. "He's come here because a lot of you are in anguish. A lot of you are angry. A lot of you are frustrated by what you believe to be the CIA's involvement in bringing drugs to South Central LA. Now, I want to hear from someone who thought it did some good."

"Well, I am glad Mr Deutch was here today," said Marcine Shaw, the mayor pro tem of Compton. "I'm glad Congresswoman Macdonald had him here because that's what it took to get your cameras here, Mr Koppel."

Koppel shook his head. "Yes, but that's not the question." Koppel finished his broadcast with, "If any suspicions were put to rest or minds changed, there was no evidence of it in South Central this evening."

Originally, Pablo was in bed with the CIA through the Medellín Cartel's contributions to the Nicaraguan rebels. Traffickers who made such payments to the CIA were allowed to operate. Testifying as a US government witness at the Noriega trial, Carlos Lehder admitted contributing millions to the Nicaraguan rebels. *Narcos* tied the Medellín Cartel to the Nicaraguan government, which gave a false impression that the Communists were financing their activity with cocaine.

It hadn't gone unnoticed by Pablo that the CIA had helped to overthrow the government of Bolivia in 1980, and put cocaine traffickers in charge – detailed in my book, *We Are Being Lied To: The War on Drugs*. In the name of fighting Communism, the CIA had put Klaus Barbi – a Nazi war criminal responsible for the deaths of up to 14,000 people – in charge of the coup in Bolivia. His Argentine death squad had massacred numerous civilians. In light of what had transpired in Bolivia, Pablo probably thought that his goal of becoming the president of Colombia was realistic.

After the coup, the CIA-backed Bolivian government exported raw coca. One of its customers was the Medellín Cartel. As the anti-Communist cause was being advanced, the CIA protected this activity by obstructing investigations by other law-enforcement agencies. In doing so, it created a secure route for coca paste to go from Bolivia to Colombia. In Medellín, the Bolivian paste was processed and distributed to the US.

The Argentine intelligence services made a fortune from selling Bolivian paste. Some of the money was laundered in Miami and recycled into other anti-Communist causes, which included buying massive amounts of weapons from US manufacturers, which Bush represented, along with banking interests. That's how Bush used drug money to finance the Nicaraguan rebels.

Prompted by the journalism of Gary Webb, the CIA and Justice Department investigations confirmed that the Nicaraguan rebels had been involved in the cocaine trade throughout the 1980s. The CIA had been aware of it, and they'd steered other agencies, such as DEA investigators, away from the truth.

Despite *Narcos* holding Pablo accountable for nearly all of the cocaine entering America, CIA-protected cocaine wasn't only coming from Colombia. Pablo was used as a smokescreen for cocaine coming from various routes originating in South America. In El Salvador, the military were involved. Honduras was a major transiting point. Anti-Castro Cubans active in Costa Rica sent boatloads of cocaine to Miami. As usual, the CIA stopped all of the investigations into these areas. The mainstream media avoided it. Long after Pablo's demise, the tangled roots of this infrastructure keep the cocaine flowing to this day.

Although Pablo started out working with the CIA, the protection provided by the CIA for those contributing to its anti-Communist causes only lasted for so long. General Manuel

Noriega of Panama learned this the hard way. While contributing to the Nicaraguan rebels, Noriega turned Panama into a haven for drug money. When George HW Bush was running the CIA in 1976, the US was paying Noriega $200,000 a year. By December 1989, Noriega was no longer useful. Bush turned on Noriega, who allegedly had filmed high-ranking CIA and US officials at sex parties with underage boys and girls at his home in Panama. Lambasting Noriega for drug crimes, the Americans invaded Panama, while omitting his CIA history. Operation Just Cause involved 27,684 troops and 300 aircraft attacking Panama. In January 1990, Noriega surrendered. In the US, he was sentenced to thirty years for trafficking, racketeering and money laundering.

Somehow Pablo fell out of favour with the CIA. Researchers have speculated over the possible causes. Some believe it was a similar situation to Noriega: Pablo had become more valuable as an enemy to Bush.

Falling out of favour with someone like Bush must have been daunting. Pablo was a midget in the murder leagues compared to Bush, who authorised the bombing of some of the poorest places in the world. Bush's invasion of Panama caused approximately 4,000 civilian deaths – about the same number of deaths credited to Pablo. According to the Pentagon, Bush's invasion of Iraq caused the deaths of 100,000 soldiers and 7,000 civilians. Backed up by presidential pomp and circumstance, video-casts of precision bombing and an ability to write off the mass murder of civilians as collateral damage, Bush committed murder with panache. With God and the media on his side, he never suffered any consequences.

With Bush and the US military stepping up actions against Pablo, he needed a new strategy to emerge unscathed. It didn't take long for him to come up with one.

CHAPTER 13
DIANA TURBAY

Diana Turbay – the daughter of a former Colombian president – was a brunette with kind eyes and a magnetic personality. In August 1990, she was invited to interview a priest leading a guerrilla group called the Army of National Liberation. Due to the risks involved, her friends and family advised her against it. But Diana was not the type to shrink from danger if she thought that good could be achieved. She'd once travelled into guerrilla territory on a mule, hoping to gain an understanding of their motivations. She'd visited a camp to meet the leader of the M-19 – who'd fired a rocket that had almost hit the room containing her father when he was president – in the hope of helping the peace process along. Now if interviewing the priest would make things safer for Colombia, she'd gladly risk her life.

On August 30, an old van arrived in Bogotá to take Diana and her crew to the priest. The two young men and a woman who emerged said they were part of the guerrilla leadership. West of Bogotá, they switched from the van to two other vehicles. After eating at a tavern, they traversed a dangerous road in heavy rain, and had to stop at dawn until a landslide was cleared.

After a sleepless night, they met up with a patrol with five horses at 11 am. For four hours, Diana rode on a horse, while most of the group walked through mountain forest and a valley with houses nestled into coffee groves. Recognising Diana from the TV, some of the locals yelled greetings. In the evening, they arrived at a deserted ranch near a highway, beyond which was Medellín. A young man claimed to be with the guerrillas, but offered no more information. Perplexed as to why they weren't in guerrilla territory yet, they consoled themselves with the notion that the priest wanted to meet them in the unlikeliest of places as a security precaution.

After two hours, they stopped in Copacabana, at a small house with white walls, its roof tiles green from moss. Diana and a female companion were given the best room at the back. As its windows were boarded over, a light was kept on in the room. The guards didn't have the usual guerrilla weapons. One was even wearing a Rolex.

Three hours later, a masked man greeted them on behalf of the priest. He said that for security the women should travel to the priest first. Getting split from her male colleagues troubled Diana. One of them whispered that she shouldn't go anywhere without them. With fright in her eyes, she gave him her ID.

Before sunrise, the women were moved to a bigger house. Her male companions arrived on September 10. Diana confided that she was depressed over having led them all into what she now suspected was a trap. She said that she didn't fear for herself, but if anything happened to her colleagues, she wouldn't find any peace. Throughout the night, she was kept awake by thoughts of what her husband, children and parents were going through. The next night, Diana and two female colleagues were forced to trek along a path in the rain.

Diana's distressed parents asked the government to locate her through their channels of communication with the guerrilla groups. Seven of the groups denied any knowledge of her in a joint statement.

A guard finally came clean: "You're being held by the Extraditables. But don't worry because you're going to see something you won't forget."

On October 30, sixty-one days after Diana's kidnapping, the Extraditables announced: "We acknowledge publicly that we are holding the missing journalists."

Particularly concerned about a colleague with a heart ailment, Diana entered his room. He'd recently been in hospital and had opposed the trip. "Don't you hate me for not listening to you?" Diana said, her eyes filling with tears.

"Yes, I hated you with all my soul when we were told that we are in the hands of the Extraditables, but I've come to accept captivity as an unavoidable fate." He felt guilty for not talking her out of the excursion.

Diana and her colleagues were moved numerous times to houses with different guards and conditions. The women were mostly housed separately from their male companions. At any time, they could be uprooted from one house to another due to the volatile nature of the kidnapping business; for instance when the authorities entered the neighbourhood where they were being held. They often found themselves rushed along muddy paths, going up and down hills in the rain. Sometimes they were moved around Medellín by taxis, whose drivers skilfully avoided checkpoints and police patrols.

In the houses, plates, glasses and sheets were generally unwashed. Toilets could only be flushed a limited amount of times each day. Guards urinated in the sinks and showers, and slept in padlocked rooms, as if they too were prisoners. Every so often, hooded bosses showed up to instruct their underlings and take reports. The mood the boss was in set the tone for the house.

Breakfast was usually a corn cake with a sausage and coffee. Lunch was beans in grey water, shreds of meat in a grease-like slop, a little rice and a soda. Cutlery was banned except for spoons. With no chairs, the captives dined on their mattresses. In the evening, they ate anything remaining from lunch. Vigilant for any updates on their disappearance, they passed time watching TV, listening to the radio and reading newspapers.

The man delegated to oversee Diana's kidnapping was don Pacho, a thirtysomething who brought gifts, books, sweets, music cassettes and occasionally hope during his rare appearances. His underlings didn't wear hoods and went by comic-book names.

Some of the guards armed with machine guns were teenagers. Displaced from the countryside, many had ended up in the slums of Medellín, where they had learned to kill. They wore T-shirts, sneakers and cut-off shorts. Starting a new shift, two would arrive at 6 am. They were supposed to alternate their sleep, but sometimes they drifted off together. A fifteen-year-old boasted about how many police he'd killed after Pablo had put a bounty on the police force, offering two million pesos for each killing. In response, the police were snatching young people off the street to torture and murder. Resigned to dying young, they consoled themselves by buying motorbikes and new clothes, and being able to send money to their mothers. They hated authority and the lives they'd been born into. They viewed crime as the only ladder up in a cruel world.

Attempting to steady their nerves, the young guards smoked marijuana at nights or drank beer laced with a tranquilliser called Rohypnol. They played with their guns and sometimes fired them by accident. One bullet went through a door and hit another guard in the knee. When the radio announced that Pope John Paul II wanted the hostages to be freed, a guard called the Pope "a nosy son of a bitch," which provoked a near shootout among the guards. Many of them prayed daily to Jesus and Mary, and asked for protection, forgiveness and success in their criminal endeavours.

Diana was unsettled by the guards bragging about sexually assaulting strangers, and their perverse and sadistic tendencies. Occasionally, they watched movies with extreme violence and pornography, which created tension with the hostages, especially when they needed to use the toilet. Guards insisted on leaving the toilet door partially open. Sometimes they caught the guards peeping at them.

Initially, the guards stressed Diana out by strolling around in their underwear and blasting music, which prevented her from sleeping. Over time, she convinced them to dress properly and to lower the music. When one tried to sleep next to her, she had him leave the room. With the guards, she sometimes played Parcheesi: an Indian cross and circle board game. She helped the guards make shopping lists. They boasted that there was no shortage of money, and they could satisfy any request within twelve hours.

The hostages sometimes found comfort in messages brought from couriers who travelled from house to house. They delivered newspapers, toiletries and sweat-suits, which the hostages were required to wear.

At night, Diana and her friend, Azucena, who worked on Diana's newscast, sought solace from each other. They discussed the news and politics, which helped distract them from their situation. They photographed each other in bed and tried to sleep until lunch arrived. They spent most of the time in a house belonging to a cartel boss, which was far more spacious than the other houses. They had a table to eat at. They listened to CDs.

Watching TV, Diana saw a show filmed in her Bogotá apartment. Realising she'd failed to lock a safe, she wrote to her mother, "I hope nobody is rummaging around in there." Through a TV program, her mother gave her reassurance.

Assorted people visited the house. Unfamiliar women gave the hostages pictures of saints for good luck. Sometimes families with children and dogs showed up.

As the news reported the kidnappings of journalists, celebrities and members of the wealthy class, Diana realised she was part of Pablo's plan to pressure the government into giving him the terms he desired for his surrender, including the end of extradition.

At night, Diana kept a secret diary of whatever was on her mind, which ranged from thoughts on politics to things happening around her. Her first entry was dated September 27, 1990: "Since Wednesday the 19th, when the man in charge of this operation came here, so many things have happened that I can hardly catch my breath." During the early weeks of her captivity, no one had publicly claimed responsibility, which Diana believed, according to her diary, was to enable the kidnappers to kill her quietly when she was redundant to them. "That's my understanding of it and it fills me with horror." As usual, she was more concerned with the safety of her colleagues than herself.

Leaning on religion gave her strength. She wrote prayers such as the Our Father and Hail Mary. When she wanted to speak to God or her family, she wrote the words down. She even prayed for Pablo: "He may have more need of your help. May it be your will that he see the good and avoid more grief, and I ask you to help him understand our situation." When the guards found out about the diary, they gave her more paper and pencils.

Diana's ex-president father was doing everything in his power to try to get the government to negotiate a peaceful settlement with Pablo, which public opinion had moved in favour of. After the first round of bombings and assassinations, the outraged public demanded retribution and imprisonment. During the next round, the public still supported extradition. But now the bombings had gone on for so long that the public wanted peace.

The president's security adviser offered an idea: if a trafficker surrendered and confessed to a crime, he would earn a sentence reduction, with a further sentence reduction available if property was turned over to the state. With the help of the justice minister, a draft was made: "Capitulation to the Law."

Even though Pablo's nemesis, General Maza, feared that Pablo would continue running his operation while incarcerated, he didn't object to the draft, but he did say, "This country won't be put right as long as Escobar is alive." After the Council of Ministers signed the decree, Maza described it as a fallacy of the times.

As the decree didn't guarantee non-extradition, Pablo was dissatisfied: "Because it must be in writing, in a decree, that under no circumstances will we be extradited, not for any crime, not to any country." He wanted traffickers to be pardoned in the same way as the M-19, which had been allowed to become a political party. He also demanded safety guarantees for his family and friends, and a prison impregnable to his enemies.

Publicly, Diana's father denied getting any messages from the Extraditables, even though he had received a three-page handwritten letter: "A respectful greeting from the Extraditables," which he believed was Pablo's pseudonym. The hostages were "in good health and in good conditions of captivity that can be considered normal in such cases." The letter railed against police brutality. It included three conditions for Diana's release. Firstly, the suspension of military operations against the traffickers in Medellín and Bogotá. Secondly, the withdrawal of the Elite Corps, a special police unit fighting traffickers. Thirdly, the dismissal of its commander and twenty officers accused of torturing and murdering 400 young men from the Medellín slums. Failing these conditions, the Extraditables would engage in a war of extermination by bombing the big cities and assassinating judges, politicians and journalists. "If there is a coup, then welcome to it. We don't have much to lose." The Extraditables wanted a response within three days, sent to a room at the Hotel Continental in Medellín.

A notary took the response to the hotel. As soon as he entered the designated room, the phone rang.

"Did you bring the package?"

"Yes."

Two young well-dressed men entered the room to collect the response.

Within a week, Pablo dispatched Guido Parra to negotiate with the parents of some of the prominent hostages. The forty-eight-year-old had practised law all of his life and was considered an expert. Wearing a light suit, with a bright shirt and tie, he said he was Pablo Escobar's attorney.

"Then the letter you've brought is from him?"

"No," Guido Parra said, realising his mistake. "It's from the Extraditables, but you should direct your response to Escobar because he'll be able to influence the negotiation."

Dr Turbay and another parent of a hostage, Santos, took the latest response from the Extraditables to the president, who met them in a small room adjacent to his private library.

The president said that Guido Parra was a bad emissary. "Very smart, a good lawyer, but extremely dangerous. Of course, he does have Escobar's complete backing." After studying the letter, the president cast doubt on its authenticity. Maybe it was somebody playing a trick pretending to be Pablo. He said that the intelligence agencies had been unable to ascertain the locations of the hostages. The two parents left the meeting disheartened.

For weeks, Diana's parents had requested evidence from the kidnappers to show that she was alive. In October 1990, a cassette tape arrived. "Daddy, it's difficult to send you a message under these conditions, but after our many requests they've allowed us to do it. We watch and listen to the news constantly."

Hoping for a progress report, Dr Turbay took the recording to Santos, and they visited the president in his library. Over whiskey, the president blamed the lack of progress on the Extraditables for demanding a more specific decree. Having worked on the decree all afternoon, he believed that tomorrow would bring better news.

The next day, the two parents found the president in a grim mood. "This is a very difficult moment. I've wanted to help you, and I have been helping within the limits of the possible, but pretty soon I won't be able to do anything at all."

Dismayed, Dr Turbay stood. "Mr President, you are proceeding as you must, and we must act as the fathers of our children. I understand, and ask you not to do anything that may create a problem for you as the head of state." Pointing at the president's chair, he said, "If I were sitting there, I'd do the same."

Afterwards, Dr Turbay said to the other parent, "We shouldn't expect anything else from him. Something happened between last night and today and he can't say what it is."

After having four children with Dr Turbay, Diana's mother, Nydia, had remarried. With Dr Turbay making no progress with the president, Nydia became more active. She arranged masses across the country. She organised radio and TV newscasts, pleading for the release of the hostages. She had soccer matches open with the same plea. She went to meetings attended by the family members of the hostages.

An informant contacted the Colombian Solidarity Foundation,

claiming that a note from a friend found in a basket of vegetables had stated that Diana was at a farm near Medellín, protected by drunken guards incapable of standing up to a rescue operation. Petrified that a rescue attempt meant certain death for her daughter, probably from police bullets, Nydia asked the informant to suppress the information.

The clue about Medellín prompted Nydia to visit Martha Ochoa – Jorge Ochoa's sister who'd been kidnapped by the M-19 – who Nydia believed was capable of contacting Pablo directly. The Ochoa sisters listened to Nydia sympathetically, but said they couldn't influence Pablo. They complained to Nydia about the heavy-handedness of the police, and gave harrowing stories of their family's suffering.

Having attempted to send a letter to Pablo via Guido Parra, and received no response, Nydia asked if they'd give Pablo a letter from her. Worried that Pablo might accuse them of creating problems for him, the sisters politely declined. Nydia viewed the encounter with optimism. Having felt that the sisters had warmed to her, she believed that a door had been opened that might lead to Diana's release and the surrender of the Ochoa brothers.

Meeting with the president, she described her visit to the Ochoa sisters. She asked him to use his power to prevent a rescue attempt and to give the Extraditables more time to surrender. He said that his policy was not to attempt any rescue without the families' authorisation. Nydia left concerned that another entity might attempt to rescue the hostages without presidential approval.

Nydia continued her dialogue with the Ochoa sisters. Visiting one of Pablo's sisters-in-law, she heard more details of police brutality. Hoping to provoke an emotional response from Pablo, she gave the sister-in-law a letter for him in her own handwriting that she'd constructed meticulously from many drafts. She addressed Pablo as "a feeling man who loves his mother and who would give his life for her, who has a wife and young innocent defenceless children whom he wishes to protect." She said that

Pablo had achieved his goal of drawing attention to his plight, and requested that he "show the world the human being you are, and in a great humanitarian act that everyone will understand, return the hostages to us."

After reading the letter, Pablo's sister-in-law said that she was sure he'd be moved by its content. "Everything you're doing touches him, and that can only work in your daughter's favour." She sealed the letter. "Don't worry. Pablo will have the letter today."

Returning to Bogotá, Nydia was convinced that the letter would achieve its desired effect. As Dr Turbay hadn't asked the president to stop the police from searching for the hostages, she decided to do so. The president declined, believing that it was OK to offer an alternative judicial policy to the Extraditables, but ceasing police operations meant stopping the hunt for Pablo. Enraged, she listened to the president harp on about the police not needing permission to act, and that he couldn't order them not to act within the limits of the law. She felt that the president didn't care about Diana's life.

The families of the hostages formed a group called the Notables, which included two former presidents. After lengthy discussions, they decided to adopt the strategy of the Extraditables by issuing public letters. In the hope of achieving progress in the negotiations, they proposed that trafficking become a collective unique crime, and the traffickers be treated as political offenders, just like the M-19.

Pablo's interest had been piqued. One of his lawyers asked the Notables to obtain a presidential letter guaranteeing his life, but they refused to ask the president.

The Notables issued a letter redefining themselves: "Our good offices have acquired a new dimension, not limited to an occasional rescue, but concerned with how to achieve peace for all Colombians."

The president approved, but made his position clear: the

capitulation policy was the government's only position on the surrender of the Extraditables.

Enraged, Pablo sent a letter to Guido Parra: "The letter from the Notables is almost cynical. We are supposed to release the hostages quickly because the government is dragging its feet as it studies our situation. Can they really believe we will let ourselves be deceived again?" Since their first letter, the Extraditables' position hadn't changed. "There was no reason to change it, since we have not received positive replies to the requests made in our first communication. This is a negotiation, not a game to find out who is clever and who is stupid."

In a letter to Guido Parra, Pablo detailed his goal of having the government grant him a secure prison camp. While negotiating their surrender terms, the M-19 had achieved this. He'd already chosen a location. "Since this requires money, the Extraditables would assume the costs... I'm telling you all this because I want you to talk to the mayor of Envigado, and tell him you represent me and explain the idea to him. But the reason I want you to talk to him is to get him to write a public letter to the justice minister saying he thinks the Extraditables have not accepted Decree 2047 because they fear for their safety, and that the municipality of Envigado, as its contribution to peace for the Colombian people, is prepared to build a special prison that will offer protection and security to those who surrender. Talk to him in a direct clear way, so he'll talk to Gaviria [the president] and propose the camp." Pablo wanted a public response from the justice minister. "I know that will have the impact of a bomb... This way we'll have them where we want them."

After the minister said no, Pablo offered more, including resolving trafficker conflicts, guaranteeing that more than a hundred traffickers would surrender and an end to the war. "We are not asking for amnesty or dialogue or any of the things they say they cannot give." He wanted to get on with surrendering "while everybody in this country is calling for dialogue and for treating us as politicals... I have no problem with extradition since I know that if they take me alive they'll kill me, like they've done with everybody else."

Diana's father and some of the Notables confronted Pablo's lawyer. "Don't fuck with me. Let's get to the point. You've stalled everything because your demands are moronic, and there's only one damn thing at issue here: your boys have to turn themselves in and confess to some crime that they can serve a twelve-year sentence for. That's what the law says, period. And in exchange for that, they'll get a reduced sentence and a guarantee of protection. All the rest is bullshit."

"Look, Doctor," Guido Parra said, "the thing is that the government says they won't be extradited, everybody says so, but where does the decree say it specifically?"

They agreed that Decree 2047 needed to be revised because it was too open to interpretation.

"How soon after the decree is amended will the hostages be released?"

"They'll be free in twenty-four hours," Guido Parra said.

"All of them, of course?"

"All of them."

On November 26, 1990 – the beginning of the fourth month of Diana's captivity – Pablo decided to release one of Diana's team. When the guards told Juan Vitta he was being freed due to illness, he thought that he was being tricked into going somewhere to be shot.

"Shave and put on clean clothes."

After dressing, he was instructed on what to say to the police and the media. If he gave any clues about his location, which led to a rescue operation, the other hostages would be killed. He was blindfolded and transported on a maze-like journey through Medellín. His captors left him on a street corner.

Another of Diana's colleagues, Hero Buss, was told he would be freed on December 11. The owners of his house of captivity were a couple who spent their bags of expense money provided by Pablo on constant parties and lavish dinners, attended by assorted family members and friends. They'd treated the large German as a celebrity, having seen him on TV. At least thirty visitors had posed for photos with him, obtained his autograph and even feasted and danced with him. At a time when the couple had no money and the wife of the house had gone into labour, Hero Buss had lent them 50,000 pesos for her hospital bill.

The day of his freedom, they returned his camera equipment and paid him back the 50,000 pesos plus 15,000 pesos for an earlier loan. Unable to find the correct shoes for his large feet, they got him a small pair that didn't fit. He'd lost thirty-five pounds, so they bought him a shirt and trousers smaller than those he wore before captivity. His only wish that they'd never granted was his request to interview Pablo.

Carrying his bags on his back, he was left by the headquarters of a newspaper, *El Colombiano*, with a letter from the Extraditables, praising his human-rights activism and emphasising that the capitulation policy should guarantee the safety of the Extraditables and their families. The first thing he did was ask a passer-by to take his photo.

The release of two hostages lifted Diana's spirits, which were further boosted when the guards told her and her companion, Azucena, that they were next. But as they'd heard that before, part of them refused to believe it. Assuming that one would be freed before the other, they each wrote a letter for the other to deliver to their family.

On December 13, whispers and noise in the house roused Diana, who leapt out of bed, expecting to be freed. Suddenly energised, she woke Azucena, and they both packed. While Diana showered, a guard told Azucena that only she was going. Azucena got dressed.

After emerging from the shower, Diana gazed at her companion, her eyes glistening with anticipation. "Are we going, Azu?"

Breathing deeply, Azucena lowered her head. "No, I'm going alone." Azucena started crying.

Even though she felt as if she'd been stabbed in the heart,

Diana mustered the courage to say, "I'm so happy for you. Don't worry. I knew it would be this way." She gave Azucena a letter for her mother, asking Nydia to celebrate Christmas with Diana's children. Diana hugged Azucena. They walked to the car and hugged again. Azucena got inside. Diana waved.

On the way to the airport, Azucena heard her husband on a radio broadcast. Asked what he'd been doing when he found out that she was going to be released, he said he'd been writing a poem to her. On December 16, they celebrated their fourth wedding anniversary together.

On December 17, Diana's cameraman, Orlando, was in a room he'd recently been moved to. Ruminating on the cause of the fresh blood stains on the mattress – either a stabbing or torture – was making him feel ill.

His door opened. In walked don Pacho, the boss in charge of Diana's house. "Put clothes on. You're leaving now."

With hardly any time to dress, convinced he was going to be killed, he was given a statement for the media and his eyes were covered. Don Pacho drove him through Medellín, gave him 5,000 pesos for a taxi and dropped him off at 9 am. Unable to hail a taxi, he called his wife. "Slim, it's me."

At first, she didn't recognise his voice. "Oh my God!"

During Orlando's captivity, they'd decided to have a second child when they were reunited. After a couple of nights of being around too many people wanting to speak to Orlando, they got lucky right away.

Diana kept abreast of the news via TV, radio and newspapers, but missed the enjoyment of discussing it with Azucena. In her diary, she wrote, "I don't want and it isn't easy to describe what I feel at each moment: the pain, the anguish, the terrifying days I've experienced." Increasingly, she mulled over dying in a rescue attempt, while hoping her release would be "pretty soon, now."

Don Pacho stopped having long conversations with Diana and bringing her newspapers. Having requested to meet Pablo, she rehearsed what she would say to him, convinced she'd be able to get him to negotiate. Hearing her mother on TV or radio gave her hope. "I have always felt she was my guardian angel." She was convinced that her mother's determination would result in a Christmas release.

On Christmas Eve, a party at the house holding Diana included barbecued meat, alcohol, salsa music, coloured lights and fireworks. Assuming it was her leaving celebration, she expected to be told to pack her belongings. On Christmas Day, the guards gave her a lined leather jacket, which she believed was to keep her warm in the cold weather during her imminent freedom. She envisioned her mother getting supper ready and a wreath of mistletoe at home with a welcome message for her. But watching all of the holiday lights getting turned off crushed her hope.

The next day, her family appeared on a Christmas TV show, including her two children – who had grown in her absence – and brothers and sisters. Even though the family hadn't been in a celebratory mood, it had been arranged due to her letter delivered by Azucena. Nydia, too, had anticipated Diana's release that day.

Diana wrote, "I confess my sorrow at not being there, not sharing the day with all of them… But it cheered me so. I felt very close to everyone, it made me happy to see them all together."

As usual, her thoughts shifted to her situation. Why wasn't the government more actively pursuing the surrender of the Extraditables if it had satisfied their requests? "As long as that is not demanded of them, they will feel more comfortable about taking their time, knowing they have in their power the most important weapon [the hostages] for exerting pressure on the government." She compared the negotiations to a game of chess. "But which piece am I? I can't help thinking we're all dispensable." She'd lost faith in the Notables: "They'd started out with an eminently humanitarian mission and ended up doing a favour for the Extraditables."

Since Christmas, Diana had been housed with another hostage, Richard. Their nocturnal existence consisted of listening to the radio and talking.

In January, a guard burst into the room of a hostage. "It's all fucked up! They're going to kill hostages!" Due to the murder of the Priscos – a group close to Pablo – by the authorities, Pablo had decided to kill a hostage every three days.

Diana overheard the guards discussing the death of the Priscos. One was crying.

"And what do we do now with the merchandise [hostages]?" a guard said.

"We'll get rid of it."

The words instilled Diana with so much fear that she couldn't sleep. She was told that they would soon be changing houses.

The first on the kill list was Marina Montoya, who'd been missing for half a year and was presumed dead. Her brother had been the president's secretary general, and had endured the kidnapping of his own son, who was released, only to be followed by the kidnapping of his sister nine months later. Once a stately figure, old Marina had withered from illness and worry. She'd charmed some of the guards who treated her as a grandmother figure.

On January 23, 1991, a guard called the Monk entered the room where Marina was watching TV with two younger female hostages. "We came to take Granny to another house."

Marina was in bed, cold and pale, her white hair a mess.

"Get your things together, Granny. You have five minutes."

He stooped to help her up. Her mouth opened but emitted no sound. She stood, grabbed her bag and floated towards the bathroom like a ghost.

While she was in there, a hostage said, "Are you going to kill her?"

"You can't ask anything like that! I told you: she is going to a better house. I swear."

After the two hostages asked to speak to a boss, another guard arrived and confiscated the TV and radio, which the hostages viewed as a bad omen for Marina. The guards said they'd collect Marina in five minutes.

Taking her time, Marina emerged in a pink sweat-suit, men's socks and her original shoes, mildewed and too large for her shrunken feet. Under the sweat-suit, she wore a scapula with a plastic cross. "Who knows, maybe they're going to release me."

"Of course they are."

"That's right. How wonderful!"

Marina asked if they had messages for their families. She put some aftershave behind her ear and rearranged her majestic hair with no mirror. Sat on the bed, she smoked slowly as if resigned to her fate.

"If you have a chance to see my husband and children," a hostage said to prevent herself from crying, "tell them I'm well and love them very much."

"Don't ask me to do that," Marina said, gazing into space. "I know I'll never have the chance."

The two women gave Marina water and powerful sedatives, but she was unable to hold the glass with her shaking hands. One of the women held the glass, so Marina could swallow the sedatives. They gave her a pink wool hood. They hugged and kissed and said goodbye.

With a stoic expression, Marina approached the guards. They rotated the hood, so that she couldn't see. The Monk steered her out of the house with her walking backwards.

On January 24, 1991, a corpse was discovered north of Bogotá, sat in an upright position against a barbed-wire fence, with her arms extended. Her outfit was intact except for her shoes, which had been stolen. The pink hood, still positioned with its eyeholes at the back of the head, was blood encrusted due to six bullets fired from a close distance. Most of the bullets had entered the left side of the face and the top of the skull. One had entered the forehead.

The crowd watching the magistrate examine the corpse was impressed by the white hair, the well-manicured hands and nails and even the quality of the underwear.

Unable to identify Marina, the Institute of Forensic Medicine sent the corpse to a recently dug mass grave, holding 200 people.

The beginning of 1991 saw violence escalate across Colombia. As well as cartel violence, guerrilla groups were bombing and kidnapping and murdering. Pablo issued a statement condemning the police for their practice of kidnapping young men from the Medellín slums. He claimed that at any time of the day, ten boys would be kidnapped at random, taken to a basement or an empty lot and shot dead without any questions asked. The police were operating under the assumption that the boys worked for Pablo, or eventually would, or supported him in some way. To back his claims up, Pablo referred to international human-rights organisations that were documenting the abuses committed by the Colombian authorities.

Desirous of insulating themselves from the escalating mayhem, the Ochoa brothers turned themselves in, which gave the impression of a division in the cartel. At the behest of the concerned females in the family, their surrender had been negotiated by Martha Ochoa. Each brother surrendered a month or so apart from the other, from December 18, 1990 to February 16, 1991. They ended up in Itagüí maximum-security prison.

Pablo was still holding out. Even though Decree 3030 – issued on December 14, 1990 – established that a prisoner convicted of multiple crimes would serve the amount of time for only the crime carrying the longest sentence, there was still ambiguity over extradition. Technically, the Ochoa brothers could have been extradited, which was unacceptable to Pablo. The new decree was criticised by many parties, including family members of the hostages, which led to the drafting of a third decree.

Diana's mother viewed the surrender of the Ochoa brothers as a positive development. As soon as the first Ochoa, Fabio, had turned himself in, Nydia, her daughter and granddaughter, went to visit him in prison, accompanied by five members of the Ochoa family, including Martha.

In Fabio's cell they were greeted by Fabio's father. Now seventy but with a face that still exuded charm, Fabio Sr lavished Nydia with praise for her brave efforts to free Diana. He wanted her to ask the president to extend the time limit for surrender in the new decree. Unable to do so, she recommended that they put the request in writing. He offered to help her however he could.

When it was time for her to leave, the younger Fabio said to Nydia, "Where there is life, there is hope."

Nydia visited the released hostage, Hero Buss, who said that after his first week of captivity, he hadn't seen Diana, but the guards had told him that she was well. His biggest concern was a rescue attempt. "You cannot imagine the constant threat that they'll kill you. Not only because the law, as they call it, is there, but because they're always so edgy they think the tiniest noise is a rescue operation." He recommended that she continue to lobby against a rescue and for a change to the time limit on surrender.

Since Pablo's announcement about killing hostages, Nydia had been envisioning the worst for Diana. She pressed senior government officials to rely on intelligence agencies rather than launch a rescue. But her efforts were unable to fix her shattered heart, a pain aggravated by a feeling that something bad was imminent and a radio broadcast by the Extraditables pledging to wrap the hostages' corpses in sacks and drop them off at the presidential palace if the decree remained unchanged.

She left a message: "I implore you to ask the president and the members of the Council on Security if they need to find bags of dead hostages at their door before they change the decree."

When the president said that Decree 3030 needed more time, Nydia replied, "A change in the deadline is necessary not only to save the lives of the hostages, but it's the one thing that will make the terrorists surrender. Change it and they'll let Diana go."

The president refused because he didn't want to reward the Extraditables with what they wanted by taking the hostages. "Democracy was never endangered by the assassinations of four presidential candidates or because of any abduction," the president said later. "The real threat came at those moments when we faced the temptation or risk or even the rumour of a possibility of an amnesty."

Disappointed in Dr Turbay for not being more proactive, Nydia decided to write a letter to the president in the hope of inducing him to take more action, but she needed divine inspiration first. Cloistered in a room with a statue of the Virgin Mary and candles, Nydia prayed all night. At dawn, she started writing multiple drafts – some of which she tore up – while sobbing endlessly.

"I don't pretend to be composing a public document. I want to communicate with the president of my country and, with all due respect, convey to him my most considered thoughts, and a justifiably anguished plea… The country knows, and all of you know, that if they happen to find the kidnappers during one of those searches, a terrible tragedy might ensue…" If the president didn't amend the decree, "This would mean that the distress and anguish suffered not only by the families, but by the entire nation would be prolonged for endless months… Because of my convictions, because of the respect I have for you as First Magistrate of the Nation, I would be incapable of suggesting any initiative of my own devising, but I do feel inclined to entreat you, for the sake of innocent lives, not to underestimate the danger that time represents."

The Extraditables issued a statement about the murder of the Prisco gang, which included two brothers and the man in charge of Diana's captivity, don Pacho. They claimed that the police had used the usual excuse of a gunfight to kill Pablo's associates in cold blood. One brother had been slain in front of his young children and pregnant wife; the other in his wheelchair – he had been paralysed during a previous assassination attempt. Within a week, a second captive would be murdered.

The statement was the realisation of Nydia's fears. She had a sense that they were going to kill her daughter, and there was nothing that she could do to move the people who could prevent it.

The father of one of the hostages called the president. "You have to stop these raids."

"No," the president said. "That isn't why I was elected."

Slamming it down, the father almost broke the phone.

Former presidents joined the Notables in their call for a peaceful solution.

Around dawn on January 21, 1991, Diana wrote, "It's close to five months, and only we know what this means. I don't want to lose faith or the hope that I'll go home safe and sound."

Around 11 am on January 21, the mechanical noise of propellers intensified as four combat helicopters homed in on the house holding Diana. Acting on anonymous tips about armed men in the area, a military-style raid had been arranged in the hope of capturing senior cartel members.

A guard appeared at Diana's door. "The law's all over us." The four flustered guards appeared incapable of standing up to the authorities.

With the guards yelling at her to hurry, Diana brushed her teeth and put on the clothes she'd been captured in, all too large now due to her weight loss. With the helicopters buzzing, she was pushed towards an exit and given a large white hat to make her look like a farmworker. They put a black shawl over her. Her colleague Richard was wearing his leather jacket and carrying his camera equipment.

"Head for the mountain!" a guard yelled.

Running, the guards fanned out, ready to train their weapons on the helicopters.

With the sun beating down upon them, Diana and Richard traversed a steep rocky path. Helicopters appeared. Gunfire erupted. Richard dived down.

"Don't move! Play dead!" Diana said and fell facedown. "Please look at my back. Before falling, I felt something like an electric shock at my waist."

Raising her shirt, Richard saw a hole in her body above the left hip bone. "You've been shot." A high-velocity explosive bullet had shattered her spinal column. She had life-threatening internal bleeding.

The shooting grew louder. "Leave me here. Go save yourself."

Richard fished a picture of the Virgin Mary out of his pocket and put it in Diana's hand. To a chorus of gunfire, they prayed together.

With their guns pointed at Richard and Diana, two troops approached them.

"Don't shoot!" Richard said.

"Where's Pablo?"

"I don't know. I'm Richard Becerra. I'm a journalist. This is Diana Turbay. She's wounded."

"Prove it."

Richard displayed an ID. Some farmhands emerged from the vegetation and helped them put Diana on a sheet and carry her, conscious and in agony, to a helicopter.

Dr Turbay's phone rang. A military source said that Diana had been rescued by the Elite Corps. Listening to the radio, he heard no news. He soon found out that Diana had been seriously wounded.

The first Nydia heard was that Diana was safely hospitalised, undergoing routine medical treatment. Whereas everyone else was optimistic, Nydia responded, "They've killed Diana!" Heading for Bogotá in a car, fixating on radio updates – the last of which said Diana was in intensive care – Nydia sobbed.

After changing clothes, she went to the airport and made a call. "They killed Diana, Mr President, and it's your doing. It's your fault. It's what comes of having a soul of stone."

"No, Señora," the president said calmly, happy to share the good news. "It seems there was a raid and nothing is confirmed yet, but Diana is alive."

"No. They killed her."

"How do you know that?"

"Because I'm her mother and my heart tells me so."

The Turbay family boarded a thirty-year-old presidential plane for Medellín. When they landed, a presidential adviser came on board with an update. In the helicopter to Medellín, Diana had lost consciousness. They'd cut her chest open and massaged her heart manually. Hours of emergency treatment had failed to stop the bleeding. She was dead.

At the hospital, Nydia almost collapsed upon seeing her naked daughter drained of colour on a bloodstained sheet with a massive incision on her chest. Afterwards, tortured by grief, she held a press conference. "This is the story of a death foretold." She detailed her appeals to the president. While holding the Extraditables responsible, she said that the guilt should be shared equally by the government and the president, "who, with lack of feeling, almost with coldness and indifference, turned a deaf ear to the appeals that there be no rescues and that the lives of the hostages not be placed in danger."

The media reported her statement. The president called a meeting. He wanted to issue a denial of Nydia's claims, but instead it was decided that all of the senior members of the government would attend the funeral.

Before the funeral, Nydia sent Diana's letters to the president.

In a crowded cathedral, the president got up and walked towards Nydia, intending to shake her hand, his every step followed by the eyes of the mourners and the lenses of the media. Convinced Nydia would turn away from him in disgust, he held out his hand. Cameras clicked and lights flashed. Relieved that he hadn't attempted to hug her, she shook it gingerly.

After the mass, Nydia asked to see the president to give him some new information. Although he feared she was coming to pluck out his heart, he agreed to see her.

Wearing black, Nydia entered his office. "I've come to do you a favour." Having learned that the president hadn't ordered the fatal raid, Nydia asked for his forgiveness. Convinced that he had been deceived, she'd discovered that the purpose of the raid was indeed to free the hostages, not to capture Pablo. The authorities had obtained the location of the house holding the hostages by capturing and torturing one of Pablo's gang. After taking the troops to the house, the gang member had been shot, left at the scene and accounted for as someone killed in the shootout.

The attitude of the president – which Nydia later described as a block of ice – reduced Nydia to tears and provoked her into relaunching her earlier attacks. "Just think about it. What if your daughter had been in this situation? What would you have done then?" Without giving him any time to answer, she said, "Don't you think, Mr President, that you were mistaken in your handling of this problem?"

"It's possible." Nydia shook his hand and bolted out.

The police had claimed that Diana had been shot in the spine by one of the kidnappers. Pablo's version of events concurred with Nydia's story. He said the police had tortured two of his men, whom he named and for whom he provided ID numbers. Running away from the house, Diana had been shot by the police. Several innocent farmhands had also been shot and accounted for as criminals killed in the gun battle.

On January 30, 1991, the Extraditables announced that the order to execute Marina Montoya had been issued on January 23. "If she was executed, we do not understand why the police have not yet reported finding her body."

The statement from the Extraditables caught the eye of the pathologist who'd performed the autopsy on Marina. She was located in a mass grave, next to the corpse of a boy who was wrapped in her pink sweat-suit. Her son identified her distinctive hands.

The deaths of Diana and Marina swung more people in favour of a peaceful settlement. With the president acquiescing, Decree 3030 was issued on January 29.

The Extraditables announced, "We will respect the lives of the remaining hostages." They said one hostage would be released right away. But the negotiations were stalled by Pablo's concerns about the continued killings of slum kids by the police, an alliance between General Maza and the Cali Cartel to kill Pablo's people and the safety of his family and associates after he surrendered.

CHAPTER 14
FATHER GARCIA

In predominantly Catholic Colombia, many people, including Pablo's workers, sought divine inspiration from a program called *God's Minute*. It was hosted by a white-haired priest with worldly brown eyes and a narrow face called Father Garcia, an octogenarian who'd become a living institution since his TV debut in 1955. Prior to the evening news, Father Garcia, the son of an army general, would appear in a black habit with a clerical collar and deliver a sixty-second homily with an important social message. Generations of Colombians grew up watching him.

In accordance with his teachings, he lived in a tiny room with numerous unrepaired leaks in a vicarage. He slept little, on wooden planks with a sheet provided by nuns consisting of miniature house-shaped bits of cloth sewn together. He didn't use pillows. He hardly replaced his clothing. In a restaurant, he once approached a woman with a diamond ring and told her that it was worth enough to build 120 houses for the poor. The next day, she mailed him the ring.

He'd won forty-six awards for arranging charitable events. He raised money to build *God's Minute* housing projects in the slums. During national disasters, he led fundraising campaigns. Since 1961, he had regularly hosted the Banquet for a Million, a fundraiser at which celebrities paid a million pesos for a cup of soup and a roll of bread served by a beauty queen. He once outraged the more puritanical among his flock by sending a fundraiser invitation to the actress Bridget Bardot who was renowned for her sex appeal.

On April 12, 1991, Father Garcia set off to visit Dr Patarroyo, who was famous for developing a chemical malaria vaccine in

1986 and donating its patent to the World Health Organisation. He wanted the doctor to help him set up an AIDS clinic. On the journey, he was accompanied by an old friend whom he often sought advice from, and who'd financed his chapel and many of his projects.

"Listen, Father," the old friend said. "Why don't you do something to move this thing along and help Pablo Escobar turn himself in?" Much later, the old friend would claim that his request that day had been inspired by God, and that, "It was like Father was floating. During the interview [with Dr Patarroyo] the only thing on his mind was what I had said, and when we left I thought he looked so excited that I began to worry."

With the priest in a rapturous state over what to do about Pablo, the old friend took him to rest at a holiday home in the Caribbean. But Father Garcia slept little. He jumped up in the middle of meals to go on long walks of contemplation. "Oh sea of Coveñas!" he yelled at the tide. "Can I do it? Should I do it? You who know everything: will we not die in the attempt?" After such walks, he'd return as if hypnotised and discuss the answers he'd received from God with his friend.

By April 16, a complete plan had unfurled in his mind. On April 18, Father Garcia arrived at the TV studio at 6:50 pm. Pablo's workers watched the man whom they considered a saint deliver a message to their boss:

They have told me you want to surrender. They have told me you would like to talk to me. Oh sea! Oh sea of Coveñas at five in the evening when the sun is setting! What should I do? They tell me he is weary of his life and its turmoil... Tell me, oh sea: can I do it? Should I do it? You who know the history of Colombia, you who saw the Indians worshipping on this shore, you who heard the sound of history: should I do it? Will I be rejected if I do it? If I do it: will there be shooting when I go with them? Will I fall with them in this adventure?

Afterwards, Father Garcia was inundated with messages from across Colombia. A swarm of journalists started to shadow his movements. The public was divided. Some believed he was acting on behalf of God. Others thought that he was insane and he'd crossed a line that separated beliefs in redemption from naiveté.

The next day, he showed up unannounced at the prison holding the Ochoas, who also trusted in his divine powers. As the negotiations required a degree of secrecy, the Ochoas were concerned about his high profile. They referred him to Fabio Sr, who told him that Pablo would be amenable to his idea and that the traffickers – who generally believed in the Virgin Mary, the Holy Infant and assorted saints – would be more likely to surrender if Father Garcia were to bless such activity. Two days later, the priest told journalists that the hostages would be freed soon and that he was communicating with the Extraditables.

With Pablo having kidnapped his wife and sister, Alberto Villamizar had paid close attention to the priest's broadcast. The president had commissioned Villamizar to negotiate the release of the captives. His sister had recently been freed after the murder of Marina, but the Extraditables were still holding his wife. As a politician, Villamizar had fought attempts by colleagues to pass legislation against extradition. In return, Pablo had sanctioned a hit on him in 1986. Following its failure, Villamizar was appointed as Ambassador to Indonesia, where he'd felt safe until US security forces captured a hit man in Singapore sent to kill him.

Watching *God's Minute* convinced him that Father Garcia could play an important part in the negotiations. In recent months – with media interest in Pablo's possible surrender escalating – Villamizar's letters to Pablo had achieved nothing. Pablo was still insisting on the police being held accountable for the murders of slum kids and claiming that General Maza had been behind the assassination of the presidential candidate, Luis Carlos Galán, for which Pablo had been blamed. "Tell doña Gloria that Maza killed her husband, there can be no doubt about it." Pablo continued to accuse Maza of allying with the Cali Cartel. Maza responded that he wasn't going after the Cali Cartel or even drug traffic, but after traffickers committing terrorism. Maza sensed that Pablo was going to call for his resignation as a condition of his surrender.

Many books on Pablo have portrayed his battle with Maza as one of evil versus good. The reality was far more complex. On November 25, 2010, Colombian prosecutors issued an arrest warrant for Maza for his involvement in Galán's murder. The prosecutors claimed that Maza had intentionally reduced Galán's bodyguard contingent to enable the assassination of which Pablo had been accused. Pablo had told Villamizar the truth about Maza.

Seeking advice, Villamizar – with a stern intellectual face, bags under his hazel eyes, short brown parted hair and a slight beard turning grey – visited Jorge Ochoa in prison, who sent him to the Ochoa ranch, La Loma, to see his father.

Cradling a whiskey and sitting in his throne-like chair, Fabio Sr sympathised. "We won't screw around anymore with letters. At this rate it will take a hundred years. The best thing is for you to meet with Escobar and for the two of you to agree on whatever conditions you like."

In a letter to Pablo, Fabio Sr proposed that Villamizar be transported to him in the boot of a car. Pablo responded, "Maybe I'll talk to Villamizar, but not now."

Villamizar tried to broker a month's truce from the National Police, who refused to halt operations against such a criminal as Pablo. "You're acting at your own risk and all we can do is wish you luck."

Villamizar went to see Father Garcia at the TV studio. They visited the Ochoas in prison. In a cell, the priest dictated a letter in the exact same manner he delivered his sermons on TV. He invited Pablo to join him in bringing peace to Colombia. In this endeavour, he hoped to be accredited by the government, so that Pablo's "rights, and those of your family and friends, will be respected." He asked Pablo not to make impossible demands on the government. He concluded with, "If you believe we can meet in a place that is safe for both of us, let me know."

Pablo responded three days later. He requested disciplinary sanctions against the police he'd accused of murdering the kids in the slums. He agreed to surrender and to confess to a crime even though no evidence existed anywhere in the world of any crime alleged to have been committed by him. The priest was disappointed that Pablo hadn't agreed to meet him.

After corresponding with Pablo in secrecy for five months, Villamizar was concerned about the priest's high profile, which now included journalists camped outside of his ascetic living quarters.

On May 13, 1991, Villamizar received a letter from Pablo, requesting that he take the priest to the Ochoas at La Loma and keep him there for as long as possible. It could be days or months because Pablo needed to examine every detail of the operation. If any security issues arose, negotiations would collapse.

On May 14 at 5 am, Villamizar showed up at the priest's study where he was hard at work. "Come, Father, we're going to Medellín."

Fabio Sr was away, so the Ochoa sisters welcomed the priest. After breakfast, Martha Ochoa said that Pablo would be seeing the priest soon. He was delighted until Villamizar clarified what that meant.

"It's better for you to know from the very beginning, Father. You may have to go alone with the driver and nobody knows where he'll take you or for how long."

The prospect of danger upset the priest. Pacing, he prayed and fumbled with his rosary beads. Occasionally, he glanced out of the window in case Pablo had sent a car for him. Resisting the urge to make a call, he said, "Fortunately, there's no need for telephones when you talk to God." He refused a sumptuous lunch. Resting on a canopy bed, he couldn't sleep.

At 4 pm, he appeared in Villamizar's room. "Alberto, we'd better go back to Bogotá."

With difficulty, the Ochoa sisters convinced him to stay. As the sun set, he insisted on leaving but was rebuffed by the majority.

Although Father Garcia was adept at many things, he was useless at removing his contact lenses. That job was entrusted to his faithful secretary, Paulina, who'd been working for him since she was a teenager and even after marrying and having a son, had continued to attend to his daily needs. She usually travelled everywhere with him and handled the delicate matter of his lenses. On this occasion, the Ochoa sisters helped the troubled priest extract his lenses.

Expecting Pablo to send a car in the dead of night, Father Garcia and Villamizar couldn't sleep. In the morning, despite many attempts, nobody was able to put the priest's contact lenses in, which upset him so much that he didn't sit for breakfast. Finally, a woman in charge of the ranch managed to get them in.

After gazing out of the window in a bad mood, Father Garcia sprang from his chair. "I'm leaving! This whole thing is as phoney as a rooster laying eggs." Persuaded to stay until lunch, he regained his composure and resumed eating and talking in a friendly way. He announced that he was going to take a nap. "But I'm warning you, as soon as I wake up, I'm leaving." Hoping to come up with a strategy to retain the priest beyond his nap, Martha Ochoa made some calls, but none were productive.

Around 3 pm, a car arrived.

Villamizar went to the priest's room. "Father, they've come for you."

The half-awake priest shook his terror off and made the sign of the cross. "Kneel down, my boy. We'll pray together." After praying, he stood. "Let's see what's going on with Pablo."

Outside, Villamizar told the driver, "I'm holding you accountable for the father. He's too important a person. Be careful what you people do with him. Be aware of the responsibility you have."

The driver's face pinched with disdain. "Do you think that if I get in a car with a saint anything can happen to us?" The driver had the priest don a baseball cap to disguise his snowy hair.

In the passenger seat, the priest removed his baseball cap, tossed it out of the window and yelled at Villamizar, whose face was crinkled with concern, "Don't worry about me, my boy. I control the waters."

It rained so much on the journey that they breezed through all of the police checkpoints not under Pablo's control. After being on the road for over three hours and changing cars three times, they arrived at a house with a massive swimming pool and sports facilities. In a garden, Father Garcia was approached by twenty armed men, whom he berated for not surrendering and for living sinful lives. On a terrace, Pablo was sporting a long beard and casual clothes.

"Pablo, I've come so we can straighten this out."

In the living room, they sat opposite each other in armchairs. A drop of whiskey steadied the priest's nerves, whereas Pablo drank fruit juice. Due to his age and bad memory, Father Garcia asked Pablo to jot down his conditions. When Pablo was finished, the priest examined the list and crossed some conditions out, stating that they were impossible. With a stroke of a pen, the priest had eliminated things Pablo had been stuck on for months, such as his grievances with the police accused of killing slum kids. The document ended up a combination of Pablo's conditions modified by the priest's scrawl, with the addition of further clarifications by Pablo.

"Are you responsible for killing four presidential candidates?" Father Garcia said.

"I've not committed all of the crimes attributed to me..." Pablo said. "The Extraditables have Maruja [Villamizar's wife] in normal conditions and good health. The hostages will be released as soon as the terms for surrender are arranged... I acknowledge the president's good faith and willingness to reach an agreement."

When the priest stood to leave, a contact lens fell out. He struggled, but couldn't put it in. Pablo tried and failed. As did the staff. "It's no use. The only one who can do it is Paulina."

"I know who Paulina is and exactly where she is," Pablo said, taking the priest by surprise. "Don't worry, Father. If you like, we can bring her here."

Eager to go home, Father Garcia opted to depart with one eye minus a lens.

"Will you bless this little gold medal?" Pablo pointed at it around his neck.

In the garden, surrounded by bodyguards, the priest blessed Pablo's medal.

"Father," a bodyguard said, "you can't leave without giving us your blessing."

Around the priest, they all kneeled, including Pablo. After blessing them, he urged them to renounce crime and help to bring peace.

At 8:30 pm, the priest arrived at La Loma on a tranquil night with the stars shining bright. After the car parked, he sprang out with athletic dexterity into the hands of Villamizar. "Take it easy, my boy. No problems here. I had them all on their knees."

For the rest of the evening, Father Garcia remained in a sprightly mood. He wanted to jump on a plane and meet the president, but the Ochoa sisters convinced him to rest. In the middle of the night, he paced around the house conversing with himself and God.

On Thursday May 16 at 11 am, Father Garcia and Villamizar landed in Bogotá, where Villamizar told his son that his mother would be released in three days.

The priest was besieged by journalists. "If we don't defraud him [Pablo], he'll become the great architect of peace. Deep down, all men are good, although some circumstances can make them evil." Contradicting the media's portrayal of Pablo for the previous two years, Father Garcia said, "Escobar is a good man."

The Extraditables issued a statement the day before the presidential meeting: "We have ordered the release of Francisco Santos and Maruja Pachón." Journalists descended on Villamizar's house.

Pablo sent a message to Villamizar, confirming that his wife would be released on Monday at 7 pm. On May 21 at 9 am,

Villamizar would have to return to Medellín as part of Pablo's surrender.

On Monday, the 6 am news announced that Father Garcia would be hosting a press conference at noon after meeting the president.

Up early, the president had adjusted his schedule to meet his advisers, whom he told, "OK, let's finish this assignment."

One adviser conveyed General Maza's belief that Pablo would not surrender without a pardon from the Constituent Assembly, but added that such a pardon would be useless to Pablo, whose enemies such as the Cali Cartel had condemned him to death. "It might help him, but it's not exactly a complete solution." Pablo's main concern was being housed in a prison that would protect him and his people.

Worried that the priest might convey an impossible demand from Pablo that would sabotage the negotiations, the advisers recommended that the president not attend the meeting on his own, and that he issue a statement immediately after the meeting to quell speculation.

The special meeting commenced at noon. Father Garcia was accompanied by two clerics and Villamizar, who brought his son. With the president were his private secretary and a senior politician.

While the meeting was photographed and videoed, Father Garcia detailed his discussion with Pablo, and expressed a belief that Pablo would surrender and free the hostages. He produced the notes from the meeting – rumours of which had achieved great heights in the media. Pablo's main condition was that the prison be the one he'd selected in Envigado.

Studying the notes, the president expressed dismay over Pablo not promising to release the hostages but only agreeing to bring the matter up with the Extraditables. Villamizar smoothed things over by pointing out that it was Pablo's strategy to not provide any written evidence that could be used against him.

The priest wanted to know what he should do if Pablo requested his presence at the official surrender.

"You should go, Father," the president said.

"Who would guarantee my safety?"

"No one can provide better guarantees than Escobar for the safety of his own operation." The president asked Father Garcia to tread lightly with the media to prevent them from quoting anything that might upset Pablo.

The priest agreed. "I've wanted to be of service in this, and I am at your disposal if you need me for anything else…"

The meeting lasted for twenty minutes and there was no press release.

Anticipating his wife's return, Villamizar took a shower.

At 6 pm, his phone rang. "She'll arrive a few minutes after seven," a stranger said. "They're leaving now."

In the living room, he waited with family members and journalists.

After 7 pm, Maruja called from a house near to where she'd been dropped off by the kidnappers. Villamizar sped over there. He sprinted into the house and embraced his malnourished wife, whose large brown eyes gleamed with love and relief.

CHAPTER 15
THE CATHEDRAL

Behind the scenes, lawyers for both sides distilled the negotiations down to three issues: the location of the prison, the prison staff and the involvement of the police and the army. As the prison holding the Ochoas was susceptible to car bombing, Pablo had refused that suggestion. He had wanted to convert a convent in El Poblado into a prison, but the nuns had refused to sell it to him. A proposal to reinforce a Medellín prison had also been rejected.

The remaining option was the Municipal Rehabilitation Centre for Drug Addicts on property called La Catedral del Valle, stationed on a mountainous slope over the Honey Valley, 7,000 feet above sea level, which would give the guards and the occupants a bird's-eye view of any threats. The area was foggy in the evening and at dawn, which made a surprise raid from the air more difficult and provided a means for the occupants to slip away unnoticed if they needed to flee. They could easily lose their pursuers in the surrounding forest, which was teeming with wildlife, such as armadillos, sloths and huge iridescent butterflies.

The building and 30,000 square metres of land had been registered in the name of one of Pablo's friends, a trusted old ironmonger. Pablo wanted only local guards and for the police and army to have nothing to do with it. The mayor of Envigado approved the transfer of the building into a prison called the Cathedral.

The building had cement floors, tile roofs and green metal doors. Formerly a farmhouse, the administration section included three little rooms: a kitchen, a courtyard and a punishment cell. It had a big dormitory, library, study and six cells with their own bathrooms. The large dayroom included four showers, a dressing room and six toilets. Motivated by Father Garcia's blessing of the project, seventy men had been working around the clock, remodelling it. Due to its inaccessibility, furnishings had arrived on mules: water heaters, military cots, tubular yellow armchairs, potted plants...

Despite its secure location, Pablo wanted a standing army of bodyguards inside the prison, just in case anything unexpected happened. "I won't surrender alone." He stated that he wouldn't abandon his associates to be slaughtered by the Elite Corps, while omitting to say that by keeping his network close, he could continue to run his operation. As added insurance, Pablo and Roberto buried weapons near their designated cells. "One day we'll need them," he told Roberto.

The night of his wife's release, Villamizar stayed up until dawn chatting with her. After an hour's sleep, he set off for Medellín. At La Loma, he met the Monkey, one of two men, including Jorge Ochoa, whom Pablo had authorised to finalise the negotiations. The Monkey was tall, blonde and had a golden moustache.

The phone rang. "Dr Villa, are you happy?" Pablo asked Villamizar. "I thank you for coming. You're a man of your word and I knew you wouldn't fail me. Let's start to arrange how I'll turn myself in."

The Monkey and Villamizar visited the Cathedral and discussed security concerns as they examined a double fence over nine feet high, with fifteen rows of electrified barbed wire. Out of the nine watchtowers, the two at the entrance were being reinforced. Villamizar frowned upon the Italian tiles in Pablo's bathroom, so they were changed. After the inspection, Villamizar said, "It seemed to me a very prison-like prison."

An arrangement with Pablo had been made whereby Villamizar would receive an anonymous call: "In fifteen minutes, Doctor." Then he'd go to his upstairs neighbour, Aseneth, and take a call from Pablo. As her house was a stronghold of writers and artists, who came and went throughout the day and night, it was considered a safe place for Pablo to call.

One evening, Villamizar didn't get to the phone on time. Aseneth answered, "He doesn't live here."

"Don't worry about that," Pablo said. "He's on his way up."

Villamizar tried to tell Aseneth what was going on. She covered her ears. "I don't want to know anything about anything. Do whatever you want in my house, but don't tell me about it."

At La Loma, Villamizar's wife thanked the Ochoas for facilitating her release. Villamizar mentioned that her emerald and diamond ring, taken by her kidnappers, had not been returned as promised. The Monkey's offer to buy a new one was declined because Maruja wanted the original due to its sentimental value. The Monkey said he would refer the matter to Pablo, who tracked the ring down and returned it.

The president's fear of the priest saying a word that might threaten the negotiations at the last minute was realised during a broadcast of *God's Minute*. Father Garcia called Pablo an unrepentant pornographer and demanded that he return to God's path. The about-face astounded the viewers. Pablo thought that something seismic must have occurred behind the scenes. As the priest's blessing had cajoled Pablo's devout underlings into mass surrendering, Pablo was now faced with a rebellion. Pablo refused to surrender unless there was an immediate public explanation.

In response, Villamizar hustled the priest over to La Loma to speak to Pablo on the phone. Out of the various explanations he offered, the one that satisfied Pablo was that an editing error had made him appear to say pornographer by mistake. Having recorded the conversation with the priest, Pablo played it to his underlings, which squashed the rebellion.

Demands imposed by the government presented the next challenge. They wanted more say in the selection of the guards. They wanted army and National Guard troops to be on patrol outside the Cathedral. They wanted to cut down trees to make a firing range adjacent to the Cathedral. Citing the Law on

Prisons, which prohibited military forces from going inside a jail, Pablo rejected the idea of combined patrols. Cutting down trees would permit helicopter landings and a possible assault on the prison, which Pablo found unacceptable. He changed his mind after it was explained that the removal of the trees would provide greater visibility, which would give him more time to respond to an attack. The national director of Criminal Investigation was insisting on building a fortified wall around the prison in addition to the barbed wire, the prospect of which infuriated Pablo.

On May 30, 1991, newspapers began reporting the terms of surrender. What caught the public's attention the most was the removal of General Maza and two prominent police leaders. After meeting the president, Maza sent him a six-page letter, saying he was in favour of Pablo's surrender: "For reasons known to you, Mr President, many persons and entities are intent upon destabilising my career, perhaps with the aim of placing me in a situation of risk that will allow them to carry out their plans against me." He suspected that the government had negotiated his position away, even though there was no official evidence of them doing so.

Pablo informed Maza that their war was over. There would be no more attacks. His men were surrendering. He was turning in his dynamite. He listed the hiding places for 700 kilos of explosives. Maza was sceptical.

Losing patience with Pablo, the government appointed an outsider as the director of the prison, not a local person as Pablo had requested. They assigned twenty National Guards to the prison, who were also outsiders.

"In any event," Villamizar said, "if they want to bribe someone it makes no difference if he's from Antioquia or somewhere else."

Not wanting to make a fuss, Pablo agreed that the army could guard the entrance. The government offered assurances that precautions would be taken to ensure that his food wasn't poisoned.

Policies and procedures for the prison were determined by the National Board of Prisons. Prisoners had to wake up at 7 am. At 8 pm, they had to be locked in their cells. Females could visit on

Sundays from 8 am until 2 pm. Men could visit on Saturdays. Children could visit the first and third Sunday of each month.

On June 9, 1991, Medellín police troops started to implement security measures, including removing people from the area who didn't live there.

Two days later, Pablo asked for a final condition: he wanted the prosecutor general to be present at the surrender.

Pablo lacked the official ID necessary for a surrendering person. To get citizenship papers, he was supposed to go to an office at the Civil Registry, which was impossible for a man with so many enemies. His lawyers asked the government to issue citizenship papers without him having to make an appearance. The solution proposed was for him to identify himself with his fingerprints and to bring an old notarised ID, while declaring that his new ID had been lost.

On June 18, the Monkey called Villamizar at midnight, waking him up. Villamizar took the elevator up to Aseneth's apartment, where a party with accordion music was in full swing. Wrestling his way through the revellers, he was stopped by Aseneth.

"I know now who's calling you. Be careful because one false step and they'll have your balls." She escorted him to her bedroom, where the phone was ringing.

Above the ruckus, Villamizar heard, "Ready. Come to Medellín first thing tomorrow."

At 5 am, Villamizar appeared at the dwellings of Father Garcia, who was in the oratory finishing mass. "Well, Father, let's go. We're flying to Medellín because Escobar is ready to surrender."

On the Civil Aeronautics plane were representatives of the government. Travelling with the priest was his nephew, who assisted him. They were met at the Medellín airport by Martha Ochoa and Jorge Ochoa's wife, Maria Lia. The officials went to the capitol building. Villamizar and Father Garcia headed for Maria Lia's apartment.

Over breakfast, the arrangements for Pablo's surrender were

finalised. The priest was told that Pablo was on his way, employing his usual evasive techniques, travelling sometimes by car and at other times walking around checkpoints. Pablo's imminent surrender unnerved the priest so much that one of his contact lenses fell out and he stood on it. To remedy his despair, Martha Ochoa took him to an optician to get a pair of glasses. On the way there and back they were stopped at numerous checkpoints, where the guards saluted Father Garcia for bringing peace to Medellín.

At 2:30 pm, the Monkey showed up and said to Villamizar, "Ready. Let's go to the capitol building. You take your car and I'll take mine."

At the capitol building, the women waited outside. Putting on dark glasses and a golfer's hat, the Monkey disguised himself. Misidentifying the Monkey, a bystander called the government to report that Pablo had just surrendered at the capitol building.

About to leave the building, the Monkey received a call on a two-way radio notifying him that a military plane was heading for the city, carrying injured soldiers. To keep the airspace open for Pablo, Villamizar had the military ambulance rerouted and repeated his order to keep the sky clear.

"Not even birds will fly over Medellín today," the defence minister wrote in his diary.

After 3 pm, a helicopter lifted from the capitol building's roof with the government's representatives and a popular journalist. Ten minutes later, an order was despatched to the Monkey's radio. A second helicopter took off with the Monkey, Villamizar and Father Garcia. As they flew, a radio broadcast announced that the government's position on extradition had been defeated in the Constituent Assembly by a vote of fifty-one to thirteen, with five abstentions. It was official confirmation of Pablo's demand for non-extradition.

The reversal on extradition had come about at a time when President George HW Bush was mustering support for the invasion of Iraq. Colombia had used its seat on the United Nations Security Council to vote against the attack. Bush had wanted the

Colombian government to reverse its position. Dozens of traffickers had been extradited to America, which was still providing arms and soldiers to Colombia. In a quid pro quo, the Colombian president had voted to attack Iraq, while reversing its policy on extradition.

The Monkey directed the helicopter to Pablo's location, a mansion behind a grove, with a soccer pitch and tropical-flower gardens. "Put it down over there. Don't turn off the engine."

As the helicopter descended, the armed bodyguards on the field became apparent, encircling a bearded man with long hair. Over a dozen approached the helicopter. Wearing tennis shoes and a light-blue jacket, the man walked with a carefree stride. Thick-set and tanned, Pablo said goodbye to and hugged the nearest bodyguards. He told two of his closest bodyguards, Otto and Mugre, to come with him.

In the helicopter, he offered his hand to Villamizar. "How are you, Dr Villamizar?"

"How's it going, Pablo?"

Smiling, Pablo thanked Father Garcia. He sat next to his bodyguards. Upon noticing the Monkey, he said, "And you, in the middle of this right to the end." His friendly tone left the passengers wondering whether he had praised or chastised the Monkey.

Smiling, the Monkey shook his head. "Ah, Chief."

Based on Pablo's tranquillity and self-control, Villamizar's first impression of Pablo was that he possessed a dangerous level of confidence bordering on the supernatural.

The Monkey was unable to close the helicopter door, so the co-pilot did it.

"Do we take off now?" the pilot said.

"What do you think? Move it!" Pablo said, briefly dropping his polite mask. As the helicopter ascended, Pablo said to Villamizar, "Everything is fine, isn't it, Doctor?"

"Everything's perfect."

After fifteen minutes, the helicopter landed next to the first helicopter on a prison soccer field with broken goalposts and rocks everywhere. Pablo got out. Fifty men in blue guard uniforms aimed their guns at him.

He responded like thunder: "Lower your weapons, damn it!"

The guns were lowered before their commander issued the same order.

They walked to a house containing the official delegation, more of Pablo's men who'd surrendered and his wife and mother.

"Take it easy, Ma," Pablo said, patting his mother on the shoulder.

The prison director shook Pablo's hand. "Señor Escobar. I'm Lewis Jorge Pataquiva."

Pablo pulled up a trouser leg, revealing a Sig Sauer 9 mm pistol with a gold monogram inlaid on a mother of pearl handle. The spellbound crowd watched him remove each bullet and throw it on the ground. The gesture was designed to show confidence in the warden whose appointment had worried Pablo. On a portable phone, Pablo told his brother that he'd surrendered. Addressing the journalists present, he said his surrender was an act of peace. "I decided to give myself up the moment I saw the National Constitutional Assembly working for the strengthening of human rights and Colombian democracy."

Journalists wrote about Pablo:

"I had thought that he was a petulant, proud, disciplined man, one of those who is always looking over his shoulder. But I was wrong. On the contrary, he is educated. He asks permission if he walks in front of a person and is agreeable when he greets someone."

"You can see that he is someone who worries about his appearance. Especially his shoes. They were impeccably clean."

"He walks as if he had no worry in the world. He is very jovial and he laughs a lot."

"He had a bit of a belly, which makes him look like a calm man."

Pablo acknowledged everyone.

"I'm here," the special prosecutor said, taking Pablo's hand, "Señor Escobar, to make certain your rights are respected." Pablo thanked him.

Pablo took Villamizar's arm. "Let's go, Doctor. You and I have a lot to talk about."

In an outside gallery, they both leaned against a railing. Pablo thanked Villamizar and apologised for the pain he'd caused him and his family. He said both sides had suffered in the war.

"Why was Luis Carlos Galán killed?" Villamizar said, referring to the presidential candidate.

"The fact is that everybody wanted to kill Dr Galán. I was present at the discussions when the attack was decided, but I had nothing to do with what happened. A lot of people were involved in that. I didn't even like the idea because I knew what would happen if they killed him, but once the decision was made, I couldn't oppose it. Please tell doña Gloria that for me," Pablo said, referring to Galán's widow.

"Why was an attempt made on my life?"

"A group of friends in Congress had convinced me that you were uncontrollable and stubborn and had to be stopped somehow before you succeeded in having extradition approved. Besides, in that war we were fighting, just a rumour could get you killed. But now that I know you, Dr Villamizar, thank God nothing happened to you."

"Why did you kidnap my wife and sister?"

"I was kidnapping people to get something and I didn't get it. Nobody was talking to me. Nobody was paying attention, so I went after doña Maruja to see if that would work." Pablo said that the negotiations had convinced him that Villamizar was a brave man of his word, and he was eternally grateful for that. Even though he was not expecting them to ever be friends, Pablo assured Villamizar that nothing bad would ever happen to his family. "Who knows how long I'll be here, but I still have a lot of friends, so if any of you feels unsafe, if anybody tries to give you a hard time, you let me know and that'll be the end of it. You met your obligations to me, and I thank you and will do the same for you. You have my word of honour." Pablo asked Villamizar if he'd have a word with his mother and wife, who were having sleepless nights as they suspected the government had arranged for Pablo to be murdered in prison.

Forty-one-year-old Pablo underwent the medical examination required for new prisoners. His health was documented as that of "a young man in normal physical and mental condition." Pablo said that the scar on his nose was due to an injury from playing football as a child. The only abnormality found was congestion in the nasal mucous membranes.

To obtain imprisonment, Pablo cited a crime that he had been found guilty of by the French authorities: acting as a middleman in a drug transaction arranged by his cousin, Gustavo. He issued a statement: "That country's penal code… gives one the right to apply for a revision of their case, when they appear before their national judge, in this case a Colombian judge. This is precisely the objective of my voluntary presentation to this office, in other words, to have a Colombian judge examine my case." Rather than plead guilty to a crime, he had surrendered to appeal the French conviction.

In court in Bogotá, Pablo declared his job title as "livestock farmer," and added, "I have no addictions, don't smoke, don't drink." He said he'd done an accounting course and, while incarcerated, he was going to obtain a college degree. "I wish to clarify that there may be people who might try to send anonymous letters, make phone calls or commit actions in bad faith under my name in order to harm me. There have been many accusations, but I've never been convicted of a crime in Colombia."

"Do you know where they got the 400 kilos of cocaine?" the judge said, referring to Pablo's conviction in France.

"I think Mr Gustavo Gaviria was in charge of that."

"Who is Mr Gustavo Gaviria?"

"Mr Gustavo Gaviria was a cousin of mine."

"Do you know how Mr Gaviria died?"

"Mr Gaviria was murdered by members of the National Police during one of the raid-executions, which have been publicly denounced on many occasions."

"Let's talk about your personal and family's modus vivendi and the economic conditions you've had throughout your life."

"Well, my family is from the north-central part of Colombia, my mother is a teacher at a rural school and my father is a farmer. They made a great effort to give me the education I received, and my current situation is perfectly defined and clear before the national tax office... I have always liked to work independently and, since my adolescence, I have worked to help sustain my family. Even when I was studying, I worked at a bicycle rent shop and other less important jobs to support my studies... Later on, I got into the business of buying and selling cars, livestock and land investments. I want to cite Hacienda Nápoles as an example of this – that it was bought in conjunction with another partner at a time when these lands were in the middle of the jungle. Now they are practically ready to be colonised. When I bought land in that region, there were no means of communications or transport and we had to endure a 23-hour journey. I say this in order to clarify the image that people have that it's all been easy..." Asked if he'd originally started in business with other people, Pablo said, "No. It all began from scratch, as many fortunes have started in Colombia and in the world."

"Tell the court what disciplinary or penal precedents appear on your record."

"Yes, there have been many accusations, but I've never been convicted of a crime in Colombia. The accusations of theft, homicide, drug-trafficking and many others were made by General Miguel Maza, according to whom every crime that is committed in this country is my fault."

After he denied any involvement in the cocaine business, the judge insisted that he must know something about it.

"Only what I see or read in the media. What I've seen and heard in the media is that cocaine costs a lot of money and is consumed by the high social classes in the United States and other countries of the world. I have seen that many political leaders and governments around the world have been accused of narco-trafficking, like the current Vice President of the United States [Dan Quayle], who has been accused of buying and selling cocaine and marijuana. I have also seen the declarations of one of Mr Reagan's daughters in which she admits to taking marijuana, and I've heard the accusations against the Kennedy family, and also accusations of heroin dealing against the Shah of Iran, as well as the Spanish president. Felipe González publicly admitted that he took marijuana. My conclusion is that there is universal hypocrisy toward drug-trafficking and narcotics, and what worries me is that from what I see in the media, all the evil involved in drug addiction is blamed on cocaine and Colombians, when the truth is that the most dangerous drugs are produced in labs in the United States, like crack. I've never heard of a Colombian being detained for possession of crack because it's produced in North America." Pablo had a point: the journalist Gary Webb discovered that the CIA had facilitated the importation of tons of cocaine into America, some of which had contributed to the crack epidemic. George HW Bush and other senior politicians were deeply involved in such covert activity while using Pablo's operation as a smokescreen (all explored in my books *American Made* and *We Are Being Lied To*).

"What is your opinion, bearing in mind your last few answers, on narco-trafficking?"

"My personal opinion, based on what I've read, I would say that cocaine [will continue] invading the world… so long as the high classes continue to consume the drug. I would also like to say that the coca leaf has existed in our country for centuries and it's part of our aboriginal cultures…"

"How do you explain that you, Pablo Escobar, are pointed out as the boss of the Medellín Cartel?"

Avoiding the question, Pablo referred the judge to a statement he'd submitted on videotape. "Another explanation I can give is this: General Maza is my personal enemy... [He] proclaimed himself my personal enemy in an interview given to *El Tiempo* on the eighth of September, 1991. It is clear then that he suffers a military frustration for not capturing me. The fact that he carried out many operations in order to capture me, and they all failed, making him look bad, has made him say he hates me and I am his personal enemy..."

The court heard a list of traffickers who'd claimed that Pablo was their boss.

"I don't know any of these people," Pablo said. "But through the press, I know about Mr Max Mermelstein. I deduce that he is a lying witness, which the US government has against me. Everyone in Colombia knows that North American criminals negotiate their sentences in exchange for testifying against Colombians... I would like to add to the file a copy of *Semana* magazine, which has an article about Max Mermelstein, to demonstrate what a liar this man is: 'Escobar was the chief of chiefs. The boss of cocaine trafficking wore blue jeans and a soccer shirt, was tall and thin.'" Pablo stood to display his short stout body. "I ask you to tell me, am I a tall and thin person? For a gringo to say that one is tall, you would suppose that man to be very tall."

By spending some of the millions he'd smuggled into the prison, it wasn't long before Pablo started to modify his surroundings to suit a man of his stature. He kept his cash in milk cans inside containers of salt, sugar, rice, beans and fresh fish, which were permitted inside because they were classified as food rations. Excess money was buried near the soccer field and in underground tunnels accessible by trapdoors in the cells. When his employees needed paying, helicopters transported cash out of the Cathedral.

He added a bar, lounge and disco, where he hosted parties and weddings. Famous people, models, politicians and soccer players danced and cavorted in the Cathedral. He installed a sauna in the gym, and Jacuzzis and hot tubs in the bathrooms. In his bedroom, he had a circular rotating bed and two other beds for his family. One of the biggest benefits to Pablo of no longer being on the run was the time he could spend with his family. Above his bed was a gold-framed portrait of the Virgin Mary.

Large items such as computers and big-screen TVs – on which they watched *God's Minute* – were smuggled in by Roberto's son, who drove a truck laden with crates of soda disguising the contraband. The truck brought women in, too. Despite rules restricting visits to official days, people were always sneaking in. Vans with fake walls held up to twenty people. This method of entry was ideal for people who wanted to keep their visits a secret, such as criminals and politicians.

Pablo's extensive record collection was there, including albums signed by Frank Sinatra from when Pablo had visited him in Las Vegas, and Elvis records purchased during a Graceland trip. His books ranged from Bibles to Nobel Prize winners. He had novels by Gabriel García Márquez and Stefan Zweig, a prominent Austrian writer from the 1920s. His movies on videotape included *The Godfather* trilogy and films starring Chuck Norris. Most of the prisoners had posters on their walls, whereas Pablo hung valuable paintings on his. His closet was full of neatly pressed jeans, shirts and Nike sneakers, some with spikes on in case he had to flee. Pablo never tied the laces of his sneakers – it was said that if he did, then something life-threatening was imminent. In case of danger from above the prison, a remote control allowed Pablo to turn off all of the internal lights.

Further up the slope, cabins were built for privacy with female visitors and as hideouts in case the prison was attacked. They were painted brightly and had sound systems and fancy lamps. Paths were made into the forest to allow a quick getaway and to enable the prisoners to walk where the air was freshest.

As the location included a direct sightline to his family's home, he mounted a telescope so he could see his wife and children while talking to them on the phone. A playhouse was constructed for his daughter and filled with toys.

The soccer field was renovated, night lights installed and wires positioned above it to sabotage helicopter landings. Despite having a bad knee, Pablo played centre forward; his associates made tactful allowances for this such as passing him the ball to score winning goals. The professional teams who came to play against Pablo and his men were careful never to win. Pablo had a replacement on standby in case he grew tired. When he regained his energy after resting, he'd join back in. The guards served the players refreshments. Sometimes his lawyers had to wait hours to see him if he was playing soccer.

The introduction of two chefs known as the Stomach Brothers addressed Pablo's concerns about getting poisoned. He enjoyed beans, pork, eggs and rice. He'd installed exercise equipment such as weights and bikes for the prisoners to get in shape, but as they were no longer on the run and had access to endless food and alcohol, they started to gain weight.

The Cathedral became known as "Club Medellín" or "Hotel Escobar." *Hustler* magazine published an illustration of Pablo and his associates partying in prison, throwing darts at a picture of President George HW Bush. Pablo obtained the illustration and hung it on his wall.

Communications were a priority. Pablo had cell phones, radio transmitters, a fax machine and beepers. Roberto has denied allegations by other authors that Pablo used carrier pigeons.

With the government protecting him instead of hunting him down, Pablo's cocaine business thrived. Father Garcia tried to help Pablo make peace with the Cali Cartel. He arranged for Pablo to speak to its leaders, but little progress was made as they were too stubborn. "I don't believe a word of those two," Pablo told Roberto. A DAS agent working as prison security discovered that the Cali Cartel had bought four bombs from El Salvador, and was attempting to buy a plane to drop them on the Cathedral. From then on, the guards fired at any planes flying too close to the prison.

To address legal problems, Pablo had thirty lawyers working for him almost full-time. He was facing an indictment for being the intellectual author of the murder of the presidential candidate,

Galán. One of Pablo's men, La Quica, was arrested in New York for traveling with a fake passport, and was accused of being a player in the bombing of Avianca Flight 203. During a raid of one of Pablo's properties, the authorities found paperwork linking Pablo to the assassination of the journalist, Guillermo Cano.

When he wasn't meeting his lawyers, Pablo was usually on the telephone or reading. He tried to learn Mandarin. At nights, he sat in a rocking chair and watched the lights come on in Envigado, while thinking about his family.

He received endless letters from people asking for help, business advice and money. If their stories checked out, Pablo often sent them cash. A teenager sent a photo of herself in a wedding dress and a letter offering her virginity in exchange for Pablo paying her college fees, so she could become a lawyer. After her story was confirmed, he paid the fees, without taking her offer up. People also gathered at the prison gate with notes for Pablo, seeking his assistance.

On December 1, 1991, Pablo celebrated his forty-second birthday with a party in the Cathedral, where his guests ate caviar and pink salmon while listening to live music. His gifts included a Russian fur hat from his mother. Photographed wearing it, he declared it would be his trademark.

Pablo took trips to watch soccer games at the stadium he'd built in Medellín. The police diverted traffic to allow his vehicles access. He went Christmas shopping at a mall. He spent the one-year anniversary of his surrender at a nightclub with family and friends.

When the government attempted to build a maximum-security prison based on the American model to transfer Pablo to, no construction company would accept the job. One said, "We're not going to build a cage with the lion already inside." Finally, a company owned by an Israeli security expert attempted to build it, with supposedly incorruptible workers from afar. Watching the work crew, Pablo's men started writing down their license-plate numbers, and eventually attacked them, causing many to quit. The project was abandoned.

In early 1992, the attorney general's office published photos taken at Hotel Escobar, including waterbeds, Jacuzzis, big-screen TVs… The embarrassed president commissioned an investigation, but the justice minister found that the furnishings were legal because each prisoner was allowed a bed and a bathtub, and TVs were permitted for good behaviour.

"I want all of these things taken out immediately!" the president said. "Tell the army to go in there and take everything. Escobar has to know we're not kidding."

No government department wanted the job. "No way," the minister of defence said. "I cannot do it because I don't have the people." When it was pointed out that he had 120,000 troops, he still refused the assignment.

Due to the deal struck with Pablo, the police couldn't do it. The DAS said that they couldn't act because they were only allowed inside the prison in the event of a riot.

In the end, a lawyer was told to take a truck and some workers, and to go to the prison and get the goods. "What have I ever done to you?" the lawyer responded. "Why'd you give me this assignment?"

Banking on the truck not being allowed to enter the prison, so he could turn around and go home, the lawyer set off. When he arrived, the prison gate opened and Pablo waved them in.

Upon being told why they were there, Pablo said, "Certainly, Doctor. I didn't know these things bothered you. Please, take everything out." Pablo and his men helped them carry the goods until everything was gone.

The lawyer rushed to his boss with photos of the bare prison. While the president was examining the photos, all of the goods were heading back to the Cathedral.

Pablo claimed that his imprisonment was a personal sacrifice for the good of all of the traffickers – for whom he'd single-handedly got rid of extradition. Due to the benefits they were receiving, they were expected to compensate him by paying a tax. In prison, Pablo was tuned into everything going on outside thanks to his extensive communications network. Those who tried to cheat him out of the tax or were perceived to have swindled him in any way were dealt with harshly.

Pablo's friends, Fernando Galeano and Kiko Moncada, ran two of the biggest trafficking groups that Pablo taxed. They were smuggling cocaine into America via a route that Pablo had established through Mexico. Word trickled back to the Cathedral that they'd been short-changing Pablo, who viewed their deceit as a prelude to a takeover of his organisation. Pablo learned where they stashed their money. His men confiscated $20 million. After denying Pablo's allegations, Galeano and Moncada asked for it back. He told them that he wanted to discuss it in person at the prison.

Pablo gave Galeano and Moncada a lecture about everything that he'd done for them. According to Roberto, they were killed after they'd left the Cathedral: Popeye killed Moncada and Otto shot Galeano. Within days, their brothers were also killed. Their distraught families begged for their corpses to give them proper burials, so Pablo told them where to find them.

Pablo wanted all of the property belonging to their organisations. Their employees were told that they worked for Pablo. Their key people were smuggled into the Cathedral through a secret tunnel to attend a meeting, many of them thinking they would die.

"I'm declaring an emergency," Pablo said. "Your bosses are already dead. Now you'll turn over all their resources to me. If you lie, you'll die very painfully." He reminded them that he was the boss. He said that they'd all be safe provided they paid him the tax.

The DEA recorded a version of events based on an informant's statement:

Escobar argued that while he and his close associates were in jail and needed money for their expensive war with the Cali Cartel, Galeano and Moncada preferred to store money until it became moldy rather than use it to help their friends… Escobar convinced cartel members who genuinely liked Moncada and Galeano that if the two men were not killed, the Medellín Cartel would be in a war with itself, and they would all perish.

Word got out about the murders of Galeano and Moncada, which made the president appear weak for not taking any action. Two of Pablo's biggest enemies – George HW Bush and the Cali Cartel – were putting relentless pressure on the government to eliminate Pablo once and for all by moving him to another prison, where he could be assassinated, or by extraditing him to the US, where he would never get out of prison.

Roberto told Pablo that he felt something bad was imminent. He asked Pablo to look into it. Government and army people on Pablo's payroll confirmed that he needed to abandon the Cathedral. He was told that George HW Bush was threatening to invade Colombia on the grounds that the government was incapable of extraditing Pablo.

Military trucks were spotted heading for the Cathedral. Pablo received a message that officials were coming to speak to him.

Aiming to transfer Pablo to Bogotá, the president told the deputy justice minister, Eduardo Mendoza – a thin young man with a boyish face – to go to the Cathedral and liaise with an army general, whose troops were already raiding the Cathedral.

"Shall I bring Pablo back to Bogotá?" Mendoza said.

"Yes," the defence minister said. "We're moving him to a military base in Bogotá. Now run!"

On the way to the airplane, Mendoza picked up Colonel Navas, the military director of prisons.

"This is totally crazy," Navas said. "You cannot do this to Escobar and get away with it." Navas viewed the action as a violation of the government's agreement with Pablo and a resumption of war. "Lots of people will die."

"Colonel, this isn't my decision," Mendoza said. "We've been ordered to go and we're going to put him on a plane and bring him back."

At the airport, they were told that their military plane had no fuel.

Waiting around, Mendoza decided to seek further clarification from the justice minister. "I don't understand what's going on. Tell me again, what am I supposed to do?"

"Look, if the prisoners give you any trouble, tell them it's because of the construction. Tell them we're having problems because they've been bullying the workers, so we have to move them temporarily out of the way."

The sun was setting over snowy mountain crests when they landed. It was getting cold. Ascending a dirt road, Mendoza was expecting to hear gunfire from the raid in progress. He translated the silence to mean that the raid was over and Pablo had been captured. Bringing Pablo back would be easy now.

When the jeep pulled up at the prison, a general in green battle garb approached Mendoza. "What are your orders?"

"General, my orders are to take Escobar back to Bogotá."

"I have different orders."

Mendoza was dismayed to learn that the general hadn't raided the prison. The troops were still outside.

"If they want Escobar," the general said, "I'll go in there myself and get that bandit and tie him up and bring him out! But until my orders change…"

Mendoza explained that he'd been told that the raid was underway. A press release had been issued stating that Pablo was at another prison.

"This is very confusing," the general said. "Do you think we should do this tonight or shall we wait until tomorrow morning?"

"General, I have no idea. I was sent to do this immediately. I thought it was done. I don't have the authority to tell you to wait until tomorrow. If it would be easier for you to do it in daylight, maybe we should wait, but I'm not a military officer. I don't know. Let's call Bogotá."

The general got on a radio phone. "I'm here with the vice minister. He wants me to do this thing tomorrow." The general hung up and invited the dumbfounded Mendoza to dinner.

A presidential military aide called Mendoza and chewed him out for interfering with a military operation by postponing it until tomorrow – which hadn't been Mendoza's idea. Troops gathering around the Cathedral was a hot media story. Pablo might be escaping.

Attempting to get things back on track, Mendoza turned towards the general. "You must do it tonight. Immediately."

After getting off the phone, the general said that the new plan was to send Colonel Navas into the prison to assess the situation.

"I should be the one to go in, not you," Mendoza told the colonel.

"No, Doctor, don't worry about it." The colonel marched to the prison gate. "Open up!" Almost an hour later, he returned. "Well, the situation is under control, but these people are very scared. They told me that they'll start blowing the place up if the army tries to come in and take Escobar, which is what they hear on the radio is about to happen. Doctor, if you were to go in there and explain what is going on and calm them down, we may be able to save lots of lives."

Exasperated and cold, Mendoza opted to go in. The gate opened. The guards lined up in formation.

"Señor Vice Minister, welcome to the Cathedral!" After declaring the numbers of prisoners and guards, the captain said, "All is quiet."

In jeans, a dark jacket and sneakers – with the laces untied – Pablo emerged with Roberto to discuss the situation. "Good evening, Doctor," he said to Mendoza.

Despite being protected by fifteen armed prison guards,

Mendoza trembled as he said that the army had been ordered to search the rooms.

"I'm sorry, but I've made a deal with the government," Pablo said. "The police and the army are not permitted inside. If you want, you can bring the regular prison officials to do this search, but I will not allow the army and even less the police. Please remember, gentlemen, I fought a war with the police and this policy is the result." Watching Mendoza turn pale and agitated, Pablo said, "I'll allow some soldiers inside, but without their weapons."

Mendoza made a call. Refusing to accept Pablo's offer, the president demanded that the army enter with weapons.

"They can't come inside with weapons," Pablo said. "No one's coming here armed to kill us. We don't know what their intentions are. I don't trust them with my life."

An army general called Pablo, and stated that the president intended to kill, capture or extradite him. Pablo told Roberto that he was going to keep Mendoza and the colonel hostage. Wearing jackets with concealed weapons, a dozen bodyguards arrived and formed a semicircle around Pablo.

"You've betrayed me, Señor Vice Minister," Pablo said. "The president has betrayed me. You're going to pay for this and this country is going to pay for this because I have an agreement and you're breaking it."

"You have nothing to fear for your life. You're only being transferred."

"You're doing this to deliver me to the Americans."

"No, we–"

"Kill them!" Popeye yelled with a cruel expression on his round face. "Sons of bitches."

Mendoza steered his eyes towards the prison guards and gazed as if imploring their help. They looked away.

"You're going to deliver me to Bush, so that he can parade me before the election, just like he did with Manuel Noriega. I'm not going to allow that, Doctor."

"We should have killed this one during the campaign!" Popeye said. "It would have been easy."

"Look," Mendoza said. "It would be unconstitutional for us to send you to the United States."

"Then you're going to kill me. You're going to take me out of here and have me killed. Before I allow that to happen, many people will die."

"Let us kill them, boss!"

"Do you really think they're going to send someone like me to kill you?" Mendoza said. "There are hundreds of soldiers outside and other officials. Do you think we would send for this many witnesses if we were going to kill you? This is just not reasonable. I'll stay with you, if you want, all night. Wherever you go, you're a prisoner and we're obliged to guarantee your safety. So you don't have anything to worry about."

Pablo glowered.

"All we have to do is finish the prison," Mendoza said, "and we can't do that with you here."

"No, Doctor," Pablo said. "That problem we had with the workers was just a misunderstanding."

"Look, I'm going to walk out of here. I'll be right out there." Mendoza pointed at the dirt road. "We're going to deliver the prison to the army. I'll be out there and I'll stay with you guys wherever you're going."

As if making a decision, Pablo scanned the area beyond the fence.

"I'll talk to you later." Mendoza, the colonel and the prison guards advanced towards the gate.

"Boss, that son of a bitch is going to betray us. We should kill them all! Are you going to let them walk out?"

The officials were almost at the gate, when Pablo's bodyguards rushed after them with their guns drawn. Mendoza expected the prison guards to defend him. Instead, they pulled out their weapons and pointed them at him. Wondering what to do next, Mendoza glanced at the colonel, who looked like he wanted to vomit.

"Boss, look, look! They are sending messages to each other. Kill him! Kill him, the son of a bitch!" Popeye said, stamping his feet.

Bodyguards shoved the officials towards the prison.

"I'm sorry," Pablo said, "but you can't leave right now. We need you to ensure our own safety while we figure out what to do."

At the warden's house, Popeye threw Mendoza through the doorway and aimed a gun at the side of his head. "I'm going to kill the guy! I've always wanted to kill a vice minister." With his face right up to Mendoza's, he yelled, "You son of a bitch. You motherfucker. You've been trying to get us for years. Now I'll get you."

"Popeye, not now," Roberto said. "Maybe later. Relax. He's worth more alive."

Mendoza was instructed to sit on a sofa in the warden's room.

"Señor Vice Minister," Pablo said, brandishing a gun. "From this moment, you're my prisoner. If the army comes, you'll be the first to die."

"Don't think by holding me you'll stop them," Mendoza said. "If you take us hostage you can forget about everything. They have heavy machine guns, lots of them. They'll kill everybody here! You can't escape!"

Pablo smiled. "Doctor, you still don't understand. These people all work for me." Pablo called his wife. "We're having a little problem here. We're trying to solve it. You know what to do if it doesn't work." He gave Mendoza the phone. "Call the president."

"The president won't take the call," Mendoza said.

"Get somebody to take the call because you're about to die."

Mendoza got through to a staff member at the president's office.

"Are you being held hostage?"

"Yes."

The staff member hung up. Trembling, Mendoza imagined himself dying in the raid.

"Let me kill him, boss," Popeye said.

To make a private call, Pablo left the room for five minutes. He returned with a gun tucked into his pants. "Doctor, you're detained, but you're not going to be killed. If anyone touches you, he'll have to answer to me."

"You can't escape from here," Mendoza said. "The army has the prison surrounded."

"You had an agreement with me and you're breaking it. Doctor, I know you guys are bothered about those killings," Pablo said, referring to Galeano and Moncada. "Don't worry. They were problems among Mafioso. They don't concern you."

Mendoza and the colonel were escorted to Pablo's lavishly furnished cell, where Popeye and a bodyguard kept watch. They were given ponchos to wrap around themselves to keep warm. Popeye kept pumping his shotgun near Mendoza, who was still ruminating on his own slaughter at the hands of the troops.

The colonel picked up a bottle. "This could be the last whiskey I'll drink in my life." After swigging some, he reached for a Bible and read Psalm 91. He asked for and was granted a telephone. He told his family goodbye.

"How do you stay so thin?" a bodyguard asked Mendoza.

"I'm a vegetarian."

"What should I eat to lose weight?"

"More fruits and vegetables."

The bodyguard fetched a plate of apple slices. "Now I'm going to start a healthy diet."

Popeye shook his head. "What are you going to do that for? We're all going to be dead by seven o'clock."

The weapons buried by Roberto and Pablo – prior to their arrival at the Cathedral – were unearthed. In addition to the pistol in his pants, Pablo slung an Uzi over his shoulder. Approaching the perimeter, they relied on the fog for cover. With soldiers nearby, Roberto used wire cutters on the electrified fence, making a gap big enough for a person to slip through.

While preparing to escape, Pablo kept trying to contact the

president. His lawyers and Father Garcia were rebuffed by the president's office.

"Either we flee or we all die," Pablo told his men. He and Roberto entered a hidden room and grabbed lots of cash. To thwart the spy planes, Roberto used his emergency remote control to plunge the prison into darkness, which terrified everybody inside, including the hostages.

Pablo listened to radio stations report different stories. One claimed he'd been captured and was on a plane to America. Another said the military had taken over the Cathedral and lives had been lost.

Concerned about his family hearing these reports, he called them. "Don't worry. Don't listen to the news. The situation is being resolved directly with the president." After hanging up, he called and reassured his mother. Pablo crouched down, grabbed his shoelaces and finally tied them. "Roberto, let's put our radios on the same frequency."

Pablo returned to his room to check on the hostages. "Try to remain calm. The situation will be resolved without anyone getting killed. I'm going to sleep. I'll see you in the morning."

With darkness, fog and rain providing cover, Pablo told his men to simply walk out through the hole that Roberto had cut in the fence, one after the other, five minutes apart. Hoping to blend in with the military units surrounding the prison, most of the men had put on army fatigues. Pablo went first. He positioned himself to watch the others emerging and everything going on around them.

Due to the poor visibility, Roberto got lost. After wandering around afraid, he found the hole in the fence at around 2 am.

The group set off down a wet slippery surface that presented a risk of injury or death. Confronted by a rock face, the brawniest went first and allowed the others to stand on their shoulders. While thorny vegetation prickled them, they held hands going down another slope. After two hours, visibility improved as the fog thinned. Realising they'd gone in a circle and hadn't achieved much distance from the prison, they traded expressions of shock and frustration. They needed to keep moving because they could easily be shot. Pablo estimated that they had two hours left to evacuate the area.

The sun was up when they reached a neighbourhood called El Salado. People were going to work and children to school. In filthy ripped clothes, Pablo and his men emerged like vagrants. They headed for a farm belonging to Memo, a trusted friend.

They knocked on the door. The groundskeeper answered, but didn't recognise them. Once it dawned, he let them in. They stripped off the soaked clothes compressed to their weary bodies. While their clothes were washed, they finally rested.

Almost an hour later, there was frantic banging at the door. Bracing for a gunfight, they grabbed their weapons and took aim. The door opened. In came the neighbours with a hot breakfast for the visitors. Other neighbours patrolled the streets to watch out for the army. Pablo and his men cleaned themselves, shaved and put on fresh clothes.

After the general outside the Cathedral had refused to launch an assault, the president had ordered in special forces. A press release was prepared, stating that Mendoza and the colonel had died in a shootout. At first, the plane carrying the troops couldn't land due to the fog. In the morning, the troops travelled up the slope in trucks. The army units already there gave the truck drivers the wrong directions and they ended up back at the airport.

In Pablo's room, the captives and the guards watched the news report the set-backs with the raid. Through a shortwave radio, they listened to the preparations outside as various units prepared to launch an assault. One of the units – trained by the Americans – was infamous for once having killed everybody in a building on behalf of an emerald dealer. Knowing this, the colonel started praying.

"Can I go outside for a look?" Mendoza said.

Bodyguards allowed him onto the porch. The rising sun was illuminating the fog. Due to the poor visibility, Mendoza's imagination ran wild with visions of his executioners closing in. Hoping that they'd recognise his business suit and not shoot him, he dropped his poncho and succumbed to the chilly air.

Gunfire. Explosions. Screams.

The commander of the prison guards was opening a door as the special forces launched their assault. A hailstorm of bullets dropped him dead. Of course, it was later reported that he'd opened fire on them.

Bodyguards dragged Mendoza back inside. "Doctor, please! They're going to kill us! Help us!"

"I've been telling you that all night! Now it's too late!"

Mendoza crawled to the bathroom and coiled his body behind the toilet, hoping it would shield him. Realising the glass would shatter and injure him, he crawled back to the living room and joined the colonel who was crouched next to a prison guard. The commotion grew louder. Mendoza attempted to leave the room.

"Get on the floor unless you want to be killed!" a prison guard yelled.

Mendoza and a guard tried to raise Pablo's mattress to hide under, but it was too heavy to move. He got down on the floor and braced to die. A grenade detonated nearby. As he twisted away from the explosion, his forehead met the barrel of a gun held by a black muscular man. With gunfire and bangs and blasts erupting all around, the special-forces sergeant holding the gun chucked Mendoza against a wall and sat on him.

"We're going to try to get out of here," the sergeant said. "Just look at my boot. Don't think of anything. Just look at my boot." They crawled onto the porch and behind a wall. "When I tell you to run, run."

With the raid raging and smoke stinging his eyes, Mendoza sprinted uphill towards the gate with the sergeant behind him yelling, "Run! Run! Run!" Mendoza had never moved so fast in his life. He accidentally hit a wall and broke two ribs, but the pain didn't register as his adrenaline propelled him. He bolted out of the main gate, where the general was awaiting his return.

After catching his breath, Mendoza said, "General, is Escobar dead?" The look on the general said it all. "Oh my God!" Mendoza said. "He got away! How could he get away?"

The raid netted five of Pablo's men. Twenty-seven guards were charged with suspicion of cooperating with Pablo.

Drinking coffee at Memo's house, Pablo listened to the radio reports, while helicopters buzzed overhead. Roberto's son called a radio station and stated that they were hiding in a tunnel under the prison with weapons and food. He told a reporter that Pablo would surrender and return to the Cathedral if the original terms were reinstated.

Hoping to unearth the tunnel, the government sent construction equipment to the prison, so that the troops could start digging. Explosives were detonated in the fields.

Pablo gazed at the activity through a window. "The only thing they'll find is the money in the barrels," he said, referring to $10 million that had been buried.

The radio reported that Pablo had ordered the assassination of all of the top government officials. Hoax bomb threats and evacuation drills at schools were widespread.

On TV in the evening, the president called for calm and promised to protect the escapees' lives if they surrendered, but he never mentioned reinstating Pablo's original deal.

Some US news outlets reported that Pablo and his men had stormed out of the prison in a hail of gunfire, with their weapons blazing. These stories increased support for George HW Bush to send soldiers to Colombia to apprehend Pablo and to incarcerate him in America.

When darkness came, the men left Memo's and trekked through the woods. At the Cathedral, explosions were still going off as the troops searched for the tunnel. At another farm, Pablo called his family and urged them to ignore the news. They ate and set off again.

Outside a farm, five German shepherds launched at them. They couldn't shoot the dogs because the noise would have alerted the authorities. One bit El Mugre on the leg, drawing blood. Pablo threw some snacks at the dogs, which distracted them. He stayed with the dogs while the others moved on and then followed everyone.

At 3:30 am, they arrived at a friendly farm. A driver took Roberto to see his mother, so that he could explain the situation. He didn't want to stay long, but she insisted on making some food for him and Pablo. Unable to say no, Roberto positioned himself at a window and watched out for the police.

When Roberto returned to the farm, some of the group had moved on because Pablo felt they'd be harder to find if they split up. More soldiers were constantly arriving in the area around the Cathedral, hoping to flush them out. For two days, they stayed at the farm, watching TV reports and listening to the radio.

On July 24, 1992, Pablo recorded a statement, offering to surrender if he could go back to the Cathedral. He said the arrival of the troops had taken them by surprise. He called Mendoza a liar as he had never been kidnapped or threatened. "As for the aggression carried out against us, we won't take violent actions of any nature yet and we are willing to continue with the peace process and our surrender to justice if we can be guaranteed to stay at the Envigado jail [the Cathedral], as well as handing control of the prison to special forces of the United Nations."

At the end, he said he was in the jungles of Colombia, which prompted the government to send soldiers and helicopters there.

They had been at the farm for twenty days when 5,000 soldiers were dispatched to the area. With helicopters arriving, they ran into the forest and escaped into the jungle. Unable to ascertain their location, the army kept dropping bombs, but missing them. For twelve days, they slept on hammocks, occasionally awakened by the explosions going on around them.

CHAPTER 16
ON THE RUN

Pablo's escape had embarrassed the president, who was appearing on TV daily, trying to explain the situation. He told the American ambassador that he didn't have a problem with US troops on Colombian soil. He wanted all of the help he could get to quickly fix the Pablo situation.

Grateful to have miraculously survived the raid, Mendoza flew back to Bogotá, where the president told him, "We must hide nothing in this. Don't take time to prepare a response. Just get out there and tell people exactly what happened."

Mendoza brought the Americans up to speed. They were delighted that they could resume the hunt for Pablo. It was an opportunity for George HW Bush to distract the public from domestic issues and to boost his popularity. Catching the person he'd labelled the biggest cocaine trafficker in the world would surely increase his chances of re-election. The DEA in Bogotá sent a cable to Washington:

The BCO [the local US embassy] feels that Escobar may finally have overstepped his self-perceived illegitimate boundaries and has placed himself in a very precarious position. Escobar's gall and bravado may lead to his ultimate downfall. But then again, the GOC [government of Colombia] has always bowed to Escobar's demands in the past. This current situation again provides the GOC with an opportunity to demonstrate its dedication to bring all narco-traffickers to justice, including the most notorious and dangerous cocaine trafficker in history, Pablo Escobar.

Amid hyped-up threats that Pablo might assassinate him and set bombs off in America, George HW Bush dispatched Delta Force, Centra Spike, the DEA, the FBI, the ATF, the CIA, the Bureau of Alcohol, Tobacco and Firearms, the army, navy and the air force after Pablo. Out of all of the agencies, Centra Spike quickly obtained results by flying planes over Medellín with technology that picked up Pablo's calls.

Pablo responded to America's involvement with a fax:

We, the Extraditables declare: that if anything happens to Mr Pablo Escobar, we will hold President Gaviria responsible and will again mount attacks on the entire country. We will target the United States Embassy in the country, where we will plant the largest quantity of dynamite ever. We hereby declare: the blame for this whole mess lies with President Gaviria. If Pablo Escobar or any of the others turn up dead, we will immediately mount attacks throughout the entire country. Thank you very much.

George HW Bush approved a $2 million reward for information leading to Pablo. The US Embassy in Colombia offered $200,000 and relocation to America for any useful information. Advertised on TV, the reward program included pictures of Pablo and his henchmen.

The Centra Spike eavesdropping enabled the authorities to determine that Pablo was using at least eight cell-phones. He viewed himself as a victim of a violation of his agreement with the government and wanted to return to the Cathedral.

Centra Spike overheard Pablo tell a lawyer that he feared the raid on the Cathedral was a US-sponsored assassination attempt: "The situation arose because they went in there shooting and all, and we were defending our lives, but our intention was to comply with the government until the end... It is possible that one or two persons were smuggled into the jail. I won't deny it... that happens in jails all over the country and the world, and, in reality,

I am not to blame. The person to blame is the person who lets them in… So that if people entered shooting and all, and we had information that Americans were participating in the operation, we have to put our lives first. We have families!" He said that incarceration outside the Cathedral was unsafe.

"Yes," a lawyer said. "That was the first issue that I explained to the president."

Pablo criticised Mendoza's attempt to construct a new prison at the Cathedral. "There was a delineation of the jail. It had been arranged. We made the design. We reworked the map, so the only thing that we didn't bargain for was a jail different from that one. And we need a public guarantee from the president that he will not take us out of the country… The problem is, I have some information… that there were some gringos [Americans] looking for Bush's re-election, so we need their [the Colombian government's] guarantee in this respect… Do me a favour. Tell Señor President that I know he's misinformed. Now, they say that I am perpetrating crimes from jail." Even if he were found guilty of committing a crime while in jail, Pablo said that they could have extended his stay up to a maximum of a life sentence, but they had no legal right to move him from the Cathedral.

"Perfect," the lawyer said. "We'll see that all this works out."

"Anyway, accept my apologies," Pablo said. "There'll be no more acts of violence of any nature, although some resentful people have been making some phone calls. People want to create chaos. But anyway, we are well disposed and we want to get this thing resolved… Tell the president that we were very uneasy because the gringos were going to be a part of the operation."

Another lawyer told Pablo, "We saw the tapes of the grey uniforms [CIA] and all that."

"Of the gringos?" Pablo said. "And how many were there?"

"Well, we could see some uniforms on TV. This afternoon we asked for tapes from the evening news programme."

Pablo wanted to parlay CIA and American involvement into trouble for the Colombian president.

"There are two things that are very important," Pablo said to another lawyer. "When you have a chance of making a statement, say that what caused the biggest concern to us was the presence of the gringos. The fact that the army would be going along with the gringos. What explanation can be given for that?"

"Yes. The press is already after that. We're on top of that."

"OK. And another thing. The president has to say it officially and make an official commitment. Everything is a contract. Now it's going to be a contract signed by the minister who makes the commitment that if tomorrow or the day after tomorrow I kill the warden and get thirty more years, they don't transfer me from here. This is a commitment."

The Colombian police converted the Cathedral into their headquarters, with the commander based in Pablo's room. Delta Force members used Pablo's observation tower at the prison. They were fed map coordinates from Centra Spike when Pablo got on a phone. They started to home in on a neighbourhood called the Three Corners. The next time Pablo made a call, his location was located and photographed. Upon receiving the information from Delta Force, the Colombian commander dismissed it. The Americans contacted the president and suggested he send a small covert unit. Instead, he ordered a full assault by Search Bloc special forces.

From the Cathedral, Delta Force watched the headlights of the special-forces convoy ascending a hill towards the Three Corners, while another set of headlights descended on the other side, which they assumed was Pablo and his men escaping. Troops spent four hours searching the empty ranch.

No matter what information the Americans provided to the Colombians, the response was always inept, which allowed Pablo to escape time after time. With General Maza out of the loop, the Americans needed someone just as gung-ho whom to liaise with. That person was Colonel Martinez, the head of the Search Bloc, whose troops had killed Pablo's beloved cousin, Gustavo.

Prior to the Cathedral, Martinez had been hunting Pablo for two years. Having been unsuccessful, Martinez hadn't received the promotion he'd hoped for. Just like with Maza, Pablo had made many attempts on his life. In 1991, he was on a flight to Spain with his family when a bomb was found on-board. The plane had to make an emergency landing otherwise the bomb would have exploded at a certain altitude. In 1992, a car bomb had been found by the Colombian embassy on the route Martinez took to work. Afterwards, the embassy asked Martinez to avoid their building.

With Pablo free, Martinez jumped at the chance to finish the job. The Americans provided him information they had received through their reward program. An informant had located Tyson, one of Pablo's hit men who resembled the boxer Mike Tyson.

To trigger the raid, "The party has begun" was whispered over a radio to Search Bloc troops. An explosive charge blew a steel door off its hinges and blasted it through a wall. The door flew into the air and dropped nine stories. Twenty-six troops charged inside. Due to the iron bars on the windows, Tyson couldn't escape. He was executed with a bullet between the eyes. His death was recorded as due to a gun battle with the National Police.

Pablo responded the same day. His hit men shot four police. Over the next two days, five more died. Pablo paid $2,000 per killing. Over six months, sixty-five police were killed in Medellín, including many of the men working for Martinez. Even though their identities were supposed to have been a state secret, many of them were executed at home or travelling to work.

Pablo infiltrated the Search Bloc headquarters. Centra Spike sent Pablo's location to Martinez and promptly overheard a call from the headquarters to one of Pablo's men: "They're on their way. They're coming for you." A recording of the call was sent to Martinez, but he couldn't recognise the voice. He fired some of his men, but the warnings to Pablo continued. The implications were so grave that Martinez tended his resignation on the grounds that he could make no progress in such a hopeless situation that was out of his control. His resignation was refused.

After Martinez returned to his headquarters, suspicion fell on a policeman who guarded the perimeter of the base. They fed him some false information, which was forwarded to Pablo. The policeman confessed to accepting money to kill Martinez. He'd been practising with a gun with a silencer.

Martinez and Pablo probed each other like chess players. Trying to shut down Pablo's ability to communicate and run his organisation, Martinez oversaw a blackout of cell-phone use in Medellín. Pablo switched to radio and couriers. Knowing that Martinez was listening to his calls, Pablo displayed a remarkable ability to use code words and numbers with his underlings. Nothing fazed Pablo. Every time Martinez tried something new, Pablo shifted his strategy with the indifference of a grandmaster.

With so many agencies after him, including foreign mercenaries wanting the reward offered by the Americans, Pablo was slowly getting backed into a corner. A Colombian judge had ruled against his claim that his escape from prison had been legitimately taken out of fear for his life. The president was resolutely against Pablo returning to the Cathedral. Even though the forces against him were increasing, Pablo felt confident enough to give a radio interview in mid-1992.

"Do you regret having surrendered a year ago?"

Pablo responded that he did, but it had been necessary to stay alive. "Does one seek escape alternatives when you have arrived at a jail to which you have voluntarily surrendered?"

"Were you the man in charge in the prison?"

"I wasn't in charge... I wasn't just any prisoner. I was the product of a peace plan, whose cost wasn't high for the government... They simply gave me a dignified prison and special conditions previously agreed to by the government with the lawyers and me."

On the subject of his extravagant living quarters in the Cathedral, Pablo said, "Even if it is the most beautiful mansion in the world, if you're limited in your movements and watched by tower guards with weapons and soldiers, then that is a prison. But I'm not going to evade responsibility in the sense that I permitted some curtains and some special furniture, and I'm willing to pay for that error in accepting the most humble cell in any jail in Antioquia as long as my rights are respected and I'm guaranteed that I'll not be moved for any reason."

"Is your head worth more than the one billion pesos offered by the government and more than the two and a half billion pesos offered by the government of the United States?"

"It seems my problem has become political, and could be important for the re-election of the president of the United States."

"At this moment, you've become once again the most sought-after man in the world. The Colombian authorities, other secret services, DEA agents, the Cali Cartel, former accomplices of your activities, deserters from your organisation, indirect or direct victims of terrorist acts. Whom do you fear the most? How do you defend yourself from them?"

"I don't fear my enemies because they are more powerful. It has been my lot to face difficult circumstances, but I always do it with dignity."

"For you, what is life?"

"It's a space of time full of agreeable and disagreeable surprises."

"Have you ever felt afraid of dying?"

"I never think about death."

"When you escaped, did you think about death?"

"When I escaped, I thought about my wife, my children, my family and all the people who depend upon me."

"Do you believe in God and the hereafter? In heaven and hell?"

"I don't like to speak publicly about God. God, to me, is absolutely personal and private. I think all the saints help me, but my mother prays a lot for me to the child Jesus of Atocha, that is why I built him a chapel in Barrio Pablo Escobar. The largest painting in the prison was of the child Jesus of Atocha."

"Why have you been willing to risk having yourself killed?"

"For my family and for the truth."

"Do you accept that you have ever committed a crime or had someone killed?"

"That answer I can only give in confession to a priest."

"How do you think everything will end for you?"

"You can never foretell that, although I wish the best."

"If it depended on you, how would you like to end your life?"

"I would like to die standing in the year 2047."

"Under what circumstances would you commit suicide?"

"I have never thought about those types of solutions."

"Of all the things that you have done, which ones are you most proud of and of which are you ashamed?"

"I am proud of my family and my people. I'm not ashamed of anything."

"Whom do you hate and why?"

"In my conflicts, I try not to end up hating anybody."

"What advice have you given your children? What would you do if either of them dedicated themselves to illegal or criminal activities?"

"I know that my children love me and understand my fight. I always want the best for them."

"What do your wife and children mean to you?"

"They are my best treasure."

"Do you accept that you are Mafioso? Does it bother you that someone says that about you?"

"The communications media has called me that thousands of times. If it bothered me, I would be in an insane asylum."

"What is it that most angers you and gets you out of control?"

"You can get angry, but you cannot lose your control. I get angry at hypocrisy and lies."

"Do you accept that they say you are a drug dealer or a criminal or don't you really care?"

"My conscience is clear, but I would respond as a Mexican comedian once said, 'It's completely inconclusive.'"

"People say that you always get what you want."

"I have not said that I have always gotten what I wanted. If I had always gotten what I wanted, everything would be rosy and I would calmly be drinking some coffee in the Rionegro Plaza or the park at Envigado. I fight tirelessly, but I have suffered too much."

"What is the key to your immense power?"

"I don't have any special powers. The only thing that gives me strength to keep on fighting is the energy of the people who love and support me."

"Corruption. To what extent has it taken hold in the government?"

"Corruption exists in all the countries of the world. The important thing would be to know the causes of corruption in order to avoid it and stop it."

"Of what do you repent?"

"All human beings make mistakes, but I don't repent of anything because I take everything as an experience and channel it into something positive."

"If you were born again, what would you do? What would you repeat and what would you dedicate yourself to?"

"I would not do those things that I thought would turn out right, but which came out wrong. I would repeat everything that has been good and nice."

"What did your wife and children say when you were in prison and what did they think of your activities?"

"They have loved and supported me always. And they accept my cause because they know it and understand it."

"Do you consider yourself an ordinary man or someone of exceptional intelligence?"

"I am a simple citizen, born in the village of El Tablazo of the municipality of Rionegro."

"Have you personally ever taken drugs?"

"I am an absolutely healthy man. I don't smoke and I don't consume liquor. Although, with respect to marijuana, I'd have the same reply that the president of Spain gave when he was asked about it."

"Do you consider it a mistake on your part to have entered politics?"

"No, I do not accept it as a mistake. I am sure that if I had participated in other elections, I would have defeated everyone in Antioquia by an overwhelming majority."

"Why so much money? What do you do with it? Is your fortune as large as the international magazines say?"

"My money obeys a social function. That is clear and everyone knows about it."

"If you had to make a profile of yourself, what would you say about you, Pablo Escobar?"

"It's very difficult to portray oneself. I prefer that others analyse me and that others judge me."

"Why did you enter drug trafficking?"

"In Colombia, people enter this type of activity as a form of protest. Others enter it because of ambition."

"Do you feel bigger than Al Capone?"

"I'm not that tall, but I think Al Capone was a few centimetres shorter than I am."

"Do you consider yourself to be the most powerful man in Colombia? The richest? One of the most powerful?"

"Neither one nor the other."

"Did you feel complimented when the magazine *Semana* presented you as Robin Hood?"

"It was interesting and it gave me peace of mind."

"By temperament, are you violent and proud?"

"Those who know me know that I have a good sense of humour and I always have a smile on my face, even in very difficult moments. And I'll say something else: I always sing in the shower."

During Christmas 1992, Pablo wrote to two senators, offering to surrender if he could be housed at a police academy in Medellín, under the supervision of the military. He wanted the Search Bloc to be disbanded and claimed that Martinez was torturing people to get information. He said he was going to respond to the war in kind with kidnappings and bombings: "What would the government do if a 10,000 kg bomb were placed at the Colombian prosecutor general's office?"

CHAPTER 17
PEOPLE PERSECUTED
BY PABLO ESCOBAR

Unable to catch Pablo, the Americans stepped things up with a two-pronged strategy. As Pablo had targeted the family members of his enemies, the CIA proposed doing the same to him:

Escobar does seem to have genuine paternal feelings for his children, and the young daughter Manuela is described as his favorite. His parents were once kidnapped by a rival group and Escobar apparently spared no effort or expense rescuing them. Whether his concern for his parents or his children would overcome his stringent security consciousness is not clear.

The other prong was to employ a method that the CIA had used for decades in South America: arming and training death squads. It was a policy described succinctly by Bill Hicks, the comedian and social critic: "… the reason I didn't vote for Bush is because George [HW] Bush – along with Ronald Reagan – presided over an administration whose policies toward South America included genocide. So yeah, ya see? The reason I didn't vote for him? 'Cause he's a mass murderer. I'll pay the extra nickel on petrol, just knowing brown kids aren't being clubbed to death like baby seals in Honduras, so Pepsi can put a plant down there."

On January 30, 1993, Pablo orchestrated a car bombing in Bogotá by a bookstore. It destroyed part of the building and sent human limbs flying. Twenty-one died and seventy were injured.

The next day, a ranch belonging to Pablo's mother was torched.

His family's dwellings were bombed, injuring his mother and aunt. Days later, one of his ranches was burned. A DEA cable described a vigilante group – ideal raw material for the death squad the CIA had in mind:

The CNP [Colombian National Police] believe these bombings were committed by a new group of individuals known as "Los Pepes" (Perseguidos por Pablo Escobar) [People persecuted by Pablo Escobar]. This group... has vowed to retaliate against Escobar, his family, and his associates, each and every time Escobar commits a terrorist act, which injures innocent people... Obviously the CNP and the GOC [Government of Colombia] cannot condone the actions of "Los Pepes," even though they may secretly applaud these retaliatory acts.

The government's response to Pablo's bookstore bomb was to make him "public enemy number one" and to offer over $6 million for information leading to his capture. The Search Bloc and Los Pepes – many members of the latter were from the former – started to execute any of Pablo's underlings they could get their hands on. Murders were reported as "Killed in a gun battle with the Colombian police."

Los Pepes included former members of the Medellín Cartel and, in particular, the Moncada and Galeano families, with whom Pablo had remained at war. The Cali Cartel joined forces with Los Pepes by providing money and intelligence.

The CIA didn't want to get caught training and arming a death squad that was getting financed by the Cali Cartel, which wanted to expand its cocaine business at Pablo's expense. To circumvent the law, the CIA trained the Los Pepes members who were police and special forces. With $2,000 bounties on their heads, many of the police had become frustrated by the limits of the law that prevented them from responding to Pablo with the same deadly force he'd used on them. In their official capacity, these police were trained by the CIA in torture and assassination techniques.

Rodolpho Ospina was a descendant of Colombian presidents. After getting involved in trafficking, Pablo had attempted to kill him twice. After turning informant, he gave the Americans some advice, which the DEA relayed in a cable:

[Ospina] states that Pablo Escobar's apprehension should be planned by accomplishing five goals. First... key Escobar organization members... should be arrested or killed, if there are no charges pending against them in Colombia. [Second], [Ospina] then named attorneys who handle Escobar's criminal problems and whose deaths would create havoc for Escobar. Third, the informant named prop-erties and important assets belonging to Escobar which should be destroyed...

Ospina stated that the five lead attorneys who handled Pablo's criminal and financial activities were worse than Pablo and should be killed. "These attorneys negotiate with the Colombian government on [his] behalf and are fully aware of the scope of [his] activities since [he] consults them before he carries out any action." Step five was the destruction of Pablo's property and possessions to make Pablo angry.

[Ospina] claimed that in order to bring Escobar out of hiding, he needs to be provoked or angered and made desperate so that he wants to strike back. The informant claimed that Escobar may then make mistakes.

Ospina suggested using the media as a weapon. "He [Pablo] controls the media through fear and payments and has confused the Colombian public by having himself portrayed as a wronged Colombian citizen, not really as dangerous as he appears to be in the foreign press." To obtain invaluable information about Pablo, he recommended cutting deals with incarcerated traffickers.

The Americans employed Ospina's strategy on Carlos Lehder, who was claiming that Pablo had played a role in his capture and extradition. Lehder detailed Pablo's habits:

Escobar is strictly a ghetto person, not a farm or jungle person. He fears more the communist and nationalist guerrillas than the army, so he remains in the Magdalena Medio Valley, a non-guerrilla region. Since the guerrillas remain in the high mountains one could disregard the mountains as Escobar's hiding place... Escobar always tries to keep within distance range for his cellular phone to reach Medellín's phone base. That's approximately 100 miles, so he can call any time.

Generally, P. Escobar occupies the main house with some of his hit men, radio operator (Big High Frequency radio receiver), cooks, whores and messengers. For transportation they have jeeps, motorcycles and sometimes a boat. I have never seen him riding a horse. Escobar gets up at 1 or 2 pm and goes to sleep at 1 or 2 am.

Fugitive Escobar uses from 15 to 30 security guards, with arms and WT (walkie-talkies). Two shifts of 12 hours each. Two at the main road entrance, some along the road, the rest around the perimeter of the main house (one mile) and one at his door... The main house always has two or three gateway paths which run to the forest and thus toward a second hideout near a river where a boat is located, or a tent with supplies and radios. Escobar is an obese man, certainly not a muscle man or athlete. He could not run 15 minutes without respiratory trouble. Unfortunately, the military-police has never used hunting dogs against him.

The only realistic de facto solution, as I analysed it, is a new military government or, at the very minimum, a freedom fighters brigade, controlled by the DEA, and independent of the Colombian politicians, police or army... There are a great number of Colombian people from all walks of life that are genuinely willing to assist, support, finance and even participate in the effective forming of a civilian militia… The rich, the poor, the peasant, the political left, center and right are willing to cooperate. Every day Escobar remains at large, he becomes more powerful and dangerous.

Thanks to all of the insider knowledge and terror methods taught by Delta Force, Los Pepes went on the rampage; kidnapping, bombing, torturing and murdering anyone associated with Pablo, regardless of whether they had committed a crime. Prime targets were family members, his workforce and especially his lawyers and accountants. Many of his employees defected to the Cali Cartel, which was flourishing and tightening its grip on the Colombian government through bribery. The Americans claimed to be in Colombia waging a War on Drugs, yet they were sharing intelligence with Los Pepes and the Cali Cartel, who were increasing the cocaine supply to America.

In a note, Pablo blamed Colonel Martinez:

Personnel under your supervision set car bombs at buildings in El Poblado, where some of my relatives live. I want to tell you that your terrorist actions will not stop my struggle under any circumstances. Your threats and your car bombs against my family have been added to the hundreds of young people that you have murdered in the city of Medellín in your headquarters of torture in the school Carlos Holguin. I hope that the Antioquian community becomes aware of what you do with the dynamite you seize, and of the criminal actions undertaken by men who cover their faces with ski masks. Knowing that you are part of the government, I wish to warn you that if another incident of this nature occurs, I will retaliate against relatives of government officials who tolerate and do not punish your crimes. Don't forget that you, too, have a family.

The warning from Pablo didn't deter Los Pepes, who were just getting started on annihilating his personnel. Using Medellín Cartel organisational charts provided by the CIA and Centra Spike, Los Pepes knew exactly who to target to maximise the damage. They offered rewards for information and caused a stir in the media by announcing what they were going to do to Pablo's associates.

In February 1993, a manager low down in the cartel hierarchy was found dead with a sign attached to his neck: "For working for the narco-terrorist and baby-killer Pablo Escobar. For Colombia. Los Pepes." They started to kill up to six of Pablo's employees and associates a day, including a director of the National Police of Colombia who was on Pablo's payroll. They shot the man in charge of financing operations multiple times in the head. Pablo's warehouse stocked with antique cars worth $4 million was torched. On February 28, 1993, the Search Bloc killed a brother-in-law of Pablo.

Rattled by Los Pepes, Pablo desperately wanted to get his family out of the country. Knowing that his family was his weakness, the US authorities intervened to prevent them from leaving.

Los Pepes killed the brother of a man who dealt real estate for Pablo. They bombed properties belonging to Pablo's bankers and lawyers. On March 4, 1993, the corpse of one of Pablo's lead lawyers was discovered with a note from Los Pepes threatening the rest of his lawyers, two of whom were swiftly killed. They killed Roberto Escobar's lawyer as he exited the prison he'd been visiting. They tortured and killed one of Pablo's lawyers and his eighteen-year-old son. Kidnapped by fifteen men with machine guns, the father and son were found in the trunk of a car, shot in the head, their hands taped together, with a note from Los Pepes: "Through their profession, they initiated abductions for Pablo Escobar. What do you think of the exchange for the bombs in Bogotá, Pablo?"

The rest of Pablo's lawyers resigned. One thought he could outsmart Los Pepes by continuing to work undercover. In

Medellín, he was strolling with his brother when Los Pepes shot him twenty-five times. One lawyer fled the country.

Pablo responded with bombs, but he was losing his ability to retaliate as the violence spiralled out of control and eroded his organisation. No one dared to stand up to Los Pepes, including the authorities who made up so many of their membership.

On April 29, 1993, Pablo wrote a letter to the attorney general:

Los Pepes have their headquarters and their torture chambers in Fidel Castaño's house, located on El Poblado Avenue near the country club... There they torture trade unionists and lawyers. No one has searched the house or confiscated their assets... The government offers rewards for the leaders of the Medellín Cartel and for the leaders of the guerrillas, but doesn't offer rewards for the leaders of the paramilitary, nor for those of the Cali Cartel, authors of various car bombs in the city of Medellín.

The state security organisations have zero victories in the matter of the assassinations of the lawyers, zero victories in the El Poblado car bombs, zero victories in the investigation into the deaths of the trade unionists and zero victories in the investigations into the massacres in which thousands of young Antioquians have died. I remain disposed to turn myself in if given written and public guarantees...

Pablo had referred to Fidel Castaño's house because the Castaño brothers, including Carlos and Vicente, were key players in Los Pepes. After their father had been kidnapped by guerrillas, the brothers had formed their own army, which had thousands of troops with a reputation for extreme violence. Carlos believed that Pablo wanted him dead because his army was taking over cocaine labs in the jungle. DEA cables documented Fidel Castaño's role in the hunt for Pablo:

As a result of a disagreement with Escobar, Castaño contacted the... [Search Bloc] and offered his help in attempting to locate Escobar. Castaño advised... that his disagreement with Escobar stemmed from his (Castaño) telling Escobar that he (Castaño) was not in agreement with his (Escobar) terrorist campaign, i.e., bombs, police killings. Castaño was also concerned that Escobar could have him (Castaño) killed at any time as had been the case with the Galeano/Moncada brothers.

Fidel Castaño had made telephonic contact with the incarcerated Ochoa clan (Jorge, Fabio and Juan David). Castaño asked the Ochoas to leave Escobar and join sides with him. Castaño explained that Escobar would have them killed just like the Moncadas and Galeanos. The Ochoas stated that they had recently given Escobar $500,000, however, they were thinking of abandoning him.... Castaño told the... [Search Bloc] that the Ochoas would never abandon Escobar for reasons of fear and that they "always lied in order to stay in neutral with everybody."

Due to the uproar, the Colombian government pretended to clamp down on Los Pepes. In response, Los Pepes announced that they had disbanded, but the killings didn't stop. On July 14, 1993, Los Pepes castrated Roberto Escobar's prize stallion and executed its rider and trainer.

CHAPTER 18
DEMISE

"Colonel, I'm going to kill you. I'm going to kill all of your family up to the third generation, then I will dig up your grandparents and shoot them and bury them again," Pablo notified Martinez. Three police bodyguards were on the way to pick up one of the colonel's sons from school when hit men assassinated them. Despite the threat to his family and the stress they were all under, Martinez refused to back down.

One of his sons, Hugo, was a member of a special unit of the Colombian police, which had been experimenting with new technology to locate Pablo. Martinez didn't want Hugo working on the case in Medellín, where members of the police were constantly murdered due to the $2,000 per hit offered by Pablo. But Hugo insisted that he wanted to help stamp out the threat to their family by tracking Pablo down with a device provided by the CIA.

Hugo's team went out in vans. Parked on hills with their antennae raised, the vans could triangulate a location. Once a signal had been received, Hugo would race off in an undercover vehicle with a monitor that made a noise as it picked up the signal's strength. As the technology was new, the team was having a hard time getting used to it. Hugo ended up chasing signals that led nowhere.

Due to the threat from Los Pepes, Pablo was in contact with his family more than usual. After being blocked from leaving the country, they were housed in a government building, worried about Los Pepes coming to kill them at any moment. Pablo's wife wrote him a letter:

I miss you so very much I feel weak. Sometimes I feel an immense loneliness take over my heart. Why does life have to separate us like this? My heart is aching. How are you? How do you feel? I don't want to leave you my love. I need you so much, I want to cry with you… I don't want to pressure you. Nor do I want to make you commit mistakes, but if our leaving is not possible, I would feel more secure with you. We'll close ourselves in, suspend the mail, whatever we have to. This is getting too tense.

Martinez and his son were relying on Pablo calling his family, so that they could trace the calls. Pablo made numerous calls to his son, Juan Pablo, a strapping six-foot teenager who used binoculars to watch out for Los Pepes. One day, he saw a man fire a rocket-propelled grenade at the building housing Pablo's immediate family. Juan Pablo photographed suspects and jotted down license-plate numbers. Pablo sent him letters written in code, with instructions about dealing with lawyers and officials. Pablo received a response from his son:

Dear Father,
    I send you a big hug and warm wishes.
    I see that Corrales [from the attorney general's office] is in high spirits, fighting Los Pepes. He doesn't have a choice anyway… The prosecutor played the fool about us leaving the country… to test us, to check what we were going to say and how we were going to react. I have been firm about your conditions and I have persuaded them. I even told them that you had planned to deal with the Cali people after turning yourself in, because you were willing to have peace back in the country.
    Corrales was very rude to me. We were talking and he started to tell me, "I have to look for your father because that is my mission. I'm not from here or there [allied to any side], I am a righteous person and he (you) knows that I am

serious about that." So I told him that there was no need for him to tell me that to my face every time he came around here because he has been here three times and all three times he has said the same thing – that I knew that was his job, but that he had to respect me, because it was my father he was talking about, and I told him he should calm down because my father was also after all those who were looking for him, and that destiny will say who finds whom.

He answered, "I'm afraid, because it's my job and no one has told me to stop looking for your father, because there are forty arrest warrants against him." I answered: "This is not for you to be afraid, but for you to show me some respect because I am with him [Pablo] and I support him," so he'd better cut it out or else. Then I told him that the prosecutor was the most fake guy in this country, that how did he expect us to believe him regarding you turning yourself in if he wasn't a man who kept his word, and that he had protected us so far only to trick us with false promises. And he answered: "I don't allow anyone to speak about my boss at my table," and I told him, "I, like a member of this family, cannot allow you either to say bad things about my boss, who is my father."

It would be good to tease the TV people, so they won't make the building [housing Pablo's family] stand out so obviously, because when they came here they told me they were going to erase the tape and they didn't do it.

Take care of yourself.

I love and remember you.

Your son.

The letter detailed where Juan Pablo suspected Martinez stayed in Medellín and described suspicious people lurking around their building.

Centra Spike and the Search Bloc tuned into Pablo's calls to his son. Initially, the code words used and the alternation of radio frequencies presented problems. Hugo led his team on so many wild goose chases that they almost gave up on him and the technology.

With the help of the CIA, Hugo learned that Pablo spoke to his son for an hour each evening, commencing around 7:15 pm. By listening to the calls, Hugo decoded the words used to indicate that it was time to switch frequencies. He was so convinced that he had located Pablo that raids were launched on the wrong buildings. Hugo ended up demoted from his position as a commander of a surveillance team.

Despite the setback and fifteen months of searching, Martinez was convinced that Pablo would soon be found. The eavesdropping technology was accumulating more information and its location techniques were being refined.

Not everybody supported the efforts of Martinez. The press attacked him for taking too long to find Pablo. The attorney general wanted Martinez removed and prosecuted with Los Pepes for all of the murder and mayhem of which Pablo was accusing them. The DEA – whose mission statement was to combat drug trafficking – learned that Martinez was on the payroll of the Cali Cartel. The DEA noted that "[Gilberto José] Rodríguez Orejuela [a Cali Cartel leader] told [an informant] they had bandits working within the Search Bloc... The informant advised that Rodríguez Orejuela states they had made an arrangement with PNC [Colombian National Police] General Vargas and Colonel Martinez regarding a reward for Escobar's capture. According to Rodríguez Orejuela, the Cali Cartel will pay a total of $10 million immediately following Pablo's capture and/or death. Of this, $8 million has been promised to the Search Bloc and $2 million for the informants who provide the information that leads to a successful operation."

The Americans knew that if this information leaked it would embarrass the DEA, but they decided it was worth the risk. They lobbied against the attorney general for trying to remove Martinez.

In October 1993, the government threatened to withdraw the guards protecting Pablo's family, which would have left them at the mercy of Los Pepes. Pablo's terrified wife asked the attorney general to visit their building and give Pablo more time to surrender, which she was encouraging him to do. She said she wasn't a criminal and she shouldn't be getting punished.

Juan Pablo sent the attorney general a letter stating how worried and desperate the family was getting. He noted that several of his close friends, a maid and a personal tutor had been kidnapped and killed in recent weeks and that some of the kidnappers were policemen.

In November, Juan Pablo negotiated a deal with the attorney general for Pablo's surrender. The conditions were that Roberto Escobar would be moved out of lockdown and into a part of the Itagüí prison housing the Ochoa brothers and other Medellín traffickers. Upon surrendering, Pablo wanted to be housed with Roberto and to be allowed twenty-one family visits each year. The final requirement was for his wife and children to be flown out of the country. The attorney general promised to help them move to a safe country, but only after Pablo had surrendered. In the end, Pablo gave his word that he would surrender as soon as his family was flown overseas. Accepting Pablo's word, the attorney general started to make arrangements for Pablo's family to leave the country.

The Americans were desperate to prevent Pablo from surrendering. Pablo tried to distract the Americans by starting a rumour that he was in Haiti, while arranging for his family to fly to either London or Frankfurt. The authorities asked the Spanish, British and German ambassadors to refuse Pablo's family entry into their countries.

After his family was airborne for Germany, Pablo found out that they were going to be denied access. Infuriated, he made a call, "This is Pablo Escobar. I need to talk to the president."

"OK, hold on, let me locate him," an operator said and contacted the National Police.

A policeman got on the phone. "We can't get in touch with the president right now. Please call back at another time." He hung up.

Pablo called again. "This is Pablo Escobar. It is necessary that I talk to the president. My family is flying to Germany at this time. I need to talk to him right now."

"We get a lot of crank calls here. We need to somehow verify that it is really you. It's going to take me a few minutes to track down the president, so please wait a few more minutes and then call back."

The president refused to speak to Pablo. The police set up a trap to trace the call.

After the phone rang, a policeman told Pablo, "I'm sorry, Mr Escobar, we have been unable to locate the president."

Pablo threatened to bomb the presidential palace and the German embassy if his family couldn't stay in Germany.

Pablo's family was flown back to Colombia and dropped off at a hotel in Bogotá without any police protection. On the phone, Pablo told them to wait there, to lobby the authorities to go to another country and to contact the United Nations.

With Pablo's family vulnerable in a hotel, Los Pepes announced that their cessation of operations – which had been initiated at the government's request – was over and they were resuming hostilities with Pablo.

Fearing a bombing, the other guests checked out of the hotel housing Pablo's family. Walking around the hotel, Pablo's daughter, Manuela, sang about Los Pepes coming to kill her and her family.

On November 30, 1993, Pablo sent a letter to the suspected leaders of Los Pepes, including Colonel Martinez, the leaders of the Cali Cartel, the Castaño brothers and members of the Search Bloc. "I have been raided 10,000 times. You haven't been at all. Everything is confiscated from me. Nothing is taken away from you. The government will never offer a warrant for you.

The government will never apply faceless justice to criminal and terrorist policemen."

Now they had Pablo worried about his family's safety, the authorities relied on him calling the hotel housing his family. Hugo Martinez came back early from a vacation to resume the hunt. In a dangerous neighbourhood, Hugo's van was spotted. A child on roller-skates approached the van and gave Hugo a note: "We know what you're doing. We know you are looking for Pablo. Either you leave or we're going to kill you."

Even though Pablo was speaking while in a moving taxi, Centra Spike traced his calls to Los Olivos, a neighbourhood in Medellín near the football stadium, consisting mostly of two-storey homes. The Search Bloc set up surveillance in Los Olivos. In a car, Hugo listened for Pablo's voice. For days, he ate and slept in the vehicle.

Roberto received a note from someone on the payroll that warned Pablo to stop talking on the phone or else he would be caught. Roberto immediately sent a note to Pablo about his phone being triangulated. He urged him to stop using it. Other sources warned that if Pablo surrendered, he would be killed.

Aware that the end was near, Pablo left a recording for his daughter telling her to be a good girl and that he would protect her from heaven. He bought his brother a copy of the *Guinness Book of Sports Records*, wrote a personal note to Roberto – who he described as his soul brother – and put it in the book.

Pablo spent his forty-fourth birthday, December 1, 1993 at building number 45D-94 on Street 79A, a two-storey house that he owned. He had one bodyguard, Limón. His cousin, Luzmila, was his cook. When Pablo wanted to make phone calls, Limón drove him around in a yellow taxi, which had given Pablo a false sense of security. Birthday congratulations kept Pablo on the phone longer than usual with his family. He celebrated with restaurant food and champagne.

Hugo picked up a signal on December 1. He sped to the location, which brought him to a roundabout with nobody there.

Convinced that he'd just missed Pablo, he was disappointed. The next day, he returned to his apartment to rest.

To throw his pursuers off his trail, Pablo had decided to hide in the jungle. He wanted to say goodbye to his mother first, so he risked going to her apartment in the early morning. He told her that it was the last time he would see her in Medellín. His plan now was to form a new group, establish an independent country and be its president. Without crying, his mother said goodbye.

On December 2, 1993, Pablo woke up around noon and ate spaghetti. He sent his cousin to buy supplies he would need in the jungle: stationery and toiletries. In a taxi, he made phone calls. On the phone, he got out of the taxi and returned to the apartment, making the mistake of speaking for longer than five minutes.

Martinez notified his son that Pablo was talking. Hugo rushed back to his team.

At 1 pm, pretending to be a radio journalist, Pablo called his family. His wife, Maria Victoria, was crying. Numerous of their family members and associates had been killed by Los Pepes. The family was distraught.

"So, what are you going to do?" Pablo said.

"I don't know," she said, still crying.

"What does your mother say?"

"It was as if my mother fainted," she said, referring to a few days ago at the airport when the family had unsuccessfully tried to flee to Germany. "I did not call her. She told me bye, and then–"

"And you haven't spoken to her?"

"No. My mother is so nervous..." Maria Victoria said the murders committed by Los Pepes had traumatised her mother.

"What are you going to do?" Pablo said softly.

"I don't know. I mean, wait and see where we are going to go and I believe that will be the end of us."

"No!"

"So?"

"Don't you give me this coldness! Holy Mary!" Pablo said. "And you?"

"Ahhh."

"And you?"

"What about me?" Pablo said.

"What are you going to do?"

"Nothing… What do you need?"

"Nothing," Maria Victoria said.

"What do you want?"

"What would I want?"

"If you need something, call me, OK?"

"OK."

"You call me now, quickly," Pablo said. "There is nothing more I can tell you. What else can I say? I have remained right on track, right?"

"But how are you? Oh my God, I don't know!"

"We must go on. Think about it. Now that I am so close, right?" Pablo said, referring to his proposal to surrender to the government.

"Yes," Maria Victoria said. "Think about your boy, too, and everything else, and don't make any decisions too quickly. OK?"

"Yes."

"Call your mother again and ask her if she wants you to go there or what…" she said. "Ciao."

"So long."

With the Search Bloc attempting to home in on the precise location, Juan Pablo got on the phone. He wanted his dad to help him formulate answers to questions from a journalist.

"Look, this is very important in Bogotá," Pablo said, hoping to present his case favourably through the media. He wanted to hear the questions first. "This is also publicity. Explaining the reasons and other matters to them. Do you understand? Well done and well organized."

"Yes, yes." Juan Pablo began with the first question: "'Whatever the country, refuge is conditioned on the immediate surrender of your father. Would your father be willing to turn himself in if you are settled somewhere?'"

"Go on," Pablo said.

"The next one is, 'Would he be willing to turn himself in before you take refuge abroad?'"

"Go on."

"I spoke with the man and he told me that if there were some questions I did not want to answer, there was no problem, and if I wanted to add some questions, he would include them."

"OK. The next one?"

"'Why do you think that several countries have refused to receive your family?' OK?"

"Yes."

"'From which embassies have you requested help for them to take you in?'"

"OK."

"'Don't you think your father's situation, accused of X number of crimes, assassination of public figures, considered one of the most powerful drug traffickers in the world...?'" Juan Pablo stopped reading.

"Go on."

"But there are many. Around forty questions."

Pablo said he'd call back later in the day. "I may find a way to communicate by fax."

"No," Juan Pablo said, concerned about a fax being traced.

"No, huh? OK. OK. So, good luck."

The Search Bloc and Centra Spike traced the call to Los Olivos. They waited for Pablo to make another call.

At 3 pm, Pablo called his son, who said that the journalist wanted to know what conditions Pablo would be satisfied with in order to turn himself in. Members of the Search Bloc started to go street to street, hoping to detect Pablo's location. Hugo's scanner led him to an office building. Convinced Pablo was inside, the troops stormed in, but Pablo was still conversing as if nothing had happened.

"Tell him, 'My father cannot turn himself in unless he has guarantees for his security.'"

"OK."

"'And we totally support him in that,'" Pablo said.

"OK."

"'Above any considerations.'"

"Yep."

"'My father is not going to turn himself in before we are placed in a foreign country, and while the police in Antioquia–'"

"The police and DAS is better," Juan Pablo said. "Because the DAS are also searching."

"It's only the police," Pablo said.

"Oh, OK."

"'While the police–'"

"Yeah."

"OK," Pablo said. "Let's change it to, 'While the security organizations in Antioquia…'"

"Yeah."

"'–continue to kidnap–'"

"Yeah."

"'–torture–'"

"Yeah."

"'–and commit massacres in Medellín.'"

"Yes, all right."

"OK," Pablo said. "The next one."

Due to the amount of time Pablo had spent on the phone, Hugo's scanning equipment had narrowed down Pablo's location. Led by Hugo, members of the Search Bloc arrived at a stream by Pablo's house.

Juan Pablo asked why so many countries had refused to allow their family in.

"'The countries have denied entry because they don't know the real truth,'" Pablo said.

"Yes."

"'We're going to knock on the doors of every embassy from all around the world because we're willing to fight incessantly.

Because we want to live and study in another country without bodyguards and hopefully with a new name.'"

"Just so you know, I got a phone call from a reporter who told me that President Alfredo Cristiani from Ecuador, no, I think it is El Salvador–"

"Yes?" Pablo went to a second-floor window and scanned the street, checking out cars.

"Well, he has offered to receive us. I heard the statement. Well, he gave it to me by phone," Juan Pablo said.

"Yes?"

"And he said if this contributed in some way to the peace of the country, he would be willing to receive us because the world receives dictators and bad people, why wouldn't he receive us?"

"Well," Pablo said, "let's wait and see because that country is a bit hidden away."

"Well, but at least there's a possibility and it has come from a president."

"Look, with respect to El Salvador."

"Yeah?"

"In case they ask anything, tell them, 'The family is very grateful and obliged to the words of the president, that it is known he is the president of peace in El Salvador.'"

"Yeah."

The length of the call had exceeded Pablo's safety limits. When asked about how the family had felt about living with government protection, Pablo said, "You respond to that one."

"'Who paid for maintenance and accommodation? You or the attorney general?'" Juan Pablo said.

"Who did pay this?" Pablo said.

"Us. Well, there were some people from Bogotá who got their expenses paid… but they never spent all of it because we supplied the groceries, mattresses, deodorants, toothbrushes and pretty much everything."

After two more questions, Pablo said, "OK, let's leave it at that."

"Yeah, OK," Juan Pablo said. "Good luck."

"Good luck."

The call had lasted for so long that Hugo and the Search Bloc were on Pablo's street, driving up and down. Hugo stopped studying his equipment and started observing the houses. He noticed a bearded man behind a second-story window, phone in hand, watching the traffic. After a few seconds, the man disappeared into the house.

Hugo leaned out of the window. "This is the house!" he yelled at the vehicle behind him. Suspecting that Pablo had noticed his white van, Hugo told the driver to keep going. He radioed his father, "I've got him located. He's in this house." Assuming that Pablo's hit men were on their way, Hugo wanted to leave.

"Stay exactly where you are!" Colonel Martinez yelled. "Station yourself in front and back of the house. Don't let him come out!"

While all units of the Search Bloc sped to the house, Hugo parked in a back alley and got his gun ready.

There have been many accounts of what happened next.

A sledgehammer knocked down the front door. Six Search Bloc members stormed inside, shooting at an empty garage with a taxi. Charging up the stairs, one member of the team fell as if shot, startling the rest, but he had only slipped.

The authorities reported that Limón had escaped through a window onto an orange-tile roof. As he fled, Search Bloc members behind the house sprayed gunfire. Shot multiple times, he careened off the roof onto the grass.

Pablo tossed his sandals and leapt down to the roof. Not wanting to end up like Limón, he stayed against a wall, which blocked clear shots at him even though marksmen were all over the place. Aiming to escape down a back street, Pablo hastened along the wall.

Shots erupted. The gunfire was so intense from all sides of the house that it tore up the bricks and the roof and some members of the Search Bloc thought they were under attack by Pablo's bodyguards and radioed for help.

Pablo fell.

The shooting stopped.

"It's Pablo! It's Pablo!"

Troops approached the blood-soaked corpse and flipped it over.

"Viva Colombia! We've just killed Pablo Escobar!"

"We won! We won!"

In the book *Escobar*, Roberto described the police barging in downstairs and Pablo sending Limón to investigate. Shot multiple times, Limón died while Pablo made it to the roof, looked around and saw he was surrounded. Having pledged to never be captured or killed, he shot himself in the head to deprive the government of being able to claim that they had killed him.

Pablo was shot three times: in his back, leg and above his right ear. Roberto believes the wound above the ear was the suicide shot.

Troops shaved a Hitler moustache onto Pablo's face and posed for pictures with him.

Shortly after Pablo's death, his mother and two sisters arrived. At first, they thought that only Limón was dead. Pablo's mother later described what happened when she found Pablo's corpse: "I felt something I have never felt in my life. It was terrible. Since then, my soul has been destroyed because there will never be anyone like Pablo again."

While the upper classes celebrated, the news devastated the poor. At the funeral, over 5,000 rushed to touch the coffin. Pablo's wife had to be evacuated. Along the streets, ten thousand joined the procession. For the first year, his grave had an armed guard.

Pablo's death had no impact on the cocaine flowing into America.

CONCLUSION

Pablo's story exemplifies the contradictions, absurdities, corruption and deaths caused by the War on Drugs.

Just like Al Capone's empire was a result of alcohol prohibition, Pablo's was a creation of US drug laws that made a by-product of the coca plant insanely valuable. The billions Pablo made attracted predators such as the Cali Cartel and George HW Bush, none of whom hunted him down for the good of humanity.

After his death, cocaine entered America through the traditional routes detailed in Chapter 12. Governments working with criminal organisations – some on friendly terms with the CIA – exported tons of it, including the Cali Cartel in cooperation with senior members of the Colombian government.

Pablo's downfall was assured after the Americans became increasingly involved following the assassination of the presidential candidate Galán, which was falsely blamed on Pablo – a crafty strategy employed by General Maza, who was later indicted as a co-conspirator in Galán's murder. Many of Pablo's domestic adversaries in the police were taking drug money from the Cali Cartel.

Pablo's power was no match for the vast resources available to George HW Bush. Once Bush had decided to make Pablo the world's cocaine bogeyman, his demise was inevitable. To this day, the CIA has refused to release information about their involvement with Los Pepes and Pablo's death.

If the hunt for Pablo wasn't about saving people from cocaine, then who benefitted? The banking, corporate and military interests represented by Bush profited, while using the War on Drugs as a cover story. All of the major players in the conflict – the cartels, the police, the Colombian troops – were fighting with weapons mostly manufactured in America.

Ex-CIA pilot Chip Tatum has alleged that some of Pablo's billions in Panama ended up in George HW Bush's hands, just like Pablo liquidated the assets of the Galeano and Moncada brothers. It was a case of a big gangster shaking down a smaller one.

With the CIA facilitating the importation of cocaine into America it was no wonder that the quantities rose after Pablo died. I document the true story of a CIA cocaine-smuggling pilot, Barry Seal, in Book 2 of my War on Drugs trilogy: *American Made: Who Killed Barry Seal? Pablo Escobar or George HW Bush.* Barry operated with the full cooperation of the Bush clan and also with the Clintons.

If the US government had followed Milton Friedman's advice by legalising cocaine – taking the market away from gangsters such as Pablo and sequestering cocaine from young people – then the black market that Pablo profited from would have ceased to exist and the deaths of hundreds of thousands of people in countries such as Colombia and Mexico would have been avoided. But Milton was ignored because fighting the Pablos of the world is big business.

GET A FREE BOOK

Sign Up For My Newsletter At:

http://shaunattwood.com/newsletter-subscribe/

REFERENCES

Bowden, Mark. *Killing Pablo*. Atlantic Books, 2001.

Bowen, Russell. *The Immaculate Deception*. America West Publishers, 1991.

Cockburn, Leslie. *Out of Control*. Bloomsbury, 1988.

Cockburn and Clair. *Whiteout*. Verso, 1998.

Escobar, Roberto. *Escobar*. Hodder & Stoughton, 2009.

Grillo, Joan. *El Narco*. Bloomsbury, 2012.

Gugliotta and Leen. *Kings of Cocaine*. Harper and Row, 1989.

Hari, Johann. *Chasing the Scream*. Bloomsbury, 2015.

Hopsicker, Daniel. *Barry and the Boys*. MadCow Press, 2001.

Leveritt, Mara. *The Boys on the Tracks*. Bird Call Press, 2007.

Levine, Michael. *The Big White Lie*. Thunder's Mouth Press, 1993.

Marquez, Gabriel Garcia. *News of a Kidnapping*. Penguin, 1996.

Massing, Michael. *The Fix*. Simon & Schuster, 1998.

McCoy, Alfred. *The Politics of Heroin in Southeast Asia*. Harper and Row, 1972.

Morris, Roger. *Partners in Power*. Henry Holt, 1996.

Noriega, Manuel. *The Memoirs of Manuel Noriega*. Random House, 1997.

North, Oliver. *Under Fire*. Harper Collins, 1991.

Paley, Dawn. *Drug War Capitalism*. AK Press, 2014.

Porter, Bruce. *Blow*. St Martin's Press, 1993.

Reed, Terry. *Compromised*. Clandestine Publishing, 1995.

Ross, Rick. *Freeway Rick Ross*. Freeway Studios, 2014.

Ruppert, Michael. *Crossing the Rubicon*. New Society Publishers, 2004.

Saviano, Roberto. *Zero Zero Zero*. Penguin Random House UK, 2013.

Schou, Nick. *Kill the Messenger*. Nation Books, 2006.

Shannon, Elaine. *Desperados*. Penguin, 1988.

Stich, Rodney. *Drugging America* 2nd Ed. Silverpeak, 2006.

Stone, Roger. *The Clinton's War on Women*. Skyhorse, 2015.

Stone, Roger. *Jeb and the Bush Crime Family*. Skyhorse, 2016.

Streatfield, Dominic. *Cocaine*. Virgin Publishing, 2001.

Tarpley and Chaitkin. *George Bush*. Progressive Press, 2004.

Valentine, Douglas. *The Strength of the Pack*. Trine Day LLC, 2009.

MY SOCIAL-MEDIA LINKS

Email: attwood.shaun@hotmail.co.uk
Blog: Jon's Jail Journal
Website: shaunattwood.com
Twitter: @shaunattwood
YouTube: Shaun Attwood
LinkedIn: Shaun Attwood
Goodreads: Shaun Attwood
Facebook pages: Shaun Attwood, Jon's Jail Journal,
T-Bone Appreciation Society

I welcome feedback on any of my books.
Thank you for the Amazon reviews!

SHAUN ATTWOOD'S
TRUE-LIFE JAIL EXPERIENCE

HARD TIME 2ND EDITION
CHAPTER 1

Sleep deprived and scanning for danger, I enter a dark cell on the second floor of the maximum-security Madison Street jail in Phoenix, Arizona, where guards and gang members are murdering prisoners. Behind me, the metal door slams heavily. Light slants into the cell through oblong gaps in the door, illuminating a prisoner cocooned in a white sheet, snoring lightly on the top bunk about two thirds of the way up the back wall. Relieved there is no immediate threat, I place my mattress on the grimy floor. Desperate to rest, I notice movement on the cement-block walls. *Am I hallucinating?* I blink several times. The walls appear to ripple. Stepping closer, I see the walls are alive with insects. I flinch. So many are swarming, I wonder if they're a colony of ants on the move. To get a better look, I put my eyes right up to them. They are mostly the size of almonds and have antennae. American cockroaches. I've seen them in the holding cells downstairs in smaller numbers, but nothing like this. A chill spreads over my body. I back away.

Something alive falls from the ceiling and bounces off the base of my neck. I jump. With my night vision improving, I spot cockroaches weaving in and out of the base of the fluorescent strip light. Every so often one drops onto the concrete and resumes crawling. Examining the bottom bunk, I realise why my cellmate is sleeping at a higher elevation: cockroaches are pouring from gaps in the decrepit wall at the level of my bunk. The area is thick with them. Placing my mattress on the bottom bunk scatters them. I walk towards the toilet, crunching a few under my shower sandals. I urinate and grab the toilet roll. A cockroach darts from the centre of the roll onto my hand, tickling my fingers. My arm jerks as if it has a mind of its own, losing the cockroach and the toilet roll. Using a towel, I wipe the bulk of them off the bottom bunk, stopping only to shake the odd one off my hand. I unroll my mattress. They begin to regroup and inhabit my mattress. My adrenaline is pumping so much, I lose my fatigue.

Nauseated, I sit on a tiny metal stool bolted to the wall. *How will I sleep? How's my cellmate sleeping through the infestation and my arrival?* Copying his technique, I cocoon myself in a sheet and lie down, crushing more cockroaches. The only way they can access me now is through the breathing hole I've left in the sheet by the lower half of my face. Inhaling their strange musty odour, I close my eyes. I can't sleep. I feel them crawling on the sheet around my feet. *Am I imagining things?* Frightened of them infiltrating my breathing hole, I keep opening my eyes. Cramps cause me to rotate onto my other side. Facing the wall, I'm repulsed by so many of them just inches away. I return to my original side.

The sheet traps the heat of the Sonoran Desert to my body, soaking me in sweat. Sweat tickles my body, tricking my mind into thinking the cockroaches are infiltrating and crawling on me. The trapped heat aggravates my bleeding skin infections and bedsores. I want to scratch myself, but I know better. The outer layers of my skin have turned soggy from sweating constantly in this concrete oven. Squirming on the bunk fails to stop the relentless itchiness of my skin. Eventually, I scratch myself. Clumps of moist skin detach under my nails. Every now and then I become so uncomfortable, I have to open my cocoon to waft the heat out, which allows the cockroaches in. It takes hours to drift to sleep. I only manage a few hours. I awake stuck to the soaked sheet, disgusted by the cockroach carcasses compressed against the mattress.

The cockroaches plague my new home until dawn appears at the dots in the metal grid over a begrimed strip of four-inch-thick bullet-proof glass at the top of the back wall – the cell's only source of outdoor light. They disappear into the cracks in the walls, like vampire mist retreating from sunlight. But not all of them. There were so many on the night shift that even their vastly reduced number is too many to dispose of. And they act like they know it. They roam around my feet with attitude, as if to make it clear that I'm trespassing on their turf.

My next set of challenges will arise not from the insect world, but from my neighbours. I'm the new arrival, subject to scrutiny about my charges just like when I'd run into the Aryan Brotherhood prison gang on my first day at the medium-security Towers jail a year ago. I wish my cellmate would wake up, brief me on the mood of the locals and introduce me to the head of the white gang. No such luck. Chow is announced over a speaker system in a crackly robotic voice, but he doesn't stir.

I emerge into the day room for breakfast. Prisoners in black-and-white bee-striped uniforms gather under the metal-grid stairs and tip dead cockroaches into a trash bin from plastic peanut-butter containers they'd set as traps during the night. All eyes are on me in the chow line. Watching who sits where, I hold my head up, put on a solid stare and pretend to be as at home in this environment as the cockroaches. It's all an act. I'm lonely and afraid. I loathe having to explain myself to the head of the white race, who I assume is the toughest murderer. I've been in jail long enough to know that taking my breakfast to my cell will imply that I have something to hide.

The gang punishes criminals with certain charges. The most serious are sex offenders, who are KOS: Kill On Sight. Other charges are punishable by SOS – Smash On Sight – such as drive-by shootings because women and kids sometimes get killed. It's called convict justice. Gang members are constantly looking for people to beat up because that's how they earn their reputations and tattoos. The most serious acts of violence earn the highest-ranking tattoos. To be a full gang member requires murder. I've observed the body language and techniques inmates trying to integrate employ. An inmate with a spring in his step and an air of confidence is likely to be accepted. A person who avoids eye contact and fails to introduce himself to the gang is likely to be preyed on. Some of the failed attempts I saw ended up with heads getting cracked against toilets, a sound I've grown familiar with. I've seen prisoners being extracted on stretchers who looked dead – one had yellow fluid leaking from his head. The constant violence gives me nightmares, but the reality is that I put myself in here, so I force myself to accept it as a part of my punishment.

It's time to apply my knowledge. With a self-assured stride, I take my breakfast bag to the table of white inmates covered in neo-Nazi tattoos, allowing them to question me.

"Mind if I sit with you guys?" I ask, glad exhaustion has deepened my voice.

"These seats are taken. But you can stand at the corner of the table."

The man who answered is probably the head of the gang. I size him up. Cropped brown hair. A dangerous glint in Nordic-blue eyes. Tiny pupils that suggest he's on heroin. Weightlifter-type veins bulging from a sturdy neck. Political ink on arms crisscrossed with scars. About the same age as me, thirty-three.

"Thanks. I'm Shaun from England." I volunteer my origin to show I'm different from them but not in a way that might get me smashed.

"I'm Bullet, the head of the whites." He offers me his fist to bump. "Where you roll in from, wood?"

Addressing me as wood is a good sign. It's what white gang members on a friendly basis call each other.

"Towers jail. They increased my bond and re-classified me to maximum security."

"What's your bond at?"

"I've got two $750,000 bonds," I say in a monotone. This is no place to brag about bonds.

"How many people you kill, brother?" His eyes drill into mine, checking whether my body language supports my story. My body language so far is spot on.

"None. I threw rave parties. They got us talking about drugs on wiretaps." Discussing drugs on the phone does not warrant a $1.5 million bond. I know and beat him to his next question. "Here's my charges." I show him my charge sheet, which includes conspiracy and leading a crime syndicate – both from running an Ecstasy ring.

Bullet snatches the paper and scrutinises it. Attempting to pre-empt his verdict, the other whites study his face. On edge, I wait for him to respond. Whatever he says next will determine whether I'll be accepted or victimised.

"Are you some kind of jailhouse attorney?" Bullet asks. "I want someone to read through my case paperwork." During our few minutes of conversation, Bullet has seen through my act and concluded that I'm educated – a possible resource to him.

I appreciate that he'll accept me if I take the time to read his case. "I'm no jailhouse attorney, but I'll look through it and help you however I can."

"Good. I'll stop by your cell later on, wood."

After breakfast, I seal as many of the cracks in the walls as I can with toothpaste. The cell smells minty, but the cockroaches still find their way in. Their day shift appears to be collecting information on the brown paper bags under my bunk, containing a few items of food that I purchased from the commissary; bags that I tied off with rubber bands in the hope of keeping the cockroaches out. Relentlessly, the cockroaches explore the bags for entry points, pausing over and probing the most worn and vulnerable regions. *Will the nightly swarm eat right through the paper?* I read all morning, wondering whether my cellmate has died in his cocoon, his occasional breathing sounds reassuring me.

Bullet stops by late afternoon and drops his case paperwork off. He's been charged with Class 3 felonies and less, not serious crimes, but is facing a double-digit sentence because of his prior convictions and Security Threat Group status in the prison system. The proposed sentencing range seems disproportionate. I'll advise him to reject the plea bargain – on the assumption he already knows to do so, but is just seeking the comfort of a second opinion, like many un-sentenced inmates. When he returns for his paperwork, our conversation disturbs my cellmate – the cocoon shuffles – so we go upstairs to his cell. I tell Bullet what I think. He is excitable, a different man from earlier, his pupils almost non-existent.

"This case ain't shit. But my prosecutor knows I done other shit, all kinds of heavy shit, but can't prove it. I'd do anything to get that sorry bitch off my fucking ass. She's asking for something bad to happen to her. Man, if I ever get bonded out, I'm gonna chop that bitch into pieces. Kill her slowly though. Like to work her over with a blowtorch."

Such talk can get us both charged with conspiring to murder a prosecutor, so I try to steer him elsewhere. "It's crazy how they can catch you doing one thing, yet try to sentence you for all of the things they think you've ever done."

"Done plenty. Shot some dude in the stomach once. Rolled him up in a blanket and threw him in a dumpster."

Discussing past murders is as unsettling as future ones. "So what's all your tattoos mean, Bullet? Like that eagle on your chest?"

"Why you wanna know?" Bullet's eyes probe mine.

My eyes hold their ground. "Just curious."

"It's a war bird. The AB patch."

"AB patch?"

"What the Aryan Brotherhood gives you when you've put enough work in."

"How long does it take to earn a patch?"

"Depends how quickly you put your work in. You have to earn your lightning bolts first."

"Why you got red and black lightning bolts?"

"You get SS bolts for beating someone down or for being an enforcer for the family. Red lightning bolts for killing someone. I was sent down as a youngster. They gave me steel and told me who to handle and I handled it. You don't ask questions. You just get blood on your steel. Dudes who get these tats without putting work in are told to cover them up or leave the yard."

"What if they refuse?"

"They're held down and we carve the ink off them."

Imagining them carving a chunk of flesh to remove a tattoo, I cringe. He's really enjoying telling me this now. His volatile nature is clear and frightening. *He's accepted me too much. He's trying to impress me before making demands.*

At night, I'm unable to sleep. Cocooned in heat, surrounded by cockroaches, I hear the swamp-cooler vent – a metal grid at the top of a wall – hissing out tepid air. Giving up on sleep, I put my earphones on and tune into National Public Radio. Listening to a Vivaldi violin concerto, I close my eyes and press my tailbone down to straighten my back as if I'm doing a yogic relaxation. The playful allegro thrills me, lifting my spirits, but the wistful adagio provokes sad emotions and tears. I open my eyes and gaze into the gloom. Due to lack of sleep, I start hallucinating and hearing voices over the music whispering threats. I'm at breaking point. Although I have accepted that I committed crimes and deserve to be punished, no one should have to live like this. I'm furious at myself for making the series of reckless decisions that put me in here and for losing absolutely everything. As violins crescendo in my ears, I remember what my life used to be like.

WAR ON DRUGS TRILOGY
BOOK 2

AMERICAN MADE: WHO KILLED BARRY SEAL? PABLO ESCOBAR OR GEORGE HW BUSH

CIA pilot Barry Seal flew cocaine and weapons worth billions of dollars into and out of America in the 1980s. After he became a government informant, Pablo Escobar's Medellin Cartel offered a million for him alive and half a million dead. But his real trouble began after he threatened to expose the dirty dealings of George HW Bush.

Set in a world where crime and government coexist, *American Made* is the true story of Barry Seal that the Hollywood movie starring Tom Cruise didn't dare to tell.

"A conspiracy of the grandest magnitude." Congressman Bill Alexander on the Mena affair

WAR ON DRUGS TRILOGY
BOOK 3

WE ARE BEING LIED TO:
THE WAR ON DRUGS

A collection of harrowing, action-packed and interlinked true stories that demonstrate the devastating consequences of drug prohibition.

PARTY TIME

In *Party Time*, Shaun Attwood arrives in Phoenix, Arizona a penniless business graduate from a small industrial town in England. Within a decade, he becomes a stock-market millionaire.

But he is leading a double life.

After taking his first Ecstasy pill at a rave in Manchester as a shy student, Shaun becomes intoxicated by the party lifestyle that changes his fortune. Making it his personal mission to bring the English rave scene to the Arizona desert, Shaun becomes submerged in a criminal underworld, throwing parties for thousands of ravers and running an Ecstasy ring in competition with the Mafia mass murderer "Sammy The Bull" Gravano.

As greed and excess tear through his life, Shaun experiences eye-watering encounters with Mafia hit men and crystal-meth addicts, extravagant debaucheries with superstar DJs and glitter girls, and ingests enough drugs to kill a herd of elephants. This is his story.

HARD TIME 2ND EDITION

As a teenager in an industrial UK town, Shaun Attwood covets the American Dream. He moves to Arizona with only student credit cards and becomes a millionaire. After throwing Ecstasy parties for thousands of ravers, Shaun bumps heads with Sammy the Bull Gravano, an Italian Mafia mass murderer, who puts a hit out on him.

The dream turns into a nightmare when a SWAT team smashes Shaun's door down. Inside Arizona's deadliest jail, Shaun struggles to survive against an unpredictable backdrop of gang violence and sickening human-rights violations. Over time and bolstered by the love and support of his fiancée and family, he uses incarceration for learning and introspection.

With a tiny pencil sharpened on a cell door, Shaun documents the conditions: dead rats in the food, cockroaches crawling in his ears at night, murders and riots… Smuggled out of maximum-security and posted online, his writing shines the international media spotlight on the plight of the prisoners in Sheriff Joe Arpaio's jail.

Join best-selling author Shaun Attwood on a harrowing voyage into the darkest recesses of human existence in *Hard Time*, the second book from the English Shaun trilogy.

PRISON TIME

Sentenced to 9½ years in Arizona's state prison for distributing Ecstasy, Shaun finds himself living among gang members, sexual predators and drug-crazed psychopaths. After being attacked by a Californian biker in for stabbing a girlfriend, Shaun writes about the prisoners who befriend, protect and inspire him. They include T-Bone, a massive African American ex-Marine who risks his life saving vulnerable inmates from rape, and Two Tonys, an old-school Mafia murderer who left the corpses of his rivals from Arizona to Alaska. They teach Shaun how to turn incarceration to his advantage, and to learn from his mistakes.

Shaun is no stranger to love and lust in the heterosexual world, but the tables are turned on him inside. Sexual advances come at him from all directions, some cleverly disguised, others more sinister – making Shaun question his sexual identity.

Resigned to living alongside violent, mentally-ill and drug-addicted inmates, Shaun immerses himself in psychology and philosophy to try to make sense of his past behaviour, and begins applying what he learns as he adapts to prison life. Encouraged by Two Tonys to explore fiction as well, Shaun reads over 1000 books which, with support from a brilliant psychotherapist, Dr Owen, speed along his personal development. As his ability to deflect daily threats improves, Shaun begins to look forward to his release with optimism and a new love waiting for him. Yet the words of Aristotle from one of Shaun's books will prove prophetic: "We cannot learn without pain."

ABOUT SHAUN ATTWOOD

Shaun Attwood is a former stock-market millionaire and Ecstasy supplier turned public speaker, author and activist, who is banned from America for life. His story was featured worldwide on National Geographic Channel as an episode of Locked Up/Banged Up Abroad called Raving Arizona (available on YouTube).

Shaun's writing – smuggled out of the jail with the highest death rate in America run by Sheriff Joe Arpaio – attracted international media attention to the human rights violations: murders by guards and gang members, dead rats in the food, cockroach infestations…

While incarcerated, Shaun was forced to reappraise his life. He read over 1,000 books in just under six years. By studying original texts in psychology and philosophy, he sought to better understand himself and his past behaviour. He credits books as being the lifeblood of his rehabilitation.

Shaun now tells his story to schools to put young people off drugs and crime. He campaigns against injustice via his books and blog, Jon's Jail Journal. He has appeared on the BBC, Sky News and TV worldwide to talk about issues affecting prisoners' rights.